Praise for *My Peoj*

"Dixon has that uncanny ability to convey to his readers the feelings that came along with the party's triumphs and defeats. Most readers will be amazed to discover what it took to create and then sustain the Black Panther Party's many community service programs. They will be equally shocked at how close party members were to the ever-present threat of death. Unlike previous autobiographies of BPP leaders, this one does not sugarcoat the organization's shortcomings, nor does it glamorize its hard-fought and often well-deserved victories. It does, however, provide a valuable, though painful, reminder of the high price of real change in these United States."

—Curtis Austin, associate professor of history, The Ohio State University

"*My People Are Rising* is the most authentic book ever written by a member of the Black Panther Party. Aaron Dixon does a superb job of presenting life in the party from the perspective of a foot soldier—a warrior for the cause of revolutionary change and Black Power in America. He pulls no punches and holds nothing back in writing honestly about those times as he successfully presents a visual picture of the courage, commitment, and sometimes shocking brutality of life as a Panther activist. This is an unforgettable, must-read book!"

—Larry Gossett, chair, Metropolitan King County Council

"There have been many books about the Black Panther Party but never has there been a Panther book as illuminating as this memoir by Aaron Dixon. It's the story from a different perspective than we've ever seen: the former member who has remained a long-distance runner for revolution. It's indispensable for anyone with an interest in Black politics or the politics of change in the United States."

–Dave Zirin, the *Nation*

TO EVICA

My People Are Rising

Memoir of a Black Panther Party Captain

Aaron Dixon

Foreword by Judson L. Jeffries

HaymarketBooks
Chicago, Illinois

Published in 2012 by Haymarket Books
PO Box 180165
Chicago, IL 60618
www.haymarketbooks.org
773–583–7884

ISBN: 978-1-60846-178-3

Trade distribution:
In the US, Consortium Book Sales and Distribution, www.cbsd.com
In Canada, Publishers Group Canada, www.pgcbooks.ca
In the UK, Turnaround Publisher Services, www.turnaround-uk.com
In Australia, Palgrave Macmillan, www.palgravemacmillan.com.au
All other countries, Publishers Group Worldwide, www.pgw.com

Cover design by Erin Schell. Cover image is a portrait of Aaron Dixon that appeared on the cover of *Seattle* magazine in October 1968.

Published with the generous support of Lannan Foundation
and the Wallace Global Fund.

Printed in Canada by union labor on FSC® certified stock.

Library of Congress cataloging-in-publication data is available.

10 9 8 7 6 5 4 3 2 1

Contents

A Party Divided: The Split

The End of the Line

My People Are Rising *is dedicated to the memory of my father and all the fallen comrades of the Black Panther Party.*

for a slave of natural death who dies
can't balance out to two dead flies

—Alprentice "Bunchy" Carter, "Black Mother"

Some names have been changed to protect the privacy of those individuals.

Foreword

Aaron Dixon has written an extraordinary book that is grounded in the ordinary. He tells the story of a boy's journey into adulthood. Born in the heartland of America, Dixon takes the reader on a trek that begins in Chicago, travels to Seattle, and takes a detour to the Bay Area, with stops in Texas before finally returning to the Pacific Northwest many years later.

My People Are Rising is filled with heart-pounding stories and gripping accounts of Dixon's life both as a civilian and as a member of the Black Panther Party in Seattle and the Bay Area. The product of a healthy, two-parent home, Dixon experienced a supportive and loving home life of the type that many kids, regardless of race, long for. To understand how Dixon became the leader of the first chapter of the Black Panther Party outside of California, one must have an appreciation for the history of activism within the Dixon family. Dixon's father was an admirer, student, and follower of both Paul Robeson and Dr. Martin Luther King Jr. Hence, neither Dixon's parents nor his friends were surprised when, as a teenager, he decided to join the Black Panther Party. Even if Dixon surprised himself at times, he could not escape the fact that activism was in his gene pool; it was a part of who he was. Dixon's two younger brothers followed suit and also joined the party, making their commitment to the Black Panther Party a family affair.

My People Are Rising is neither a tell-all work nor a sensational or score-settling diatribe, elements that have characterized a number of autobiographical accounts during the last twenty years or so, especially where the Black Panther Party is concerned. Nowhere in the book does Dixon denigrate or speak ill of anyone inside or out of the Black Panther Party. Instead, Dixon's book is a rich, down-to-earth story of his life, much of which chronicles the day-to-day goings-on in the most widely known of the Black Power groups and arguably the most effective Black revolutionary organization of the latter half of the twentieth century. As a member of the Black Panther Party, Dixon spends the better part of his young adult life as a soldier on the front lines of the Black Power Movement. The decision to do so, however, comes with great personal sacrifice.

Dixon puts a human face on the many young people who, like him, left the secure confines of home, risked their lives, and devoted themselves to the struggle for Black liberation. Dixon is particularly effective in enabling the reader to visualize the many women Panthers who not only helped keep the party afloat but also played an integral part in the Black Panther Party's success. The book introduces us to a number of vivid characters and stand-up men and women who have heretofore not gotten much attention from previous writers, including Leon "Valentine" Hobbs, one of the party's unsung heroes.

I would especially encourage young people to read this book, as it provides a perfect illustration of the impact that young men and women made in Black communities throughout the country during the 1960s, 1970s, and 1980s.

Dixon also paints a more complete portrait of the Black Panther Party than have most writers. The Black Panther Party consisted of more than just patrols of the police and the Free Breakfast for School Children Program. By discussing the Panthers' broad array of community-focused Survival Programs, Dixon provides the reader with an accurate and balanced depiction of the party's activities generally and in Seattle specifically.

Dixon, a stand-up guy, has written a stand-up book about his life before, during, and after the Black Panther Party. *My People Are Rising* deserves a broad hearing. This is a book that will, in fact, appeal to readers of all ages, regardless of their political persuasion or their opinions of the Black Panther Party, the most maligned and misrepresented organization of the twentieth century.

Judson L. Jeffries, PhD
Professor of African American and African Studies, The Ohio State University, and author of *Huey P. Newton, The Radical Theorist*; *Comrades, A Local History of the Black Panther Party*; and *On the Ground: The Black Panther Party in Communities Across America*.

Acknowledgments

On August 27, 1989, Huey P. Newton was gunned down on a lonely street in West Oakland, not far from one of the old National Headquarters of the Black Panther Party. Three days later a memorial service for our embattled leader was held in Seattle. At the service I was approached by Anna Johnson, the former owner of Open Hand Publishing. She asked me if I would be interested in writing a book about my experience in the party.

And thus began a journey of more than two decades, as I attempted to tell my story and the stories of so many others regarding one of the most significant, most intriguing, and brightest moments in modern American history. Writing this memoir has not been an easy task for a single parent suffering from some form of undiagnosed PTSD, raising not only my own kids but also the kids of others because the traditional family system had collapsed. It took a lot of support and encouragement, at times seemingly an entire village, to bring this project to completion. So I must acknowledge and thank all those who have helped along the way.

During the earlier years, a number of people helped the manuscript get off the ground. My first typist was from Pike Place Typing Service, which kindly provided discounted typing service, and later, my friend Pam, who worked for the City of Seattle, donated her time to typing my handwritten pages. My good friend Virginia Wyman stepped up to provide valuable assistance and support. Dean Patton worked with me as a writing coach. Deborah Green, the widow of Dr. John Green, volunteered her time to edit the first draft of the manuscript. And I am thankful to my good friend Gilda Sheppard, faculty at Evergreen Tacoma, for reminding me that I had a lot to say.

I thank all my Panther comrades. If not named directly here in these acknowledgments, my gratitude and love for my Panther comrades are in the pages of this memoir. Bill Jennings of the website It's About Time BPP fielded my constant questions and gave me ongoing reminders to finish this book. Bobby Seale had long phone conversations with me, discussing details. Emory Douglas provided steady encouragement, as did Leila McDowell. My good friend Valentine Hobbs and I had daily conversations about our years in the party. I am amazed how the memories of those days are fresh in our minds. I'd also like to thank original BSU members Larry Gossett and Gary Owens, who have become my close friends over the years.

I want to express my appreciation to Anthony Arnove and Haymarket Press for recognizing the importance and value of *My People are Rising*. I could not have asked for a better editor in Caroline Luft, who seemed to know about everything from football to music to politics. Her patience and commitment to the project were invaluable.

I thank my family for always being available for information as well as inspiration. My mother allowed me to call her day and night to ask her questions—at times redundant—about our family history and her memories of the turbulent years of the '60s and '70s. My brothers, Elmer and Michael, and my sister, Joanne, provided ever-present support. My cousin Mark shared so much valuable information about my father's side of the family. I thank my children—Aaron Patrice, Nisaa Laketa, Venishia, Aziza, Asha, and Zain—for their joyous curiosity about their dad's writing a book, and for their love and strength. Also in my heart are my grandkids Fela, Iyanna, Grace, Natasha, Daisia, Syrena, Miko, and Taliyah, and my great-grandchildren, twins Xamaria and Xavier, for the hope and peace they bring into this world of uncertainty.

And the one person who, above all, helped me and cajoled me in making this book worthy of publication is my partner, Farah Nousheen. For the past seven years we have worked together on this project as if we were one, even while she was immersed in completing her BA and master's degrees, and in post–9/11 activism in the South Asian community.

Lastly and very importantly, I express my utmost gratitude to all my friends, comrades, and the people of Seattle, especially those who kept on asking me, year after year, "Hey, Aaron, when's your book comin' out?" At last, I have an answer.

Our Family Journey Begins

The Dixon family. Back row, left to right: Mommy, Poppy, Joanne. Front row, left to right: me, Michael, Elmer. Chicago, summer 1964.

1

Ancestors

Southern trees bear strange fruit,
Blood on the leaves and blood at the root,
Black bodies swinging in the Southern breeze,
Strange fruit hanging from the poplar trees.
—Billie Holiday, "Strange Fruit," 1939

On a hot, muggy night during the tumultuous and wild summer of 1968, I crouched in waiting, along with three comrades, clutching my carbine tightly with sweaty hands. We were silently waiting for our prey. No, this was not Vietnam; it was Seattle. The riots had raged for three nights, much like the other rebellions that scorched across America that summer, from Newark to Chicago to Los Angeles. These rebellions would leave hundreds of people dead, wounded, and imprisoned, as well as endless blocks of burned-out, ravaged buildings, standing as a lasting memory of the anger of Black America. I did not know, nor did I care, whether I would survive that night or, for that matter, the many other nights we took to the streets to seek our revenge.

It was only a few months earlier that Martin Luther King Jr. had been assassinated, and just a few years since the assassinations of Malcolm X and Medgar Evers. These deaths were still fresh in our minds and hearts, as were the countless deaths of the lesser-known victims of American racism. For more than three hundred years, Black people in America had been denied basic civil rights, first when they were ripped from their African homelands and sold into slavery in the New World, then, after Emancipation, under the racist system of Jim Crow laws and segregation. The uprisings of the '60s, erupting with volcanic force throughout Black America, sent a loud and clear signal that the time of silence and complacency was at an end. Taking up arms against the racist power structure was a powerful move toward liberating our streets, our cities, our communities, not only for Black Americans in our time but also for those who had come before, and those who would follow.

Thus, my story, and the stories of so many others, begins not in 1968 but hundreds of years earlier, when the first Black slaves set foot on this sacred land of the red man. Yes, the ashes of our ancestors are long gone, and memories of them have long since dissipated. Yet their struggles, their strength, their courage, and their wisdom, along with their failings and flaws, will always be with us, pushing us, encouraging us, and watching over us as we navigate our way through the life ahead. For most of us whose ancestors were dragged ashore, shackled, bewildered, and despairing, it is difficult to tell where our stories begin or end.

I know very little of my slave ancestry, and even less about Mariah, a small, bowlegged Black slave woman in Durant, Mississippi, where she lived, toiled, and died thousands of miles away from her ancestral homeland. In 1858, under the old slave laws that did not legally recognize marriage between enslaved people, she married Frank Kimes, a half-Irish and half-Black mulatto man, as he was described by the census. They officially remarried after Emancipation. Mississippi, like most Southern states, was an inhospitable place for most newly freed slaves. Many remained in bondage or worked as indentured servants under the Black Codes, laws enacted after Emancipation by the Southern states to restrict the rights of Black people, keeping them in servitude. Worse developments were to come with the reign of terror under Jim Crow laws, starting the 1870s, which included mandatory segregation, the elimination of the rights to vote and to bear arms, forced imprisonment, and hideous acts of lynching.

My maternal great-great-grandmother, Emma, one of Mariah's four daughters, was born August 2, 1868, three years after the end of the Civil War. Emma grew up in a small house in Durant under the watchful eye of Mariah, now a free woman, free to raise her five children according to her own will. When I was a little boy, Emma would tell us stories of her childhood, such as how her mother would sit on the porch and keep an eagle eye on her children as she instructed them in the art of doing laundry. Emma also told us how, when she was a young child, the local Cherokees attempted to kidnap her, thinking she was one of their own because of her long black hair. Emma left home at eighteen to marry Mr. Joseph Ely, who worked as a brakeman for the railroad. Emma worked as a laundress, one of the few occupations available to a Black woman during the late 1800s in Mississippi. In the early 1900s, her husband died a tragic death on the job in a railroad accident. Emma went on to live a very long life, surviving uterine cancer, and she gave birth to eight children, only four of whom lived beyond childhood.

One of Emma's surviving girls was Mabel, my great-grandmother, who according to many was very beautiful. Mabel did the unthinkable— she had an affair and became pregnant by a German-Jewish man, Mr. John William Brown. This affair and pregnancy led to her being ostracized from her family and community, and resulted in the birth of a daughter, Willy Joe—my grandmother. Named after her father, later she was raised as "Josephine." Mabel departed this world far too early, at the age of twenty-three, dying of "consumption," the earlier name for tuberculosis.

Josephine was only three years old when her grandmother Emma took her in. The fact that Josephine looked more white than anything else presented problems for her grandmother. Southern social rules of the time dictated that a child who appeared to be white should not be seen in the company of an adult who was obviously Black. Soon, the decision was made that Josephine would go live with one of her mother's sisters, Aunt Marie, in Chicago, where racial rules were slightly less restrictive. Aunt Marie's husband, Uncle Milton, had graduated from Lane College, a boarding school in Tennessee. He was employed with the post office. They lived with their three kids in a big Victorian house on a large plot of land on Chicago's far Southside, where they grew much of their own food and ran a family ice cream parlor. My grandmother often talked about working long hours in the ice cream parlor and performing many other chores while the other kids played.

There was one thing that my grandmother wished more than anything else, and that was to be able to take piano lessons just as Aunt Marie's kids did. But she was denied that opportunity, something my grandmother would never forget. Her unhappy stay with Aunt Marie added to the anger and confusion she already felt. Although Aunt Marie herself was mixed, she could never really accept her sister's half-white daughter. When Josephine turned twelve, her grandmother Emma made the long train trip up from Mississippi to Chicago and took Josephine back to Durant, and eventually sent her away to boarding school.

Black boarding schools were a saving grace for those Black families who could afford to send their older kids away to be educated and prepared to enter the segregated US society. Boarding school was a place to meet others and build camaraderie during the remaining years of youth. That is where Josephine met my grandfather, Roy Sledge, a dapper, handsome young man. It is said that Roy's family history in America begins with the story of an African princess, enslaved and brought to the shores of the New World, who eventually married a Cherokee chief. Roy's father, Cyrus Sledge, was the only Black blacksmith for miles around in Como, Mississippi, and was often seen riding his white horse through the countryside.

Although Roy had only one suit, he carried himself as if he owned a whole closet full. It wasn't long before Josephine, strong-willed, and Roy, mellow and calm, married, and Josephine gave birth to my mother, Frances Emma Sledge, in 1925. They soon joined more than a million other Black Americans in the Great Migration to the North of the 1900s, looking for more opportunity and freedom than what they had experienced in the Jim Crow South.

Roy found work in Chicago as a railway porter, and Josephine, who passed as white, took a variety of jobs before finding permanent work as a waitress in a restaurant, where she eventually retired after thirty-four years. It is interesting to note that the entire time Josephine worked there, neither her customers nor her employers had any inkling that she was of mixed race. This was a common practice among Blacks light enough to pass.

Roy and Josephine struggled at times, even separating on numerous occasions. Roy's personal battle with alcohol caused him to lose his job with the railroad. Josephine had to move to St. Paul and back to Chicago before Roy, at thirty-two, was able to get a handle on his drinking and reunite with his family. With assistance from Josephine's uncle Milton, Roy landed a much-coveted job at the post office, where he worked until retirement. His tools for maintaining his sobriety were the Bible and the *Christian Science Monitor*, which he read diligently in silence every day after work.

Josephine was determined that her daughter would have the best of whatever she could provide, sending her to the best schools, starting her on the piano at age five, and finding the best piano instructors. At age seven, Frances was acknowledged as a child prodigy and began giving recitals and concerts in Milwaukee and Chicago. Josephine was relentless in her desire for her daughter to become an accomplished pianist, since the opportunity had been denied her. She would often set straight those white teachers who tried to rebuff her about teaching her brown child.

My mother graduated from high school at fifteen. After graduation, she refused to go any further on the piano. Ten years of having her knuckles swatted with rulers by stern teachers and the many hours of practice had pushed her to the point of no return. She was no longer interested in being a serious pianist. She tried modeling for a while and enrolled at Hamlin University in St. Paul before eventually settling into studies at Chicago Teachers College in 1944.

In 1943, my father was across town, preparing to graduate from Inglewood High School. Elmer Dixon Jr. was born in 1924 in Henderson, Kentucky, to Elmer and Mildred Dixon. Their family also joined the Great Migration to the North, landing in Chicago in the mid-1920s. Despite Chicago's own form of segregation and racist practices, Chicago and other northern cities would provide a launching pad for the coming Black middle class.

My paternal grandmother, Mildred West, was one of the many grandchildren of Amanda Brooks, an enslaved woman whose father was the slave master on the Arnett plantation in Henderson, Kentucky. Mildred's family traveled a different road out of slavery than did my mother's family. When the Civil War broke out, Mildred's grandfather, Richard Brooks, and her great-uncle escaped the plantation to join the Union Army, becoming some of the first slaves to join the Union forces. After the war ended, the slave master and his family abandoned the plantation and headed to Colorado. Mildred's grandfather and great-uncle each received a government allotment for having fought in the war. Combining that with the slave master's land, which Amanda Brooks inherited, the family founded their own town and gave it the family name, Brookstown.

As a young boy in Chicago, I always marveled at my grandmother's oak dressers with marble tops, the two leather rocking chairs, and the other fine antiques in her house. Many years later she would tell me that those items had once belonged to the family's slave master. My grandmother DeDe, as she was known, always talked so proudly of her family and their history. She once told me that her grandmother had her thumb chopped off for refusing the advances of a slave master. But DeDe was always happy and carefree; she did not appear to have suffered any of the effects of the slave legacy that I saw in my mother's family. The only time I saw a hint of sadness in her eyes was when she talked about her brother Clifton, whom she described as very handsome and debonair, a star athlete, and college-bound until he was killed in a tragic car accident.

DeDe's husband, Elmer the First, was a large, strong man with big olive eyes and a heart of gold. Little is known about his family. When he was just an infant, Elmer's father left Kentucky and headed for St. Louis, where he became one of the nation's few Black millionaires. But he never acknowledged his son, creating a tremendous void in my grandfather's life as well as depriving our family of any connection to the Dixon name and history. DeDe located her husband's father and wrote to him on numerous occasions with the hope that he would come forth to acknowledge his son, but he never responded.

So my grandfather took the deep pain of rejection and pushed it deep down inside, putting all his energy into his own family. He found work in Chicago with a wealthy Jewish family and did well enough that his wife never needed to work outside the home. She devoted her time to raising her son, Elmer Jr., and his older sister, Doris. DeDe also became a leader in her community and cofounded the Woodlawn Organization, which would have a long, rich history of community building in Chicago. When she wasn't spoiling my father and his sister, she hosted bridge and tea parties with friends and often spent time writing poetry.

My father grew up in this protective family and the community cocoon of Chicago's Southside, playing football with his good friend, Buddy Young, one of the first great Black college football players to come out of Chicago. My father's artistic talents led him to start taking classes at the Art Institute of Chicago, and he eventually received a scholarship to the institute, the most prestigious art school in the country. But college would have to wait.

One afternoon, my father, captain of the Inglewood High School ROTC, was sitting with his buddies in the Regal Theater. He and his three best friends, fellow ROTC classmates, were known as the "Four Feathers," after the title of the 1939 movie. As they sat watching the newsreels before the movie, on the screen came footage of atrocities committed by the Japanese against US soldiers. At the newsreel's conclusion, he and his friends jumped up and ran down to the navy recruitment center, as the navy was my father's first choice. With enthusiasm, he told the naval officer on duty that he wanted to enlist then and there. The white officer shot back, "We don't take boys like you." My father was shocked, angered, and greatly disappointed. It was a rejection he would not forget.

Just months later, on the day he graduated high school, he received his draft notice. My grandfather escorted his only son down to the induction center. A large man, my grandfather dwarfed his son as he prepared to hand him over to the unknown. Neither of them had any idea what the trials ahead would present.

My grandmother could not bear for her son to leave. She was a doting mother, and her son and daughter meant the world to her. She told me that when her son left to go to war, she let loose a sound of anguish so deep and so pained that it could be heard by many of her neighbors. The thought of her little boy, now a man, going off to war and facing possible death was almost too much for her to bear. But he was determined to go. Finally resigned to the fact that her son had gone, she penned the following poem, published in a local paper in 1943:

To My Son

Oh, how I miss you my son,
And the tricks you played in fun.
I miss your loud laughter and tumbled room
And your constant juggling of the kitchen broom.

How I miss your begging for pie,
And saying in fun, that for sweets you would die.
I miss the gang who would come to the door
Just as you started to scrub the floor.

There are many things I miss, since you went away,
As I wander through the quiet house each day;
Praying to Him, who is above
To send back to me the son I love.

At boot camp in Kentucky, my father and his friends were assigned to the famed Seventh Cavalry, a fact that made him very proud. In preparation for war, they learned about weapons and proper use in discharging them, as well as techniques of hand-to-hand combat. They were also whipped into top physical shape, running and marching in the Kentucky countryside, where my father was bitten by a rattlesnake while marching in the field. He also experienced constant haranguing from some brothers about his light-brown complexion. After boot camp, the green recruits were ready to confront the enemy. But they would soon find out that the enemy was not the one they expected. The young, exuberant Black soldiers were loaded onto a train with the windows covered and issued helmets with the letter "M" painted on them. The recruits thought the "M" meant they were being shipped out to Michigan, or maybe Minnesota. They had no idea that their destination was Mississippi. My father had never been south of Kentucky, let alone as far as Mississippi.

The legacy of slavery in the South was still intact in 1943. My father and his friends had heard the stories of lynching and brutality against Blacks, and of the segregation that was far worse than in Chicago. But for a wide-eyed young man, none of those things mattered, or maybe they sounded too extreme to be true. He and the others had no idea what shocks and dangers awaited them in the Deep South.

The segregated South and the segregated US Army presented serious problems for Black soldiers. On the army base, they were treated with disdain. Off the base, their lives were often in danger. The mere sight of a Black man in uniform could often be enough to incite violence from whites. There were three main incidents in Mississippi that reshaped my father's understanding of his country and what it meant to be Black in America.

The first trial took place on a dusty road as Black soldiers marched in formation, carrying their packs and unloaded weapons. Led by their white officers, they had been marching for hours in the hot, humid Southern sun, fighting off the aggravating mosquitoes, sweat running down their brown faces, marching across cotton fields where Black slaves had once toiled in the heat of the day for the white master. Finally they came to a large field with a faded red barn. Standing there to greet them was a white man in dingy overalls, holding a double-barreled shotgun.

"You niggers stop right there!" he barked out.

The commanding officer put up his right hand slightly for his tired troops to halt. He replied, "Sir, my men and I need to march across your field so we can avoid the swamp."

The white man's face remained emotionless. As far as he was concerned these niggers should still be in chains, heads bowed, shuffling along. Pointing his shotgun at the men as he spoke, he said, "Ain't no niggers gonna march across my field." The words came out of his mouth finite and resolute.

In other circumstances, most of the Chicago men would have rushed the gun-toting white man. They had been in their share of racial brawls in Chicago, but this was not the time or the place to fight back. And even though the white man was outnumbered, there was no doubt among the men or the officers that he would use his weapon. At the officer's command, the exhausted men turned around and marched into the swamp. Later that evening the men set up camp, ate their rations, and bedded down. Once the white officers were asleep, my father led a group of his friends back to the farmer's land and torched his field and the red barn. It is difficult for me to imagine what was going through my father's mind or the minds of his fellow conspirators. For young Black men from Chicago to commit such an act in the heartland of Jim Crow America in 1943 represented either sheer insanity or tremendous defiance.

The second incident occurred while my father was on furlough in the local town not far from the base. He had met a pretty, young Black woman who was very light-skinned and probably passed for white on occasion. They had spent the day at the edge of town enjoying the sunny weather and each other's company, as any young couple on a first date might do. As evening approached, the young lady announced that it was getting late and she had better get home before dark.

My father responded, "I'll walk you home."

His friend began to get anxious and nervously replied, "Oh, I think you better not do that."

But my father, being a true Chicago boy, brought up to respect tradition and the old-fashioned cultural values of honor and chivalry, persisted. Back home in Chicago, the proper thing to do was to escort your date home. Even though the young woman protested that he should not walk her home, my father insisted on continuing with his escort, oblivious to the line he was crossing. They set out on the walk across town, which took them out in public. My father was dressed smartly in his uniform, hat tilted to the side, smiling a happy-go-lucky grin as he often did. His young female companion was nervous and doubtful. First it was the threatening stares and the whispering from passersby. And then, there on the sidewalk stood the town sheriff, his red neck almost bursting through the stained collar of a brown shirt and his stomach bulging over the belt that held his service revolver. The sheriff wasn't quite sure what he saw. He had seen these nigger soldiers all spruced up in their brown uniforms, and had put many of them in their place, and maybe he'd done more than that. But now, this nigger appeared to be walking with a white girl.

He looked my father in the face and said, "Nigger, when I come back here, you better be gone."

My father continued walking with his date. They just happened to be passing a post office, so he and his date went inside. He wrote a postcard to his mother, describing the danger he was in and what had been happening to him and his fellow Black soldiers in the Deep South. He asked for a stamp and mailed the postcard. Then he continued across town with his date, walking toward her home. He made it back to the base unharmed but was shaken by what had occurred. When his mother received the postcard, she wrote to Eleanor Roosevelt, the wife of the president, telling Mrs. Roosevelt about her son's dire situation and that of the other Black soldiers on the army base.

Some time later came the third incident. On a Sunday morning, my father and the other Black soldiers were preparing to go on furlough when orders came that their furlough had been canceled. Instead, they were ordered to clean the latrines in the white soldiers' barracks. This was the last straw. All the incidents since they had been in the Deep South came to a head and exploded on that Sunday. Anger and rage and defiance all collided and ignited as the Black soldiers broke out in rebellion. They smashed up the furniture, beds, and anything else from the barracks they could propel out into the yard. They lit fires and refused all orders to disperse. Their rebellion continued for almost three days. Finally, a train pulled into the camp, and all the Black soldiers from that Mississippi base were taken out of the South. My grandmother always believed that Eleanor Roosevelt had played a role in relocating the Black soldiers and delivering her son to safety.

After stops for further training at Fort Lewis in Washington State and at Pearl Harbor, my father and his friends stepped aboard an amphibian craft in the Pacific, clutching their weapons, preparing to storm the beach.

They fought ferocious battles in Luzon, Philippines, and Okinawa, Japan, facing young, eighteen- and nineteen-year-old Japanese soldiers who were encountering the onslaught of the US Army, newly rebuilt and expanded following the attack on Pearl Harbor. For the young Japanese soldiers, it was their last stand, a fight of desperation, which made for an extremely tough adversary. The battles were brutal; many men perished on both sides. My father remembers that, after one battle, he found himself standing, blood splattered all over him, bodies of the enemy scattered about, and only a handful of his comrades still alive, including the two brothers who had harassed him in boot camp, trembling in fear in the trench.

He also told me a story about patrolling through the jungle and coming face-to-face with a Japanese soldier. For a split second they looked at each other, before my father was able to get off the first shot. He then rushed to the side of the young Japanese soldier, pulled out his first aid kit, and patched up the bullet wound as much as he could. He located the young soldier's wallet and opened it. Inside was a picture of the soldier with his wife and child, which my father let the soldier look at. My father comforted him and gave him water from his canteen before leaving his side.

In Okinawa, my father witnessed something that would change him forever, and almost cost him his life. After a fierce battle, during the mop-up, he saw a US Marine cut off a breast of a dead Japanese woman and hold it up on his bayonet. This barbaric act incited such rage in my father that he raised his machine gun and prepared to fire on the white marine, but his comrades stopped him. He had witnessed a lot of bloodshed by soldiers on both sides, but in no way did he expect to witness such inhumane cruelty toward civilians. Because of this incident, he went AWOL in Seoul, Korea, where Japanese families had also fled. He spent time with a Japanese family after meeting a young Japanese woman named Myoka, eventually returning to his post in order to avoid court-martial.

Finally, the war was over and my father returned home, bringing with him the spoils of war: two samurai swords, a 7.62 sniper rifle, a much-prized Japanese machine pistol, a Filipino bolo knife, several Japanese kimonos, and a picture of him and Myoka. Those first few weeks at home he said very little or nothing about his experiences until one evening at dinner, his mother asked him, "Well, son, what happened over there?" With that, all the emotions he had been holding back from Mississippi to Okinawa came flooding out, and he began to tell his many stories.

At last he was able to put the nightmare behind him, and he reunited with his Chicago friends, going out to parties, dancing and drinking at the city's great ballrooms, built in the 1920s. He joined Paul Robeson's Progressive Party and began attending their meetings. He also started school at the Art Institute of Chicago.

One evening at a party he was introduced to a young girl named Frances, my mother, and it was not long before they agreed to begin a family journey together.

2

Our Family Journey Begins

The house I live in,
The friends that I have found,
The folks beyond the railroad
and the people all around,
The worker and the farmer,
the sailor on the sea,
The men who built this country,
that's America to me.

— Paul Robeson, "The House I Live In," 1947

I entered into this world in the dead of winter, not far from the cold, windy shores of Lake Michigan, on January 2, 1949, almost four years after the bloodiest of wars and shortly before the beginning of the Korean conflict. By the time my parents finished their personal baby boom, there were four little Dixons and one who did not make it. Diane, a victim of premature birth, paved the way for my entrance. For many years I felt I was living life for both of us. I always imagined what she would have looked like if she had safely made the trip. Joanne came first, taking the crown as the oldest, then came Diane's short stay, then I arrived, and then sixteen months later, Elmer III emerged into the world. Finally, after two years had passed, Michael, the youngest, made his debut.

We lived with my father's parents for a couple of years on Chicago's

Southside, at Langley Avenue and 51st Street, while my father completed his studies at the Art Institute of Chicago. When I was about three years old we moved from Chicago to Champaign, Illinois. My father was offered a job as a technical illustrator at Chanute Air Force Base, which put his artistic pursuits on hold. We settled into Birch Village, formerly a military housing facility for air force pilots stationed at the base and their families. It would be our home for the next five years.

Birch Village was made up of dozens of cement brick blocks in clusters, each two stories high, with cold gray cement floors. Though the place looked drab from the outside, this in no way reflected the true character of the village. Many of the families were just like ours, fathered by upstart young Black men who had returned from World War II. These were men who had fought their way out of boot camp in the South just for the right to die in Europe or the Pacific. Their wives were hardworking, strong-willed women. Birch Village was like one big family. You could go anywhere in the village, any time of day, and feel secure.

Here, our family struggled through the same adjustments as most young families. Our parents strove to feed and raise four hungry, needy kids, each with a distinctive personality and specific demands, while my mother and father shifted their focus to parenthood after having spent their earlier lives worrying only about themselves. At twenty-one, my mother had been one year shy of graduating from teachers college before my sister and brothers and I came on the scene. Her time would now be devoted to washing, feeding, loving, disciplining, hugging, and teaching four inquisitive young people.

Joanne coined the names for all the elders in our family. My parents were known as Mommy and Poppy, my father's parents were called DeDe and Grandada, and my mother's parents were called Ma and Bop Bop.

Everything seemed perfect and safe during those early years of my life in Birch Village. Everyone looked out for one another. As kids, we roamed around the entire perimeter of the village without a worry or care, getting into mischief and playing hide-and-seek and "Crash the Circle." In the winter we built snow forts and snowmen, and sometimes huddled against the front door of the house, trying to stay warm, wishing Mommy would let us in. But with four kids, our staying in the two-bedroom house all day was not an option. When naptime came, all four of us had to go to our room whether we wanted to nap or not. My good friends Lyn and

Ricky lived in the end unit; their family had just arrived from Mississippi. We spent the night at each other's houses and walked to school together. It seemed like we would be friends forever.

One of the elders of the village was Mrs. Nailer, toothless and hair in disarray. We kids would sneak into her house, which was full of jars with weird things held in their confines. Everyone looked out for Mrs. Nailer. The only white people we ever saw were the milkman and the bread man, who would sometimes give us hungry kids free jelly rolls.

On a day I remember vividly, my brothers Elmer and Michael followed me down past the fence around the village's perimeter and over a set of railroad tracks to a large rock quarry. We excitedly climbed the rock mountains as our feet sank in the gravel. We got stuck in a tar pit, barely able to haul ourselves out once we heard Mommy calling us: "Aaron! Elmer! Michael!" We clambered back over the fence with tar-covered shoes and pant legs. I think that was the very first time the three of us ventured out together to do something we knew we weren't supposed to be doing.

Mommy got a part-time job playing the piano at the local church, and at night, Poppy worked a second job making pizzas. I still remember those nights when, after work, he would bring home delicious Italian pizzas to us waiting kids. And on weekends, Mommy and Poppy would go out to parties with friends from the village, drinking scotch and bourbon, dancing the Bebop and the Swing.

During the summers, Poppy worked in Champaign while Mommy and us kids went up to Chicago to spend those months with Grandada and DeDe, and Ma and Bop Bop. They happened to live around the corner from each other: Grandada and DeDe lived on 71st and Calumet and Ma and Bop Bop lived on 69th and Prairie. At night, out in the yard, we would chase lightning bugs with our cousins Mark and Keith, known as KeKe. On quiet days I sometimes went upstairs at Ma and Bop Bop's to talk to Gramma, my mother's great-grandmother Emma, and listened to her stories of old while I brushed her long, silky, gray hair, looking into her big, ancient, brown eyes and touching her leathery, wrinkled skin. I loved spending those quiet times with her. They were the only connection I had to our family's long, sometimes difficult and painful history.

When I was five years old, Gramma became very ill and requested that my mother send me from Champaign to her bedside in Chicago. Of course, Mommy thought it was rather ridiculous to summon a five-year-old from almost two hundred miles away, and so I did not go. Gramma passed away not long after at the age of ninety-four, taking with her almost a century of history encompassing the African American experience. I would miss those summer visits when I sneaked upstairs to sit in silence, holding her caramel hands. Perhaps I reminded her of someone or something from her past. She reminded me of something I could not quite comprehend, yet I understood our special connection. Her face, her scratchy voice, her sometimes cranky disposition would always be there with me, following me, whispering to me, protecting me, and guiding me.

When it came time for me to start kindergarten, I was not ready to leave my mother's side. I must have cried the whole day. First grade was easier, since I started the school year with my new friends, taking shortcuts home through the Negro League baseball field, getting chased by the old Black caretaker, barely making it over the fence, and laughing from the fear of almost getting caught. By the third grade I dreamed of someday soon running with the Birch Village Cats, the neighborhood gang. I often saw them chasing their rivals, the Alley Cats, kids who lived outside the village. That was the first time I remember yearning to belong to a group. Up north in Chicago I had seen the hastily written chalk words of the Blackstone Rangers, Chicago's largest gang, scrawled on walls and buildings throughout the Southside. I often wondered if I would join the Rangers when I got older.

One night in 1956, there was a knock on the door, and standing in the doorway were two white men dressed in dark suits. Poppy didn't let the men in. He exchanged words with them and then hastily closed the door. He later told me that these men in the dark suits were from the FBI and they had come to question him about his involvement in the Communist Party.

Poppy had been part of Paul Robeson's youth security contingent when Robeson had appeared at Soldier Field in Chicago in the '40s. Paul Robeson was an almost mythic figure in Black American history. A two-time All-American football player, he graduated from Columbia Law School, played professional football, and then went on to become a world-renowned and highly paid stage actor and singer. He toured the world as a performer and as an ambassador of social justice, and his speeches packed Soldier Field in Chicago during the '40s. Committed to justice for all working people, Robeson joined the Communist Party, which led to his being blacklisted and banned from international travel, and many recordings of his performances and speeches were destroyed. After returning from the war, Poppy, inspired by Robeson, had attended some Communist Party meetings in an effort to try to understand what had happened to him and others in the Deep South.

There was another incident of savage racism that affected Poppy deeply. In August 1955, Emmett Till, a fourteen-year-old Black teenager from Chicago, was visiting relatives in Mississippi. He made the fatal mistake of speaking to a white woman. That night, a truckload of white men abducted him from his uncle's home and took him down by the river, where they tortured and brutally beat him to death. His mother had the courage to leave his casket open during the funeral in Chicago. The pictures of little Emmett Till's tortured body were seen by millions of Black Americans, thanks to the work of *Jet* magazine and other Black publications. Finally, the terror of the Jim Crow South was exposed to the world. The murder of Emmett Till had a profound effect on Poppy. It brought back a flood of memories of his personal experiences in Mississippi and laid bare the hypocrisy of the United States.

In response to this tragic murder, Poppy wrote this poem:

Deep in the heart of Dixie
Where the cotton blooms in June
An old black man tills the field
Humming a sad tune.

His heart was heavy, his eyes were full
His body aching and sore
I wish I was dead, I wish I was dead
My heart can't take no more.

They took a little Negro boy
And chopped and smashed his eye
They tormented, teased, and cut him up
Just to make him die.

They tore off an ear, when he shed a tear
And they beat him in the face
Each mark and scar was symbolic of suffering
By the Negro race.

They threw him in the river
His hands and legs all bound.

Hoping that his body
Never would be found.

The river current surged and splashed
To free its mangled prey
But it didn't matter anymore
For it was Emmett's Judgment Day.

The two White men who did these things
Are free to lynch and kill
Now my God I pray to you
Avenge poor Emmett Till.

The hate and evil in this world
Is something sad to see
Why Oh Lord do they hate us so
Why can't we all be free?

The children played on the courtroom floor
The grownups drank cold beer
They laughed and joked, and enjoyed themselves,
Like they had no God to fear.

I'll never forget you, Emmett Till
And how you horribly died
I'll never forget the smiling jurors
And how the lawyers lied.

Well Emmett's gone, ain't nothing to do
But push this White man's plow
I guess little Emmett's made his peace
'Cause he's with his father now.

—Elmer J. Dixon Jr., Champaign, Illinois, October 1955

Poppy never spoke of this horrific crime again, but his poem was always there for us kids as a reminder of what horrible injustices Black people faced in America. By the time I was ten years old, I had memorized this poem and often took it to school to share with others.

In 1957, my father received job offers in Spain, Alabama, and a place called Seattle. I was hoping he would choose Spain, but, to my dismay, he chose Seattle, somewhere far away in the northwestern part of the country. At first I felt excitement at the thought of traveling to a distant place and the possibilities of experiencing new things and meeting new people. When it sank in that I would be leaving the only place I had known as home, this safe haven of family and friendly Black faces, I was devastated. I would have to leave all my friends, peculiar old Mrs. Nailer, and the security of Birch Village.

Most of all I would miss the trips to Chicago to visit with Ma and Bop Bop and DeDe and Grandada, as well as my cousins and other relatives scattered throughout the Chicago Southside. I would miss the family barbeques, when Grandada would cook his Kentucky-style barbeque ribs with a strong accent on vinegar. He would wrestle with us kids, letting us ride on his large back and broad shoulders before tickling us to death. On hot nights we sat on his lap while he smoked his pipe or played his harmonica, rubbing his rough, tickly whiskers against our soft brown faces. I would miss watching Bop Bop come home from work at the post office, dressed neatly in a suit and tie, bringing us his bus transfers to use as play money. He would quietly go upstairs to change, come down with his Bible and *Christian Science Monitor*, sit quietly on the corner of the black leather sofa, put his spectacles on over a serious face, and silently read. This was his way of keeping at bay the demons of alcoholism, which he had soundly defeated many years earlier.

I would miss my grandmother DeDe, who always reminisced about the old days, sharing stories of her family, demonstrating the Charleston; my father's sister, Aunt Doris, and my cousins, Mark and Keith; and Ma, dressing us like prissy rich kids, greasing our faces with Vaseline, feeding us non-fried food and wheat bread, and constantly reciting from the Bible.

My grandparents represented everything that we were and hoped to be. Now, we sadly had to leave them behind. I remember Grandada standing there with his bug eyes and thick eyelashes, his stomach bulging over his brown trousers. DeDe stood next to him in the brown flowered dress that she often wore on hot, muggy days.

"Have a safe trip, and, Brother, you be careful, you hear?"

DeDe always affectionately referred to her son as "Brother." We drove off slowly, with us kids looking out the back window at the two figures standing on the green lawn, looking back at us. I would never forget that image.

It took me many years to forgive my parents for taking us out of this haven of comfort. I carried a lot of anger for a long time, not really understanding or caring why. I never quite felt that security, that contentment, that familiarity again.

3

The Search for Home

When the night has come
And the land is dark
And the moon is the only light we'll see
No I won't be afraid, no I won't be afraid
Just as long as you stand, stand by me
                    —Ben E. King, "Stand By Me," 1961

Moving two thousand miles away was a traumatic experience for everyone, especially my mother. I remember her bursting into tears at the sight of the Lake Washington floating bridge, the portal to the Pacific Northwest. Despite her relief at being free from Ma's tight hold on her, Mommy missed her mother and father and Chicago, with its segregated neighborhoods and Midwestern culture, a distinct Black culture that enabled Black people to develop their own system of self-sufficiency. Poppy, in contrast, was an explorer, an adventurer, and an artist. He was sincerely inquisitive about the unknown, the taboo, and was excited about the possibilities that lay ahead. We kids just sat in the back of the '52 Plymouth, looking at the new topography of mountains, evergreen trees, and water, homesick for Grandada and DeDe, Ma and Bop Bop, and our first home, Birch Village.

Those first couple years we must have changed residences and schools three or four times, trying to settle down to something as secure and familiar as what we had left behind. Early in our search for a permanent home, I

23

saw Mommy and Poppy perform an act of compassion that had a lasting effect on me. We were living in a very rundown part of Seattle, on Hiawatha Street. Our two-bedroom flat was dingy and dilapidated, but it provided our family a place to rest after the long trip. One cold, rainy Sunday evening there came a knock on the door. It was an older Black gentleman, dressed in worn, tattered clothing. He had a sad, hopeless look on his face.

He asked, "Can you spare something to eat?"

Mommy and Poppy invited him in. Mommy went into the kitchen and made him a sandwich from the roast she had been preparing for supper, along with chips and cookies, packing all of it neatly in a brown paper bag, and gave him some money as well. It was something I would see Mommy and Poppy do many times over. These acts of kindness helped shape my concern for others.

In 1960, three years after our departure from Birch Village, we moved into our permanent Seattle home, in a mixed neighborhood called Madrona Hill in Seattle's Central District. Across the street from our house was a neighborhood park with a baseball field that doubled as a football field, and at its other end a tennis court. The streets of the neighborhood were lined with large maples and reddish-brown Madrona trees, native to the Pacific Northwest. On our block and the blocks west of us, most of the inhabitants were Black, Chinese, Filipino, and Japanese. We lived on 33rd Avenue. On 34th Avenue and down the hill heading east toward Lake Washington, the residents were mostly white.

Madrona was like a lot of the neighborhoods in central Seattle back then. Formerly occupied largely by Italians and Jews, these neighborhoods were now "in transition," as many Black men and women had returned from WWII and the Korean conflict and moved in. They had served their country and many had worked in munitions factories, helping the United States to victory. Now it was time to enjoy a piece of the pie—and home ownership was part of that pie.

Japanese Americans released from WWII internment camps, who had in many cases lost their homes, businesses, and possessions, also moved to the area. The Central District was the only part of Seattle where Asians, Jews, and Blacks were allowed to live, due to the racist zoning practice known as "redlining" and racial restrictive covenants. In response to the influx of Black and Asian families, many whites had moved out in droves, relocating across Lake Washington and farther south into the suburbs.

Two blocks to the north of us was a small business district with a little Chinese mom-and-pop grocery store, owned and operated by Joe and Mae, who would give credit to anyone in the neighborhood who needed it. On the corner was a Black-owned cleaner, and across the street was a Chinese drugstore. Two Black-owned gas stations stood directly across from one another on 34th and Pike. Nearby were an A&P grocery store and a Bavarian bakery that my parents were very fond of.

Madrona was a little paradise of Asian, white, and Black families, a bit removed from the rest of the city, with Lake Washington as a natural boundary to the east and the Harrison Valley to the west. The park was the hub for all the kids in the neighborhood, the focal point where much of our growth and maturation would take place. It was a battleground of sorts, a training ground for athletic endeavors, a spot to meet friends and acquaintances, and often the scene of physical confrontations.

On hot days we would go down to Collins' Soda Fountain, an old-fashioned soda shop operated by Mr. Collins, a slim, white-haired, elderly white man. We would sit on the twirling stools, surrounded by old wood and leaded glass, sipping hand-mixed sodas or malts or milkshakes. When we were done, Mr. Collins would carefully bring out a wooden box of penny candies, wrapped in waxed paper. Afterward, we would run across the street to the Rental Freezers and take refuge inside the cold store, trying to cool down from the scorching sun. Along with our newfound friends, on summer days my brothers and I would make go-carts with broken roller skates and wooden crates. Or we would make stilts, swords, bows and arrows, and slingshots. We would play marbles on patches of dirt or lag pennies against the wall, winner take all. Sometimes when we needed spending money, we would cut the grass of our neighbors' overgrown lawns.

Our house was large and spacious. Its hardwood floors were softer than the concrete floors in Birch Village. Joanne got her own room, but even though there was an extra room designated as the "TV room," Elmer, Michael, and I had to share a bedroom. The front and rear verandas, extending off the upstairs bedrooms, soon would serve as our escape route out into the night. Sometimes I caught Poppy standing and surveying his new home, beaming with pride and contentment. He brought home young trees and planted them around the house, one for each child. Seattle, especially Madrona, was much more racially and socially diverse and tolerant than the segregated Southside of Chicago had been; for Poppy, that is what his artistic soul needed to heal from the scars of war.

Poppy always sought out people from other cultures. I remember the friendship he struck up with Mr. Aschak, the old Russian man who lived down the street from one of our temporary apartments. Poppy and Mr. Aschak would get together and drink vodka and eat Russian rye bread. Even though Mr. Aschak could barely speak English, he and Poppy seemed to have a genuine liking for each other.

It was not until we got to Seattle that I had any lasting contact with a white person other than schoolteachers. Mr. Santo lived across the street from another of our temporary living quarters. A short, squat, red-faced Italian man in his eighties, he lived in his yellow house by himself. Sometimes we would trample through his well-cultivated garden on our way to raid the cherry trees next to his house, and he would give us a good scolding. I remember sitting in the yard next door with my friend Cornelius Bolton, watching Mr. Santo in the hot sun in his straw hat, working his garden of tomatoes, squash, and beans. He looked up and motioned to us with his hand to come over.

"Have you ever had fried squash?" he asked us in his accented English.

We shook our heads no, looking inquisitive.

"I'll cook you some." He got up and went inside. About three minutes later he came out with fried squash and fried tomatoes that were very tasty. After that we were much more careful of Mr. Santo's garden. Later I learned that he was the father of Ron Santo, the famous all-star third baseman for the Chicago Cubs.

Poppy and Mommy began to make friends in Madrona—artists, musicians, folk dancers, beatniks, communists, a mix of Black, Jewish, and Greek individuals. Our house sometimes resembled an international festival. Once a month the rug was rolled back and the cheese and wine put out as my parents entertained their friends, who all belonged to the same folk-dancing group. It was fun to watch the adults sipping wine and eating cheese, having political discussions before engaging in Greek, Italian, and Jewish traditional dances. On the weekends, Poppy sometimes tried to paint before taking us out on long Sunday drives to explore the natural splendor of the Puget Sound area.

Much of Mommy's time was spent taking care of the family—cooking, cleaning, serving as president of the PTA, watching over us at home, reading us classics such as Edgar Allan Poe, or keeping tabs on us at the park. Not long after we moved into the neighborhood, a couple of the local bullies took a baseball mitt that Elmer had found. They said it was theirs, and it may have been, but the way they snatched it from Elmer did not sit well with Mommy. After Elmer ran home to tell her, within seconds she was out of the house, all 110 pounds of her, yelling and chasing the bullies, Tommy and Delbert. She gave them a good tongue-lashing. They politely gave the baseball mitt back to Elmer, and from that day forward, all the kids in the neighborhood knew Mommy respectfully as Mrs. Dixon.

Even though Poppy had a good job as a technical illustrator at Boeing, Mommy finally had to go to work to help pay the monthly house note. She started working at Christmas and other holidays at Frederick and Nelson, the large department store downtown, battling subtle racism every step of the way. When she went to apply for the job, they said they didn't have an opening, even though it was posted on a sign. She insisted they give her a job and they finally relented. Customers as well as her employers often spoke to her in a disrespectful manner, and she would tell us all about her battles at work. Eventually she got a job as a doctor's assistant at Virginia Mason Hospital, where she worked for many years until retirement. She never got the opportunity to finish teachers college, which had always been her dream.

My father was gregarious and outgoing, but the war had left him hard in many ways, and he still lived in its shadows. He called himself the commander in chief of our family. Parading around the house in his military hat with a broom on his shoulder as a makeshift rifle, he would bark, "Attention!" and then "Parade rest," spreading his feet and putting his rifle out front. Poppy also frequently recited Tennyson's "The Charge of the Light Brigade" and the speech from Shakespeare's *Julius Caesar* about the great Pompey walking the streets of Rome. He taught me how to recite Shakespeare's verse, and the Pompey speech was forever etched in my mind.

My own shy, inward nature was sometimes at odds with his "get up 'n' go" style. Once, when I was in the fifth grade, he told me I was nothing but a dreamer. I did love to daydream about faraway places and fantasy worlds. I still had not gotten over being uprooted from the Midwest, taken away from the security of Birch Village and from my grandparents and all our other relatives. This anger I held on to like a piece of fungus clinging to an old dead tree. I was sometimes sullen, preferring to be by myself.

Ma, my grandmother, had told me I was a deep thinker and said that one day I would be a minister. Elders often praised me as a thoughtful and kind person. I would buy cards for birthdays and little boxes of candy for my mother, especially for Valentine's Day.

Despite these attributes I found myself in more fights than I care to remember, and I often hung out with the baddest kids in school or the neighborhood. Fighting was something I had to do once I started school in Seattle. Colman Elementary School, where Mommy enrolled us when we first got to town, was a predominantly Black school. I guess since I was a new kid, shy, and curly-haired, I was fair game. At times it seemed that Colman Elementary was a "gladiator school" of sorts, where you were trained to defend and take care of yourself. I began hanging with some of the tough crowd, feeling connected by our inner anger. When my family moved to Madrona, I continued to attend Colman but also had to fight all comers at the park across the street from our house. It seemed a fight could break out for any reason.

On the first day of seventh grade, at flag football tryouts, I got into a fight with Howard Redman. Howard was a cousin of James, Joyce, and Randy Redman, the most fearsome family of fighters in the Central District. Everyone knew and feared the Redmans. Just the name would send shivers up your spine. It wasn't until I had Howard on the ground and was beating him that I heard whispers in the background saying I was in for it, because Howard Redman was a cousin to James and the rest of the Redman gang. I immediately got off of Howard and refused to fight any further. When I came home from school that day, word had already spread to the park about what had happened. As a result, I got into two more fights while playing football.

But I was not really a fighter. I didn't like to fight, unlike some of the kids I hung out with. I did it to keep from being beaten up, which I was determined never to let happen to me. I soon began running with a Madrona gang called the Inkwells. After a few months I got into an argument with the younger brother of one of the leaders. But I refused to fight him. Ma had sent all of us siblings our own Bibles. In her letters, she was always quoting scripture. Some of the verses she quoted had connected strongly with me, and I gradually resolved to avoid fighting. At this point I was also pretty tired of it. After refusing to fight, I ran home in tears.

Poppy was very angry with me for not sticking up for myself. "You're a coward!" he yelled at me in disgust. The word "coward" rang in my head for a long time. I often wondered if that were true.

Music was one of my first loves. I enjoyed sitting and watching Mommy while she delicately played the piano, swaying from side to side, playing Beethoven and Tchaikovsky. Our house was always filled with music, and each day there was a different kind of music in the air. On Saturdays the sounds of Lionel Hampton, Dizzy Gillespie, Dinah Washington, Duke Ellington, and Errol Garner could be heard late into the night on the hi-fi. Sunday morning would be gospel, giving way to opera—*The Tales of Hoffman, Carmen,* and *Madama Butterfly.* During the week it was musicals like *Oklahoma, South Pacific,* and *My Fair Lady,* and, as we got older, artists like the Temptations, Otis Redding, and Aretha Franklin began to be heard more frequently.

When I was in the fifth grade, Joanne, Elmer, and I began to study music in school. Joanne took piano lessons from my mother, and Elmer started the guitar and later the trumpet. I was uncertain of what I wanted to play, so Ma, who was paying for the instruments, decided I would take up the violin. I loved the sound of the violin, but it was not what I wanted to learn to play. I struggled through my violin lessons, barely learning to read the notes. Mommy and Poppy would fuss and yell, trying to get me to practice. One day on the way home from school, my friends and I stopped off in the alley and traded instruments. I took Ronny Hammond's drumsticks and he took my violin, and I also played somebody's sax. We had a lot of fun. However, my violin strings broke, along with the bridge, the small piece of wood that holds up the strings. That evening, Mommy and Poppy angrily told me I couldn't play an instrument anymore. Michael eventually got my violin, and sadly the opportunity to play music was taken from me. I was the only sibling who did not learn to play an instrument.

I began hanging more with Elmer, trying to avoid the gang of tough cats who always seemed preoccupied with fighting. Elmer had transferred schools after the move to Madrona and was attending Madrona Elementary, a well-integrated school with whites, Asians, and Blacks. He had met a couple of white boys—Mark Sprague and David Booth. Mark did some professional acting work and was from a well-to-do family. In contrast, David and his older brother and sister were raised by their working mother.

Yet Mark and David lived across from one another down on 35th Avenue, a predominantly white part of Madrona. The four of us spent a lot of time playing war and archery, and we even put on our own abridged production of *West Side Story*. David was more mischievous than Mark, and, as time went by and Mark became more occupied with his acting, David, Elmer, and I began to get into pranks that weren't really Mark's style. We rang doorbells at night, wrapped houses in toilet paper, stole stuff from the drugstore, and plastered passing cars at the corner of 34th with eggs we'd swiped from the grocery store.

David was full of ideas for troublemaking. Once he told us he knew how to make a bomb—all we needed was some saltpeter and powdered sugar. Off we went to the drugstore to steal some saltpeter. We got some powdered sugar, compressed the mixture in cans and bottles, and made a fuse. To our surprise, when lit, it exploded. We did this several times, blowing up cans and other things until David came up with another idea.

Poppy had kept only one gun out of all the weapons he had brought back from the war, a 7.62 Japanese sniper rifle. He had taken out the firing pin, rendering the gun useless, or so he had thought. We had often played with the rifle, mimicking the soldiers in the countless war movies we watched. However, David had experience with hunting and knew a thing or two about guns. His idea was to take a nail and stick it into the bolt in place of a firing pin. Then we took some of the empty shell casings Poppy had, filled them with the saltpeter–powdered sugar mixture, and packed it in. Finally we melted some wax over it, making a hard, wax bullet.

We took the rifle out onto the front balcony of the house, which faced the park, and pulled the trigger. We didn't really think it would work, but to our shock it did, letting off a loud bang. Laughing, we went back into the house. Minutes later the police rang the doorbell. Mommy and Poppy had been downstairs in the kitchen, sipping highballs and listening to some jazz, oblivious to what had just transpired. Poppy answered the door.

"We just had a report that a weapon was fired from this vicinity," said the officer.

My father answered, "We don't have any weapons in this house, so it didn't come from here."

We later learned that the wax bullet had just missed the head of Peanut, one of the neighborhood bullies. We laughed for days about this incident but never revealed our secret to anyone.

In junior high, I was in need of some extra money, so I got a morning paper route, which meant getting up at six in the morning to deliver the papers before school. Sometimes I teamed with Michael Lee, one of the older, tough guys in the neighborhood, who had a route parallel to mine. On Sundays we would get our papers and head to the Laundromat on Cherry Street, climb inside the dryers, and try to warm up before going out in the cold to deliver our papers.

I hung out with an assortment of friends. One was Johnny Goodman, a red-headed white boy a year older than me. Johnny had done time at Green Hill School in Chehalis, a state juvenile rehabilitation institution, and had the muscles to prove it. He was a good baseball player who could often hit home runs.

One day, Johnny and I went down to his house near the lake. "Hey, man, my father made some blackberry wine," he said, grabbing two small beer bottles filled with his father's home brew.

We started drinking. The taste was sweet and slightly tart. In minutes we had emptied our bottles. I started to feel lightheaded and somewhat dizzy. The only wine I'd had prior to this were the sips that my siblings and I would occasionally sneak from our parents' supply. After a while, I looked at my watch and it was nearly six o'clock. I almost freaked out. I had five minutes before I was supposed to be sitting at my spot at the kitchen table. And I would have to walk six blocks up steep hills, including a climb up a three-block-long staircase. I had no idea how I would make it in my condition. Pulling myself up the steel stair banisters and stumbling the last two blocks home, I barely made it to the kitchen table in time. My drunkenness went unnoticed.

I also took to hanging with some Filipino boys who lived down the street, Danny and Jerry. They had both been to the juvenile detention center; Jerry had been specifically sent up for stealing. A good athlete, Jerry could play some football and baseball, but what set him apart from everybody else was that he was a thief and a very good one. I should have known that hanging with him would get me into some deep trouble.

One morning, on a school holiday, Jerry and Danny accompanied me on my paper route. I didn't want them to come with me because I had a bad feeling that with these two anything could happen. While I was delivering my papers, they were breaking into houses, not really looking for anything in particular, just doing it because they could. They kept trying to get me to join them, but I refused. On the way home, after I'd finished my route, they convinced me to break into one last house with them.

Jerry had a glasscutter. He cut a hole in a glass pane on the front door, stuck his hand through, and opened the door. To our dismay, when we stepped into the house we noticed someone sleeping on the sofa in the front room. That did not deter Jerry and Danny one bit. They tiptoed around the house as if it were their own, picking up whatever they wanted. They took several items, including a .22 rifle and a transistor radio, and we left. Later in the day, Danny rode his bike down to the same house and threw the rifle into the yard. The owner saw him and called the police.

Meanwhile, I was just sitting down with the family for dinner, as we did every evening at six o'clock. About midway through the pork chops and mashed potatoes, the doorbell rang. It was the police. Mommy and Poppy had never shown any fondness for the police. I remember the day I blurted out in the kitchen that I wanted to be a policeman—they had both looked at me with scorn.

"Is Aaron Dixon here?" asked one of the cops at the door. They had come to arrest me for breaking into that house. Poppy was not about to surrender me so easily to these white cops. As the two cops stood there, Poppy pulled me behind him.

"What if I say you can't take him?" Poppy said, getting into a defensive stance. Finally the cops agreed to let Poppy bring me down to the station for questioning. They decided not to charge me, but because Danny and Jerry had records, they were charged and sent up to juvenile. I did not see Danny or Jerry too much after that.

I seemed to be constantly getting in trouble, yet always just barely escaping serious consequences.

4

Rumblings in the South

Oh there been times that I thought I couldn't last for long
But now I think I'm able to carry on
It's been a long, a long time coming
But I know a change gonna come, oh yes it will
—Sam Cooke, "A Change Is Gonna Come," 1964

During this same time period, but seemingly removed from
the occasional personal drama playing itself out in my own life, there were
tremendous changes occurring in other parts of the world and in the US
South. The United States and the Soviet Union had become world super-
powers pitted against each another—Communist Russia versus the United
States, leader of the free world. Both nations possessed intercontinental
ballistic missiles with nuclear warheads. I remember the lurking fear of
the prospect of a nuclear attack, and how those who could afford to do
so built bomb shelters. The Jewish family on the corner of our block built
one, further alienating themselves from the increasing numbers of Black
families moving into Madrona.

In African colonies, Black revolutionaries, supported by Moscow,
were organizing and fighting to overthrow the European colonizers, dis-
pensing with three hundred years of imperial oppression. This revolutionary activity led to the first democratically elected African prime minister,
Patrice Lumumba of the Democratic Republic of Congo, who after only

seven months in office was assassinated with the backing of the CIA. Revolution was also brewing in South and Central America, as poor and oppressed Latin countries were tiring of the domination of American corporations and the exploitation of their people and land. Closer to home, in Cuba, Fidel Castro marched into Havana and overthrew Fulgencio Batista, the US-supported tyrant who had allowed American businessmen to use Cuba as their personal whorehouse and casino. The dynamic intensified when Castro aligned himself with the Soviet Union. The increasing probability of Russian missiles being positioned close to US soil led to a failed CIA plot to overthrow Castro, the Bay of Pigs debacle. And across the Pacific, following World War II, the Allied powers had foolishly and selfishly split Vietnam into two nations, giving North Vietnam to the French, and setting the stage for what would become America's own Waterloo.

In the Deep South of the United States, Black folks began to lay the foundation for the permanent transformation of America. I remember well sitting at home, watching the black-and-white images on TV. The sit-ins, the demonstrations, and the faces of hatred—white men beating or hosing down the protestors, Black and sometimes white, who were mobilizing against segregation, a byproduct of three hundred years of slavery, oppression, and terrorism. Change was in the air, and soon my generation would step up to play a leading role in confronting the archaic and puritanical past.

I had seen Martin Luther King Jr. on TV, fearlessly leading his demonstrators into the jaws of the enemy. He was poised for greatness, almost saintly. In November 1961, King came to Seattle to support a march against redlining. On a sunny Saturday afternoon, I found myself marching down 23rd Avenue South, walking arm to arm with thousands of other people of all colors, singing "We Shall Overcome" and other protest songs. It was a unifying moment of solidarity, a feeling of serene peace and the possibility that our world could come together to create something new, something different. You could feel the determination, the sense of purpose, the spirit of oneness engulfing us all, culminating in a large rally and a speech by Martin Luther King.

Quietly and solemnly I made my way to the bandstand at Garfield Park, watching him and listening to his words—words that I had heard on TV, on the radio, and on record albums. I took a spot on the edge of the bandstand, scanning the crowd, looking for a threat to our savior and spiritual leader—as if a thirteen-year-old could do anything to stop an assassin's bullet. But I realize now that my taking that spot, that position of defense, was symbolic. It represented an impending shift, a changing of the guard. All across the country, thousands of Black, white, Asian, Native American, and Latino kids, just like me, were slowly making an unconscious move, positioning for the big push to change America.

The integrationists were organizing and fighting for desegregation of the schools, probably the biggest strategic blunder of the Civil Rights Movement in that it forced Black kids to travel across town to hostile, racially charged environments. While white kids were able to stay comfortably in their own schools and communities, Black kids had to give up their secure surroundings and the dedicated attention and understanding of their Black, or sometimes white, teachers. But at the time school integration sounded good, and it felt right for me, personally, to work toward Martin Luther King's dream. So in 1964 I signed up for Seattle's first voluntary busing program. The timing was perfect because I felt I needed to get out of the gladiator schools in the Black community. In junior high the combat had slowly moved beyond fisticuffs to include weapons such as push-button knives and switchblades, like the ones we had seen in *West Side Story* and *Blackboard Jungle*. I owned several push-button knives and stilettos. We would play with our knives and show them off during recess, fortunately never really using them on one another.

For ninth grade, I transferred to an all-white school called Denny Blaine, located in a white neighborhood of fine homes called Magnolia, which sat on a bluff overlooking Elliott Bay. I had chosen this school partly because a friend of mine, Mike Rosetti, went there. Mike spent the summers at his aunt's house, down the street from ours in Madrona. His aunt was a madam, and at night her place transformed into a bordello. Mike was a scrawny, troubled Italian kid whose father was involved in some Mafia-type activities. Mike's dad was hardly ever around, but he showed up on occasion in his white Cadillac, with a CB radio and a snub-nosed .38, to dish out dollar bills to his son and wife. Mike's mom was definitely being abused; she often had bruises and black eyes and was clearly overwhelmed at having to raise Mike and his two sisters on her own.

I enjoyed that year at Denny Blaine. I had only a few friends, but that was okay, as long as nobody tried to mess with me. Being about the only Black kid in the school, I was looked to as an athlete. I played on the flag football team at halfback. The girls even started a cheer when I wasn't in the game: "We want Aaron! We want Aaron!" I guess they must have been disappointed at basketball tryouts, because at that point I had not played a lot of basketball and ended up not making the team. However, I did go out for track toward the middle of the season. As the school was so far from my home, I only went to a few practices, and when I did, I worked on the high jump. I loved to jump as a little kid. I would try to jump over bushes, fences, anything. At one of the practices I managed to attend, the coach approached me and informed me with a look of astonishment that I had just broken the state junior high school record in the high jump. You would think that upon such a feat, I would have felt fueled to pursue track and high jumping, but after that day I never showed up for track practice again.

I had always loved sports, especially football. I was taller than most boys my age and quicker than most my size. As I grew older, I channeled all my anger and frustration into playing football at the park. We played in the rain, snow, sleet, hail, hot weather, or freezing weather, pretending to be Gale Sayers, Jim Brown, or Dick Butkus busting through the line, throwing the halfback for a loss. In the evenings we stopped at six o'clock so Elmer, Michael, and I could go home to eat, and sometimes my brothers and I would get to go back outside to play until the sun had disappeared behind the Olympic Mountains. I played other sports as well, like ping-pong, tennis, basketball, and baseball—but football was my love and passion. I could be reckless, playing with abandon and determination, pulling out all the stops to score that winning touchdown or make that great defensive play. My friends always asked me why I never tried out for the Gil Dobie or Bantam youth football leagues. I just shrugged my shoulders and said, "I don't know."

After the year at Denny Blaine, my last year of junior high, I continued on my personal quest toward integrating Seattle's schools and enrolled at Queen Anne High School, an all-white high school on top of Queen Anne Hill, in a middle-class neighborhood of Victorian homes. Now a sophomore, I finally got the courage to try out for the football team, and made it. I remember how quietly excited I was to be issued my uniform, shoulder pads, and helmet. My confidence grew with getting my ankles wrapped and plodding out to the field in my black, high-top football cleats and lying on the ground doing calisthenics with the team. The coach had a real Southern drawl, something I had heard before only on TV, and at times he seemed to be picking on me as the only Black kid on the team, but I wasn't going to let that stop me.

Later that week, we started scrimmaging, and since I had joined late, I started on the fifth-string defense. Within a few days I had worked my way up to second string, playing middle linebacker. The next day the second string had a full scrimmage against the first-string offense. That day I played as if I had been injected with an invincibility potion, proving to myself and to everyone on the field that I had the potential to become a very good player. Every play the offense ran, I was there to stop. On one series I ran to the right, running down a halfback's sweep, and grabbed the ball carrier and threw him to the ground. They went left and I ran the ball carrier down again. He came up the middle. I met the fullback, knocking him backward. Then they tried a short pass over the middle and I intercepted it and immediately got the hell knocked out of me.

The coach recognized that I had the speed to play offense, so he gave me a try at halfback. Even though my dream was to play defense, I was glad for this chance to show him what else I could do. But every time my number was called and I ran into the line, there was no hole. I could not break through. Maybe the white boys on the line were intentionally not blocking the opposing defense; I don't know for certain. For whatever reason, the second-string center and guards were not able to break a hole through the first-string defense while I was at halfback that day. Being unable to break through represented my entire life at that moment and into the future. I would spend a lifetime trying to break through the hole, to find the opening to daylight, to freedom, to respectability.

Despite the frustration, I remember traveling home that night on the hour-long bus ride, sitting quietly by myself, feeling a kind of confidence I had never felt before. At last I had found it—that one thing I could use to ride to the top, one thing I loved that could power me up out of my sense of despair, the dungeon of nothingness.

Humbly, I walked into the kitchen. Mommy was preparing dinner, looking moody. Poppy was sipping a highball, trying to relieve the stress of working in a hostile, racist environment. I finally summoned up my courage and said, "I need twenty-five dollars for insurance so I can continue to play football and play in the game Saturday."

"We don't have twenty-five dollars for football insurance," Mommy responded. Poppy continued sipping, not acknowledging my request, tacitly agreeing with Mommy.

That must have been the most disappointing day of my youth. I felt, *I guess I didn't deserve it.* I even felt guilty for asking. However much I tried to hide it, I went into a permanent sulk. I took the hurt and anger and put it inside, pushing it down harder with the passage of time, burying it. I never went out for football again, leaving that day on the field as a memory of what could have been. I resolved never again to rely on my parents for anything but the bare necessities of life. Maybe if I had been different, maybe if I had been more outgoing, more gregarious, more confident, I could have overcome my parents' own dark shadows. But I wasn't. I was too sensitive, too quiet, and at times too rebellious. My self-esteem was too low to overcome those obstacles. This would prove to be my struggle in life, to overcome my shyness and my lack of confidence.

I continued to play sandlot football, often playing pickup games with future college and NFL players. I also played basketball in the CYO league, where all the high school ballplayers who did not make their high school teams played. And every summer, I played center field for the Parks Department softball league, frequently traveling to hostile white neighborhoods for away games. Even as much as I loved sports, there seemed to be something else calling me. I just didn't know what.

5

Sticking Together

Mom loves the both of them
You see it's in the blood
Both kids are good to Mom
"Blood's thicker than mud"
It's a family affair, it's a family affair
— Sly and the Family Stone, "Family Affair," 1971

Our family was a unit that found happiness in being together. I remember my parents' constant reminder: "You boys, stick together." At times togetherness was enforced, as when we had to do chores as a team. On summer days, before we were old enough to go out and play without asking permission, we had to stay in the house and clean up before being allowed to go out to the park. Joanne cooked our breakfast, making coffeecakes, teaching Elmer and me how to cook. Sometimes we would surprise Mommy and Poppy with a cake we had made from scratch. There were times we had to spring into action as a group, straightening up the house after we'd taken it apart, with one of us as the lookout while the rest hastily tried to put things back in order.

One Christmas vacation we broke a glass window in Mommy and Poppy's room while they were out being Santa Claus. We knew we would be in big trouble when they came home after spending their hard-earned money on our Christmas toys. So Elmer and I swung into action. We had helped Poppy enough around the house to know how to fix a broken window. We took out the broken glass, measured the window, and then ran down to the hardware store and bought a windowpane and putty knife with our Christmas money. We hurried back home, set in the glass, and puttied the edges just before Mommy and Poppy returned. Unfortunately, we left a putty knife sitting out, and had to confess.

On cold winter days during the long Christmas vacation, Elmer, Michael, and I would play sock football on our knees on the hardwood floors in the hallway of the house. It was me against them, using a sock as a football and scooting down the hall on our knees. They could never stop me from scoring a touchdown.

Elmer and I were accustomed to doing everything together, and were at times inseparable. When we were little kids in Champaign, Mommy sometimes dressed us up like twins in little blue sailor suits, and every Easter we had matching suits. During our early teen years we sneaked out of the house together by dangling from the veranda outside our bedroom and dropping the last five feet to the ground. Then we would roam the neighborhood, enjoying our secret freedom.

Through our friendship with Elmer's classmates Mark and David, we were introduced to the wilderness of the Northwest. We went camping and small bird hunting on many occasions, unsupervised by adults. Exploring along the Sauk River, among evergreens and ferns, we were free—free from our parents, free from our enemies in the city. Though we were only thirteen and fourteen, Mommy and Poppy did not seem to mind our going off into the mountains by ourselves. They were not as supportive, however, when we asked to go to a party or dance—then, the answer usually was no.

One December, David, Elmer, Michael, and I went camping at the base of Mount Si, a steep mountain with its base about forty minutes from Seattle. Mommy and Poppy dropped us off in two feet of snow. We four boys hiked up as far as we could go, carrying our equipment. We set up camp with our old army tent and prepared our meal. After eating, we got in our tent and sleeping bags and pulled out bags of candy. We told stories and laughed until we fell asleep.

We awoke at about three in the morning to find that two of our sleeping bags were soaking wet and our socks and pants were wet as well. It had been snowing all night and the packed snow on our old tent had leaked through at any points of contact. We decided to share the dry sleeping bags, trying not to move around and bump against the tent. We barely slept that night in such miserable conditions. In the morning, we tried to find some dry socks but everything was wet, and the snow outside was almost three feet deep. Without dry clothes or socks we could not go outside the tent to cook. After our candy was gone, we tried eating raw potatoes. That didn't taste too good or digest well. Finally, we decided to brave the cold, open up the tent, and cook on the Coleman stove. Our hot meal of eggs, potatoes, and bacon was delicious.

Although we had planned to camp for two nights, we decided we could not stay another night under those conditions and would have to hike out to get to a phone. Since Michael and I had the driest footwear, we struck out in our still-damp socks, walking down the mountain trail at a fast pace. Michael lagged behind but I made sure not to lose sight of him. It was a silent and beautiful walk among the snow-covered trees. The only sounds were an occasional bird chirp and the crunching of the snow beneath our every step. It seemed we walked for hours before coming across a little chalet. Inside, a couple was preparing breakfast. They let us use their phone to call our parents and then invited us to join them for breakfast. That evening we were back at home, sitting in front of the fireplace, trying to thaw out our frozen feet.

We were free to explore up in the mountains, but back at the park, we always had to be on guard. One day while David, Elmer, and I were playing, we heard five gunshots. We ran down to the corner of the park and saw three young Black men lying in three different spots. We ran to the side of one of the men. He had been shot between the eyes. Blood was pouring from his wound and we could hear a gurgling sound as he tried to breathe. We ran to the other two men and they had also been shot in the head. It seemed to take forever for the police and ambulance to arrive. We learned later that the assailant was the oldest of the several Harris brothers. The large Harris family, originally from Louisiana, was to a person quiet and respectful, never involved in any controversy, and the brothers were considered nice boys. But like most families from the South, they had a lot of experience with guns and hunting. There had apparently been an ongoing dispute among the four young men in the park.

It was the first time any of us had seen death. At the time, we didn't think too much about the shooting. It was beyond our comprehension. We had no context to help us understand what we were witnessing, but it was a stark reminder that deadly violence did not just happen on TV but was right here with us, waiting to snuff out someone's life, even the innocent. The images of those young men lying alone on the cold ground would always linger in the back of our minds.

Even before this incident, Poppy always had concerns that if he did not make the right decisions regarding us boys, we would end up in some kind of trouble. This concern had actually led to our moving to Seattle. As the influence of the Blackstone Rangers spread in Chicago, he was taking no chances on his boys' getting caught up in the gang scene. Both my cousins in Chicago had succumbed to the lure of the Rangers and their rival gang, the Disciples. To help keep us in line, Poppy made sure we were not idle during the summers.

One summer Poppy got his friend Jerry Sussman to employ us as laborers on his boat. A friend of our whole family, Mr. Sussman was Jewish, and we celebrated Passover with his family. Joanne and I also frequently babysat his three children. Mr. Sussman's boat, *The Puffin*, was a one-mast schooner, a twenty-five-footer with a cabin. We worked hard on that boat for several months, dry-docking it, scraping the hull, repainting the hull inside and out, and re-rigging the mast. It was very tedious work, and Mr. Sussman made everything a lesson, stopping to teach us the purpose and importance of each task. After our work on the boat was complete, we sailed up through the Strait of Juan de Fuca to Cypress Island, one of the San Juan Islands up north near Canada.

As we approached our destination, islands were scattered all around us, with green forests, white cliffs, rocky coastlines, and a few sandy beaches, eagles flying. Herons skimmed the water, trying to catch jumping fish, and an occasional orca streamed by in the distance. We finally reached Cypress Island, dropped anchor, loaded up the dinghy, and rowed ashore. We could hardly contain our excitement at being in this lush, deserted place.

Mr. and Mrs. Sussman and their daughter camped on the beach, while Elmer, the two Sussman boys, David and Matthew, and I camped inland. Our main job was to help Mr. Sussman build a cabin on a cliff overlooking a small bay. In between playing on the beaches and running in the forest, we spent hot days hammering, sawing, and hauling materials up the cliff using a pulley. Some days we worked long hours, laying the floor of the cabin and putting up the frame. Other days, realizing we were city kids, Mr. Sussman cut us loose to run free.

Being on the island reminded me of the book *Treasure Island*, and I imagined I was a pirate on the crew with Long John Silver. I loved being up on Cypress—no phones, no electricity, no stores, no cars, just the ocean holding countless creatures, some of which made their way to the surface. During low tide, we gathered oysters on the rocky edge of the beach. There seemed to be thousands. We ate them for breakfast, lunch, and dinner. I remember the solitude of the island, the white sand and the green forest. Everything seemed so perfect, so right, so much in harmony. Sometimes I sat on a dried-out log, watching the sun slowly set, looking up at the vast, open, clear sky, wishing I could remain there forever. Much too soon, our time was up and we had to sail away, leaving Cypress behind to go back to the city, back to everyday reality.

When Elmer was fifteen he got an evening paper route, and I, without a choice in the matter, was ordered to accompany him for a whole year. We left the house together with the papers in Elmer's bag carrier, taking turns carrying the papers to the big houses down by the lake, splitting up and dividing the route, and meeting up again before heading back up the long, steep hills of Madrona. Rain, snow, sleet, or hot weather, the two of us worked that paper route as one. There were many times I detested helping my skinny younger brother on his route. I could have been up at the park or running with my friends or—worse—getting into some trouble. Despite being forced to support Elmer's paper route, I truly enjoyed those days of the two of us working in tandem for one goal: to finish in the quickest way possible. In a few short years, we would be working in tandem for a much bigger purpose.

For my junior year, I transferred to our neighborhood high school, Garfield. I was tired of the racism at Queen Anne and the whole idea of voluntary integration. Elmer and I also began to drift apart as we got older. Mommy and Poppy eased up on their demands that we stick together. Elmer hung with his white friends, wearing sandals and a serape, riding a skateboard, listening to the Beatles and the Rolling Stones. My Black buddies from Garfield and I sipped beer and listened to the Temptations and the Four Tops, gathering in damp basements, trying to sing notes too high for our screechy voices, occasionally puffing on Pall Malls.

At some point we realized we needed to look for work. Emerson Swain, a comically wild friend, and I got jobs at the Pancake House washing dishes, making $1.25 an hour. On weekends we would get to close the place, leaving us two kids alone in an empty restaurant full of pies and ice cream. We would take a whole pie, top it with vanilla ice cream, and gorge ourselves while we hastily cleaned.

I took on a second job at Swedish Hospital up the street, making $1.75 an hour working in the kitchen. For a while I tried to keep both jobs, running from one shift to the next. I finally quit the Pancake House and concentrated on the job at Swedish. I worked with the dieticians, checking the individual patient menus to make sure the correct food was put on each patient's tray. I enjoyed working. It helped me to free myself, at least partially, from my parents. At the hospital my friend Mike Dean and I worked from 4 to 8 p.m. after school and 7 a.m. to 4 p.m. on weekends. During the summer we worked fourteen-hour days, seven days a week.

On some paydays Mike and I would have saved enough to go downtown and buy sharkskin suits, Italian sweaters, and loafers. And at Mrs. Jackson's record shop up on 34th, we'd buy the latest from Motown—Junior Walker, Ben E. King, Mary Wells, Stevie Wonder, and Smokey Robinson. No longer did I have to sit at a sewing machine under dim lighting, tapering the unfashionable baggy pants sent by Ma, as I had done on so many occasions. It felt so good to have this financial freedom from my parents. I didn't want to have to ask them for anything other than permission to go out.

At sixteen, I guess you could say I was "smelling myself." I felt like I knew a few things—and maybe I even knew enough to set Mommy and Poppy straight on a few occasions. A collision with reality was inevitable.

On one of the many evenings that Poppy chose to work overtime, Mommy and Joanne got into a little disagreement. Like many girls growing up in the '60s, Joanne was having a difficult time with her parents—Mommy and Poppy were no exception. It was two cultures clashing—the old ways of long skirts and polite, pigtailed girls who played the piano and did their arithmetic, versus the new girls of the '60s, who wanted to wear short skirts and long hair, do the Watusi and the Hully Gully, and hang with greasy-headed boys at the dance, slow-grinding to some Smokey Robinson or Etta James. Mommy's personal frustrations and battles with her own mother often surfaced in the verbal clashes between her and Joanne.

Poppy was usually the calming force, the voice of reason in these clashes, but on this particular evening he was gone. In the kitchen, Mommy verbally attacked Joanne, asserting something she assumed was true.

Joanne did not argue back. Mommy was a small, slight woman, but with a fiery disposition. She even grabbed a belt.

I was standing in the hallway, watching and listening. Suddenly I rushed in and grabbed the belt from Mommy, looked down at her, and said, "Stop. Leave her alone."

My actions and words shocked everyone, including Elmer and Michael, who were also standing by, looking on in disbelief. I had wanted to say "stop" for so long. The words had been held at bay long enough and they just came out.

Mommy looked at me with amazement and then burst into tears. "I'm going to tell your father."

Afterward I could feel the sense of doom in the house. Everyone knew that Poppy would not be happy about this. Disrespecting Mommy and Poppy's authority was not tolerated—not in this house.

The next morning, as I was quietly getting ready for school, I awaited my fate. Poppy came into the room, his fist up and anger on his face. I stood there, now almost six feet tall, looking down at a still muscular Poppy.

He blurted out, "If you ever do that again, I will knock you out."

I just stood there and listened. I had no doubt that he could knock me out with one blow, but that really didn't matter. He could knock me out a thousand times and I would still have done the same thing. I felt strongly that Mommy was wrong, and that since Joanne was eighteen it was time to treat her with respect.

The Tide of the Movement

Reading my poetry in a Links Arts contest, Seattle, 1967.

6

Slow Awakening

When you feel really low
Yeah, there's a great truth you should know
When you're young, gifted and black
Your soul's intact
—Nina Simone, "To Be Young, Gifted and Black," 1970

My sophomore year as a voluntary integrator was a disaster. Seeing my dream of being a havoc-raising linebacker extinguished was difficult enough. But running into the big brick wall of racism was a rude awakening.

It had always been there, weaving its way in and out of our family's history. I first got a glimpse of this ugly monster in the late 1950s as a seven- or eight-year-old, mostly on Friday nights after the Friday night fights on TV were over, and our fried fish dinner had long since been digested. I saw Mommy and Poppy's sad faces. They knew full well that their Black, muscular fighters, Sugar Ray Robinson, Archie Moore, and countless others, despite the thrashings they gave their white opponents, had been robbed, cheated out of victory by bigoted referees and judges. They never said anything about it to us kids. They never demeaned whites. They just continued working to provide us with a sense of freedom that they and their parents never had.

Poppy would come home from work at Boeing filled with rage from dealing with some petty racism. One day while he was driving home and stuck in traffic, someone drove by and shouted, "Nigger!" Poppy lost his

49

cool, got out of his car, grabbed rocks, sticks, anything he could throw, and propelled it all after the bastard, who was long gone. Had he been able to get to the white man, Poppy would surely have hurt him—which is exactly why Poppy never owned a functioning gun and never wanted one around. I could understand why, when he came home, he reached for a highball. It helped to defuse the anger, to hold at bay the deep rage and the memories of war.

Mommy also had her share of stories of being told lies such as "No, we don't have any jobs open," despite a sign stating the contrary. And down from our house, there was the Lake Washington Realty office on the corner of 34th and Union, with the little, skinny, pale, spectacled white lady behind the desk who let it be known that she did not do business with Blacks or Asians. As kids, we knew every other business owner in Madrona on a first-name basis, but we never ventured inside that real estate office.

For the most part, Seattle was different from a lot of places in the United States at the time. Racism was not out in the open, staring you in the face, thrusting you into confrontations or forcing you to question your own integrity. Nevertheless, it was there, hidden, mostly in faraway neighborhoods, in the souls and the hearts of misguided, miseducated, and misinformed white men and women. I remember listening to the older teenagers in the neighborhood as they shared their battle stories of venturing out of the Central District, our safe haven, going to neighborhoods like Ballard, Queen Anne, and Shoreline, and being attacked by bat-waving, "nigger"-yelling white boys—and how, afterward, they would load up in three or four cars and drive back out to seek revenge. *Always carry a bat with you*, they said, *and be ready to run*. Then there was the unsettling story of the Black lady raped by a gang of white policemen, with nothing ever said or done about it, which created a sense of helplessness in our young minds.

At the end of one of our summer trips, we were driving back from Chicago. Poppy had driven the length of Montana, a grueling stretch. We reached Deer Lodge, a small cowboy town. Poppy spotted a motel with a "Vacancy" sign, pulled into the lot, and went in. He was dog-tired and limping from a ruptured Achilles tendon, which he had injured before the trip.

When the man at the front desk told him he didn't have any rooms available, Poppy got that crazy look on his face. It was the kind of look that a man gets when he has had enough of talking and is prepared to take action, like *I will tear you and this motel apart if I don't get a room*. I'm not sure what Poppy said, but he put it to this jag-jaw cowboy in no uncertain terms that he was tired, his family was tired, and he'd better get a room or else. Later that night, as Poppy, Elmer, Michael, and I walked to a nearby store, the sheriff followed us around, peeping at us from behind corners as if we were going to blow up the town.

Up on Madrona, we kids were largely insulated from the tentacles of racism. It was only when we ventured out that it reached us. Sometimes when we had softball games in a distant, white, working-class neighborhood, things got tense. Sometimes the older kids got into fights. Or there were the questionable ball calls that always went against us. Over time, we seemingly became conditioned to such things.

The biggest slap in the face came after our tennis team qualified for the Parks Department city championship, which was held at the Seattle Tennis Club, a prestigious club on Lake Washington. Only a few years earlier the same club had denied access to the greatest Mexican American tennis player of all time, Pancho Gonzales. Everybody on our tennis team was Black, with the exception of one Jewish boy, Marty, who always wore a yarmulke. Nobody was sure where Marty went to school and we didn't know the actual location of his house. We just knew he was a heck of an athlete, and we were always glad to see him up at the park. He was a phenomenal left-handed quarterback, a solid pitcher on the softball team, and one of the better singles tennis players in our age group up at Madrona.

I don't think the Seattle Tennis Club was prepared to have a young all-minority team competing on their clean, smooth, green courts, and they were even more surprised when we took first place, soundly defeating all comers. Besides receiving trophies, we were supposed to get lunch in the club dining room and a free swim in the Olympic-sized pool. To our astonishment, with the exception of Marty they would not allow us in the restaurant or the pool. Instead, they brought hot dogs out to us and directed us down to the beach, while we watched the white kids we had defeated being led into the club dining room. In the moment, we were so excited about our victory we didn't have time to think about what they were doing to us, but Elmer and I would not forget.

At Queen Anne, my 2.5 grade point average plummeted to a 1.5. My typing teacher flunked me because my wrist, badly sprained from playing football, made typing impossible. My math teacher, who never answered my questions, gave me an E—the equivalent of an F, or Fail. Many of the kids I had known and played with at Denny Blaine the year before were now distant and unfriendly.

A turning point came in late February of my sophomore year, during the city high school basketball championship game, held at Hec Edmundson Pavilion at the University of Washington. Garfield, the predominantly Black school my neighborhood friends attended, was playing against Queen Anne, the all-white school where I was enrolled. The game seesawed back and forth, going down to the wire. I sat with my friends on the Garfield side, stomping our feet as we cheered our Black warriors to victory, holding our breath, our hearts in our throats, wondering if victory would be denied as it so often was. When Black folks competed against whites in sports, it represented much more than a sporting event—it was a declaration of equality, a silent demand that one's right to exist be recognized.

With five seconds to go, Garfield had a three-point lead and had the ball. We were all sitting there, wondering what could go wrong. Garfield had been denied the city championship so many times in the past. Then, right before our eyes, it happened. A phantom foul was called on a Garfield player, giving the ball back to Queen Anne. And the referees even added another five seconds to the clock. Queen Anne ended up winning the game by one point. We were stunned, outraged at how blatantly victory had been stolen out of the hands of the Garfield players. I went home feeling very sick about the injustice of the game.

When I went to school the next day I noticed that a lot of students were absent. I also noticed that the white kids were looking at me strangely, staring at me like I had shit on my back. During the course of the day I heard stories of how the white kids from Queen Anne were attacked and beaten after the game, some dangled from the Montlake Bridge, others chased to unsuspecting homes. The Black Garfield students had gone on a rampage, declaring through their actions that they would no longer tolerate blatant racism without there being some form of retribution. The remainder of my year at Queen Anne was very tense. The handful of Black students stayed closer to each other, everyone vowing not to return the following year. The rivalry between Garfield and Queen Anne had always been intense. After this incident, whenever we played on each other's turf, violence broke out.

In 1966, my junior year, I gave up on voluntary integration and came back to the community to attend Garfield, where Quincy Jones had honed his musical skills, where Jimi Hendrix was enrolled before dropping out to embark on his quest to become the most famous guitarist in history, and which Bruce Lee had adopted as his own. Though not an alum, Lee had developed an attachment to Garfield, with its wonderful mix of Black and Asian and white students. He lived in Seattle for several years and often came by to greet some of his martial arts students or simply to hang out.

Garfield's student body was mostly Black and the rest a mix of Filipino, Chinese, Japanese, and whites. The staff was well-blended, with whites, Blacks, and a few Asians. In many ways it was the ideal school for the '60s—a place where no matter your color or beliefs, you could feel free to express yourself. Here were the best musicians, the best athletes, some of the city's best teachers, the best example of racial harmony, and a rich tradition of openness. It was here at Garfield that my identity had an opportunity to grow and flourish. I could explore and search, discover who I was and why I was here on this earth. I found a new circle of friends, and over the next couple of years we played sports together, got drunk together, and philosophized about our future and the world.

At Garfield, there were old-school teachers and new-style, "hip" teachers. The old-school teachers, some of whom carried paddles, went around intimidating students. The new style was embodied by Mr. Peoples, the young, white, sharply dressed math teacher and track coach who was much better at teaching us about social development and dressing well than teaching math. He was very well-liked by the students and was able to set a good example for us young guys because he acted like one of us. On the other end of the spectrum was Mrs. Hundley, a tall, light-skinned Black woman who never smiled. The word was out that she did not take any mess. There was no idle chatter or laughter in her class. She got the most out of you, whether you wanted to give it or not. A throwback to the old days when Black folks relied on their own initiative, understanding that hard work paid off, she was easily the best teacher I ever had. We read the classics and through her I learned the love of literature.

Mrs. Woodson, the tall, Black, rail-thin student counselor, called me into her office one day during my senior year. I had been skipping a lot and getting into some trouble—for example, being kicked out of art class for starting a clay fight—and being sent to study hall far too often. Mrs. Woodson had never said much to me. But what she said that day angered me and woke me up.

She said, "Aaron, you are not going to college. You are just not college material."

Those words stuck in my mind like lead. Mommy and Poppy had always told us we were going to college. I guess I had just assumed that I would go. But my GPA at that point was a pitiful 2.0, not high enough for me to be accepted into college.

Not only was my GPA merely average, but I was also short on credits, meaning that if I failed or dropped even one class, I would not graduate. I knew that Mommy and Poppy would not be pleased with that. But it was the words of Mrs. Woodson that burned inside my head. I realized I had to buckle down, and the remainder of the year I did. I still worked at Swedish and had fun with my friends, but I made sure my studies were taken care of. Even so, I still did not put in a lot of time on homework, doing most of it during school so it would not interfere with those long hours up at the Madrona basketball and tennis courts.

Besides hanging out with my friends, sports were the most important activities in my life. By now, football had taken a back seat to basketball and tennis. Every warm day during the school year, the ballplayers congregated up at Madrona Park. College players from Seattle University, high school players for Garfield and Franklin, varsity rejects like me and my buddies Mike Dean and Chester and Michael Childs, we were all there, waiting for an opportunity to get on the court and show our skills, waiting for winners, sweating, pushing, shoving, jumping, scoring, rebounding— and sometimes fighting. I had become known for my rebounding, my fearlessness beneath the boards, and my tenacious defense against older and bigger opponents. Sometimes we were out playing until sunset. Some of the guys even stayed out way past nightfall. I remember lying in bed, hearing the sound of the leather ball bouncing on the concrete, and wondering who was still out on the court. Sports had become an increasingly important focus for me at this time. They gave me a sense of purpose; I could direct all my energy onto the basketball court, the tennis court, or the football field. I was fearless when playing sports—it was the one area where I had almost complete control and a healthy confidence in my abilities. But there were other, more important things on the horizon for which my skills would prove to be best suited.

Something was brewing in America, something that had begun hundreds of years earlier when Black slaves were brought to the shores of the

New World. It was something unavoidable, something that could no longer be held down. The Civil Rights Movement of the '50s had ushered in the beginning of the end of segregation and outright racial discrimination. And it was my generation—not only young Blacks, but also young whites and other young people of color—who sat at home watching the shaky black-and-white television images, steadied by rabbit-ear antennas, of Southern Blacks integrating universities, schools, buses, restaurants, movie theaters: establishments and institutions that had failed to recognize Blacks as equal human beings. These images penetrated our young minds, informing our visions of our future.

The '60s had begun with one of the most unsettling events in US history, the assassination of President John F. Kennedy in November 1963. Kennedy, the first Irish Catholic president, embodied possibility and hope, a break with the conservative '50s and President Eisenhower. To many Black people, Kennedy represented an opening, a ray of light on a dark, ugly past. Many felt that at last there was someone in the White House who understood us, who cared about us, who spoke with his own words and not those of the power- and money-hungry moguls that infested the political scene. We had been lied to for so long. Finally, we thought we would get the truth.

But Camelot was short-lived. On November 22, 1963, thousands of Americans gathered in starched dresses and pressed slacks and ties to watch their beloved president's car pass by in Dallas. Millions of other Americans were watching the parade on TV in their homes. Suddenly Kennedy slumped over onto his wife's lap with blood gushing from a bullet wound to his throat. Americans were in shock, stunned as they witnessed their president being shot in front of them, out in the open, in broad daylight. It was a heavy, terrible day. Like most of my peers, I was too young to comprehend the events that happened before our eyes, but our parents' sorrow and despair was transferred to us. It was the first and only time I saw Poppy cry, crying in anger, throwing chairs, books, barely able to hold himself up under the strain and sorrow.

Little did we know that 1963 marked only the beginning of a very violent decade. Earlier that same year, Medgar Evers was assassinated. Evers was as important to the Civil Rights Movement as Martin Luther King Jr. and had become familiar to every Black home in America. His leadership and tenacity would never be with us again. In 1966, the most feared Black man in America was assassinated: Malcolm X, tall, persuasive, sharp, strong, fearless, a brilliant man many of us had not even had the opportunity to know. It was only afterward that we realized we'd had a genuine diamond in our midst, an authentic Black American hero who could have helped shape a positive future for this country.

A year earlier, in 1965, white policemen in the Watts neighborhood of Los Angeles stopped and arrested a Black motorist, Marquette Frye, on suspicion of driving under the influence and proceeded to beat him violently as well as his mother, who lived nearby and tried to intervene. It was also rumored that, in the preceding days, the Watts police had roughed up a pregnant Black woman. These events ignited the first of many violent riots to rock the nation. The Watts Uprising woke up America. Blacks rioted for five days, burning down establishments that had exploited Black people far too long, sniping at racist cops, rampaging through the streets, liberating TVs, clothes, food, and guns, throwing Molotov cocktails, leaving behind a wasteland.

Thousands of miles away, young Americans were being sent to hostile, hot jungles, armed with M-14s, trained to kill Vietnamese men and women because they dared to fight for the unification of their country. Older boys I had grown up with were now absent from the neighborhood, no longer on the basketball court or the football field but in the trenches, muddy, bloody, and slowly becoming bloodthirsty for an enemy they did not know. Many would never return.

I managed to stay disconnected from all the chaos, yet it was slowly seeping into my subconscious. In other parts of the country, new Black organizations were sprouting up. Black Nationalism, which rejected white culture and made its primary concern the improvement of the conditions of Black people, was just beginning to emerge. Its focus was on Black independence and self-determination.

One day I was out on the tennis courts perfecting my serve and my net game, aspiring to be the next Arthur Ashe, the first Black male professional tennis player. Mommy called out from the porch as she usually did that dinner was ready. I remember walking by the TV as the six o'clock news was broadcasting. Walter Cronkite was reporting that in Sacramento some Black men with guns had invaded the California capitol building. After dinner, as I walked back out to the tennis courts, I thought briefly about the image of the Black men with guns, feeling a tinge of pride and amazement. Then I forgot about it, yet the image stayed in the back of my mind.

7

Stokely Comes to Town

We're people, we're just like the birds and the bees
We'd rather die on our feet
Than be livin' on our knees
Say it loud, I'm black and I'm proud
—James Brown, "Say It Loud—I'm Black and I'm Proud," 1968

The Civil Rights Movement, initially led by Black Southern ministers, slowly began to hear other voices—voices of young Black men and women who were starting to question the tactic of nonviolent protest. With each march, with each fallen martyr, with each crack on the head by baton-wielding, racist policemen, these voices of dissent grew louder and louder.

Two of these voices soon emerged as new leaders of the Student Nonviolent Coordinating Committee, better known by its acronym, SNCC ("snick"). Stokely Carmichael and H. Rap Brown were both fiery speakers, addressing the concerns of the emerging youth movement that was gradually picking up steam. SNCC, founded in 1960, was originally focused on desegregation and voter registration in the South, and exercised nonviolent protest methods such as sit-ins and marches. But under Stokely's leadership, "Black Power" began to replace "We Shall Overcome." Meeting violence with violence was put forth as an alternative to nonviolent protest. Stokely, who took over as chairman in 1965, and H. Rap, who succeeded Stokely in 1967, were eloquent as well as confrontational, unafraid to say aloud what many young people were feeling and thinking: "Whitey" was going to have to pay the consequences for two hundred years of slavery and one hundred years of segregation. These two young rabble-rousers crisscrossed the country, speaking to college students, high school students, and Black communities, preaching this new empowerment. It wasn't long before the clenched fist of Black Power became the new symbol of resistance, and soon the Black Power Movement took the lead from the floundering Civil Rights Movement, creating hysteria among whites and a lot of fear among older Blacks.

Stokely Carmichael came to Garfield to speak in the spring of 1967. There I was, sitting in the middle of the front row with Elmer and Mike Dean. We had gone out and bought some black Ray-Ban Wayfarer sunglasses, just like the ones Stokely was so often seen in. We were excited and feeling defiant. The tall, lean brother came onstage and began to address the crowd, punctuating his speech with shouts of "Black Power!" as he raised a clenched fist. He talked about "Whitey" having had his day, and that it was our day now. He talked about the riots breaking out in Harlem and Chicago and Philadelphia, and that we had a right to burn white, racist businesses in retaliation for the many years of exploitation. He talked about the Black revolutionary leaders, such as Kwame Nkrumah in Ghana, Julius Nyerere in Tanzania, and Samora Machel in Mozambique, who were emerging to change the colonized land of Africa. The crowd went wild with Stokely's every rebellious word. We left the Garfield auditorium with a much different view of whites than what we had before. A slow current of anger began to brew inside me, and to my mind whites were now the cause of all the problems that Black people faced.

I walked out of the auditorium transformed. I was not the same person who had entered. From that day forward, I looked at the world and everyone around me with anger and rage. I even looked at Mommy and Poppy differently. They no longer fit my frame of reality. Their views and ideas were not compatible with my new, angry, "Get Whitey" outlook. As a matter of fact, there were not many adults with whom I felt I could hold any real conversations. The anger I had held at bay for so long had now surfaced and was coming out whenever my emotions were challenged. Family conversations in the kitchen about politics often became heated, and I questioned Mommy and Poppy's political beliefs.

My job at Swedish kept me financially independent. I had even been able to save up some money. But after listening to Stokely, my job did not seem that important anymore. There were issues beyond my personal realm that now took center stage. I began to look more closely at my interactions with whites, and since most of those interactions occurred on the job, I began to scrutinize every look, every word that I received from my white coworkers. Mrs. Gannen, the head supervisor of the kitchen at Swedish, had called on the first day of my senior year to tell me they were offering me a special position if I would work full-time rather than complete my senior year of high school. I handed the phone to Mommy. She cursed out Mrs. Gannen, telling her that school was more important than some damn job, and hung up on her. I began to reflect on Mrs. Gannen. She had shown what she thought of me—to her I was only worth a buck seventy-five an hour, as opposed to my going to college and being worth twenty-five to thirty thousand a year.

For the most part, the whites my friend Mike Dean and I worked with in the kitchen were friendly. But the dynamics were changing rapidly. And I was probably changing faster than most of the people around me. I had become super-sensitized to all the events taking place, in my own life and around the nation. All the stories I had heard from Mommy and Poppy and my grandparents, all that I had seen on the evening news, and my own personal sense of righteousness were coming to a head, threatening to erupt—just like those Black folks in Watts and Newark and Philadelphia, erupting without conscience, without concern for the results. Burning, destroying, even killing, lashing out like an angry, cornered dog.

I had started wearing my Black Power shades to work. My position was the most important on the food tray assembly line—I had to read the menus so the other workers could place the proper dietary dishes on each patient's tray. With my sunglasses on, I messed up on more than one occasion. The white night supervisor was a rather rigid person, and after I'd made a few mistakes, she turned off the conveyer belt and asked me to take my glasses off. I refused; we got into a heated argument, and suddenly I exploded. All the anger I held against whites erupted like Mount Vesuvius, spewing out in words of profanity. When she threatened to send me home, I ripped off my apron, told her to kiss my ass, and called her words I had never said to an adult in my life. I stormed out of that place, never to return.

8

The Tide of the Movement

When the dog bites
When the bee stings
When I'm feeling sad
I simply remember
My favorite things
And then I don't feel so bad
    —Rodgers and Hammerstein, "My Favorite Things," 1959

In June of 1967 I graduated from Garfield High with a 2.50 GPA. I celebrated like everyone else—partying and getting drunk. I remember, a week after graduation night, sitting on the long radiator in the living room, looking out the window at the park, where my childhood years seemed to slowly disappear. My head was foggy from another night of drinking with my friends Chester, Tony, and Mike as I tried to figure out what I was going to do with my life.

"Aaron, you're going to have to get a job or go to college. You can't be sitting around here all day," Mommy said while sweeping the living room. Even though I was eighteen and now a high school graduate, I still pretty much respected my parents' words. I knew I was going to have to do something. But what, I did not know.

Without school and without a job, I had no sense of direction or purpose. Leroy Fair, one of the fastest football players in the neighborhood, and I had signed up to crew on a survey ship that traveled from Seattle to Hawaii and Alaska, but Poppy would not let me go. This made me terribly distraught. It would have been a childhood dream come true, an opportunity to travel the high seas and explore exotic, exciting new places. It seemed that every time I reached for a dream, either suddenly or gradually it disappeared from my grasp, leaving me empty and unfulfilled.

Slowly, I began to go into a deep retreat. I spent many lonely days walking the beaches of Lake Washington, sometimes in the rain, feeling empty and purposeless, yet sensing there was something in the distance, on the horizon, waiting to fill up my life. But I could not find any answers or guidance. Searching within, I only ran into my inner anger, my inner rage that also seemed directionless.

Joanne got married to a cat named Curtis Harris, who used to hang out at the Madrona basketball courts—he had a hell of an outside shot. In the meantime, Joanne moved out and Mommy and Poppy let me move into her room, which I appreciated, as I was finding that I needed more time to be alone.

Some days I just lay on the bed, thinking, contemplating, sometimes gazing out the window at the cold, light-blue mountains of the Cascades. Slowly I began to write down my thoughts. The thoughts turned into poems, and the poems began to fill up pages. Mommy and Poppy bought a new hi-fi and gave me the old one, and I started listening to a song I had heard Poppy play, "My Favorite Things" as recorded by John Coltrane. The rhythmic sounds of McCoy Tyner on piano and the melodic play of Coltrane on soprano sax seemed to touch a deep, inner part of my self. I borrowed more records from Mommy and Poppy, and even bought my own jazz records, listening to more Miles Davis and more Coltrane. The sweet, haunting sound of Miles in *Sketches of Spain* seemed to hold a hidden message, a profound piece of information that I somehow had to transcribe, translate, in order to move on with my life. I spent my days writing and listening, listening and writing, coupled with lonely walks, trying to decode the confusion, trying to understand the world and the endless, confounding contradictions in our society.

At times I seemed to be sinking into an abyss, a bottomless pit of despair and sadness, sometimes crying for no evident reason. The idea of death became a close companion, and I began writing about it, wondering about it, about the other side, wondering if that was where I belonged.

Maybe there, in eternity, I could make the connection, decode the signals, find myself, find out who in the hell Aaron was and what he was doing here on earth.

That summer I signed up for a part-time job with a theater group presenting skits that dealt with stereotypes. The theater group was one of the poverty programs initiated by President Lyndon Johnson's War on Poverty. I worked with actors around my age, putting on improv skits with characters we created such as slaves, watermelon-eating coons, white racists, uppity Negroes, and Uncle Toms. Calling ourselves The Walking Stereotypes, we performed all over town at community centers and for other poverty programs. I enjoyed doing those improv skits immensely. After they ended I started hanging out with Aaron Dumas, a playwright and one of the actors from the group. He was three or four years older than me and had written several plays. A smallish, round-shouldered brother with bug eyes and a goatee, Dumas looked like a young version of the playwright LeRoi Jones.

Dumas' first play, *General's Coup*, was about a Black revolt led by a mad Black Nationalist general, who stormed the White House with his troops, and his son, who was also his lieutenant. Dumas played the role of the general and I played his son. The lieutenant son was the voice of reason trying to convince the mad general that it was not necessary to kill all the whites, particularly a young white girl befriended by the lieutenant. Toward the end of the play the general is near insanity, while the son tries to control his father's rage. On our own, we performed this play all over Seattle, on university campuses, in coffeehouses, and at community events. Sometimes Dumas got carried away performing the fight scenes. At times he jumped off the stage and pretended to attack whites in the audience, yelling, "Kill all the honkies!" as I tried to hold him back.

Dumas and I became good friends, spending our free time listening to Eric Dolphy, Gene Ammons, Alice Coltrane, and Yusef Lateef, often discussing the musicians and their personal histories. Dumas knew a lot about jazz and the musicians who played it. Jazz seemed to contain so much within its chords. Listening closely I could make out words and hear stories of lost loves, hopes and dreams.

After we finished with *General's Coup*, we presented another play by Dumas, this one about an interracial affair, a topic extremely rare in 1960s theater. This time, we recruited other actors for the production. Our group was the forerunner of Black Arts/West, Seattle's first Black theater company (formed later, in 1969). Through my work with Dumas, I also got a part in the play *Tom Jones* with a small professional theater company in town, run by a white woman who lived in a Victorian house. I found that I enjoyed performing onstage. Even more, I enjoyed writing, and decided that someday I would go off to New York and become a famous playwright like LeRoi Jones—later known as Amiri Baraka—whose plays and books I had seen and read.

That September, three of my high school friends—Chester, Tony, and Courtney—and I were recruited for a new program, sponsored by the Urban League, designed to help Black students get into the University of Washington. They provided full scholarships, part-time employment, and tutors. A Jewish woman, Mrs. Richman, whose daughter had graduated from Garfield in my class, ran the program. This opportunity came along right after I had received a rejection letter from Tennessee State, where Poppy's sister Aunt Doris had graduated. I had thought I would go there, but my GPA was not high enough. Everyone I knew who went to college had gone away to Black colleges and universities; I had always thought I would get my higher education on an all-Black campus, like Tennessee State. Although I was disappointed, it seemed it was not meant to be.

When we started in September 1967 at the University of Washington, there were only thirty Black students. And it wasn't long before my three buddies dropped out. Sometimes, as I walked through the campus that fall, I was on cloud nine. I could hardly believe I was there. It was picturesque, with the leaves changing colors and all the big, drooping trees. When I walked into my English class, I was surprised to see Mrs. Hundley from Garfield. I was really glad to see her because, with the exception of Mrs. Green, my fourth-grade teacher, Mrs. Hundley was the only teacher who had truly believed in my abilities. Finally, everything was working out. Mommy and Poppy were very supportive and loving. College actually seemed easier than high school. My GPA was higher than it had ever been in high school, and I met a girl, Brenda Dunge, who became my first real love. Originally from Ohio, Brenda was a senior at Franklin High School, and sometimes she came to the UW campus to surprise me.

I continued writing poetry, improving with each new poem. Soon I was participating in poetry readings around town and won second place, including a $500 scholarship, in a Links Arts program. When the Watts Writers Workshop, a group of extremely gifted writers, came up from Los

Angeles to do readings and workshops, I was the only local poet they asked to read with them. Slowly I began to fill up some of the emptiness inside— writing had become my lifeline. Gradually I began to see my possibilities, my hopes and dreams, coming to fruition.

For my sociology class I had to write a term paper. With the help of my tutor and advisor, Dr. Bodemer, I decided to write a paper on Malcolm X. I spent many days with Dr. Bodemer, a short, stocky, gregarious white doctor who taught at the UW Medical School. He taught me the fine art of research, compiling information and organizing that information in a structured manner in order to create a finished product. I met with him at his home in Madrona, becoming good friends with his wife and young kids, and developing a friendship with this easygoing doctor.

For the first time I learned about Malcolm X in depth—his difficulties while growing up, his transformation from thug to righteous militant, and his powerful speeches on the racism of white America. I read about his further transformation upon traveling in the Middle East and how he returned with a broader perspective on the world as whole, rather than only Black America. I was enthralled with Malcolm and his dedication to making the uneven even.

Writing that paper on Malcolm X created a desire in me to know more about the plight of Black people. In junior high and high school I had learned absolutely nothing about Blacks, other than that we had been slaves. I remember how embarrassed I felt every time a history textbook opened up and there was a picture of a slave in tattered clothing, looking lost and disheveled, helpless and hopeless. These images did not correspond to the strength and confidence I experienced in my family and the Black community. I couldn't believe these few images of slaves represented the sum total of the historical Black experience in America. I would slide down in my chair, wishing I could disappear. Or, when the class was mostly Black, someone might crack a joke about the pictures.

I began to read James Baldwin, Richard Wright, Julius Lester, and others—books such as Baldwin's *Blues for Mr. Charlie* and *Notes of a Native Son*, *The Spook Who Sat by the Door* by Sam Greenlee, and *Nigger* by Dick Gregory. Some days I went up to the little Garvey Bookstore on 23rd and Union to browse for some good Black books. I sat with the proprietor, Mrs. Daisy Boyetta, and listened to her stories about Marcus Garvey and her involvement with the Garvey Movement when she was young. Garvey was America's first true Black Nationalist, active in the 1910s and '20s. His movement focused primarily on empowering Black people, and advocated for Black people in America ultimately to return to Africa. I knew very little about that history. Daisy Boyetta was like an old griot, sitting in her little bookshop surrounded by pictures of Marcus Garvey and other Black leaders. She could sense that something was coming, that Blacks were getting ready for the next big push for social justice. Like many Black young seekers who came to her store, I sat quietly, listening to this little old Black lady with her short natural haircut. There was a bitterness about her. Maybe it was disappointment about the unfulfilled potential of the Garvey Movement. Maybe it was the unceasing fight against racism. Maybe it was her own unresolved personal issues. But through these conversations with us young people, she could reinvigorate herself, discussing the injustices committed by the white man and suggesting ideas to counter these injustices.

Some of the older Black students on campus, including Larry Gossett, were starting up a Black student organization at the UW and asked if I would be interested in joining. Larry Gossett had been a basketball star at Franklin High School, one of Garfield's rivals. I began attending meetings of the organization, soon to be called the Black Student Union (BSU). I listened to long discussions about Stokely and Martin Luther King Jr., about Blackness and what it meant, and about the direction of the movement to change America.

The BSU also sponsored guest lecture sessions with out-of-town speakers. One of these lecturers was a young city councilman from Berkeley, Ron Dellums. He was the most engaging Black radical I had met, and he carried himself in such a distinguished manner. There was also a sense of urgency in his talks, as if he were prepping us for an as-yet-undefined mission. Berkeley seemed to be a place on the verge of a social and political transformation. We were always energized when Dellums came to the campus. I and the others around me gradually shed our young, soft skins and began to grow a new, stronger covering, developing a new way of thinking, which energized us with purpose, moving toward a mission even though we didn't yet know what this mission would be. Sometimes I felt as if Dellums were speaking directly to me.

Elmer also began to make a transformation, as did so many other youth. We started hanging around each other again. He left behind his skateboard and sandals, David Booth and Mark Sprague. He had continued playing the trumpet and was by now quite accomplished. I can take partial credit for that because I was always playing Hugh Masekela records while he was practicing, and after a while Masekela, the great African trumpeter, could be heard coming out of Elmer's horn, giving him a unique sound compared to the other trumpet players around town. It seemed that everybody who could play an instrument was in a band, and it wasn't long before Elmer had his own group. They were called the Regents, with Biggy Lewis on guitar and Dennis Blackmon on keyboards, Gary Hammon on tenor sax, and Ralph Brooks on drums. These cats were one hell of a band. Most would go on to make names for themselves. As a matter of fact, the Central District was loaded with great musicians. There must have been eight or ten bands in the area, each with its own unique sound. I sometimes traveled with Elmer's band on their gigs and developed a close friendship with the sax player, Gary Hammon. He went out and got a soprano sax and started teaching me how to play. Sometimes we would go to a dusty, funky little jazz club, both of us carrying our saxes. While Gary played a few numbers, I wished for the day that I would get good enough to sit in.

Even so, my lifelong love of music and my newfound passion for writing and the theater were slowly giving way to my studies and the demands of the BSU. Elmer and his classmate Anthony Ware organized the first high school BSU in the Northwest at Garfield. SNCC had also sent organizers to Seattle with the intention of organizing a chapter. It wasn't long before Elmer, Anthony, and I joined up with SNCC. We bought dark-blue jackets and had "SNCC" stenciled on the back. We attended SNCC/BSU study groups, usually led by E. J. Brisker and Carl Miller. E. J. Brisker, a cat from Washington, DC, could play some basketball and was also extremely intelligent. He was the only person I had ever met who read while walking. At the drop of a hat, he could break down Julius Lester and James Baldwin or discuss the death of Patrice Lumumba. He talked rapid-fire, like a machine gun, puffing constantly on Kool cigarettes, looking down over his wire-rimmed glasses. His protégé, Carl Miller, was from New York. He had good leadership skills and was elected BSU president. Under the guidance of those two and Larry Gossett, the BSU and the new Seattle SNCC chapter began organizing the youth on campus and in the community.

In time, though, Elmer, Anthony, and I started to grow weary of all the meetings and the dissecting of racism in America. Each successive, momentous world event pertaining to freedom and the rights of the oppressed—combined with the deaths of Che Guevara and Patrice Lumumba, both engineered by the CIA; the wars of liberation breaking out all over Africa and South America; intensifying American protest against the war in Vietnam; the student revolts in Mexico City; and the race riots here in the United States—made it increasingly difficult to resist taking action. We felt there had to be some type of message conveyed to the white power structure that if things did not change drastically, we too were going to explode—just as in those other big US cities.

One night Elmer, Anthony, and I decided to make a statement. Carrying a small container filled with gasoline, we sneaked into Broadmoor, a gated private community not far from Madrona. With its fine homes and private golf course, Broadmoor was a place where Black and brown people were not allowed to reside, but they could come in to clean the homes of their white employers. It was a place where young Black boys, many of them my friends, went to carry golf bags and retrieve golf balls for well-to-do white men. That was a job in which I never had any interest. We crept along quietly, looking at the expensive homes, hoping the inhabitants were fast asleep. We found a spot right in the middle of the manicured green lawn of the golf course. Hurriedly, with sticks we carved "Black Power" into the grass and poured gasoline onto the dirt words. We threw a match on the fuel and took off. We never heard of any response to this action. But deep down inside we must have known this would be the first of many acts of rebellion we would carry out in the coming years.

These were very tense times in the United States. There was an edge and a tinge of anger in the air, particularly in interactions between young Blacks and older whites, and especially with the police. I had never experienced police misconduct firsthand; I knew only the experiences of others. But that changed one night as I was leaving my sister's apartment. In front of the apartment building, I observed five police officers accosting my brother-in-law Curtis and his friend Calhoun. The cops threw Curtis down and began to beat him and Calhoun with their batons. I yelled in vain for them to stop. They paid no attention to my young voice. In shock and horror, I turned and sprinted the four blocks home. I opened the door and went into the dining room, grabbed my father's bolo knife from the Philippines, and yelled to my parents that the police were beating Curtis.

As I attempted to run out of the house with the knife, my father grabbed me and said, "Aaron, you can't leave here with that knife."

I suddenly burst into tears. The drama had caught up with me. In frustration and helplessness, I ran back down to Joanne's apartment. Joanne told me that the police had arrested Curtis and Calhoun for some minor traffic violation, and they were already long gone. I walked back home solemnly, resolving never again to experience those emotions. I never wanted to feel that vulnerable or that helpless again.

Not long after that incident, I visited Daisy Boyetta at the Garvey Bookstore. She told me about a brother that was in town. "Aaron, you heard of Voodoo Man?" she asked, peering at me over her wire-rimmed glasses.

"No, I haven't," I answered.

"You need to go see him. He's trying to get some brothers together."

I looked at Mrs. Boyetta with her big, round eyes, half smiling, quietly urging me on as she always did.

Anthony, Elmer, and I decided to pay this Voodoo Man a visit. We found the house Mrs. Boyetta had described on Olive Street, right off of 23rd Avenue, walked up the stairs, and knocked. A tall brother in his late forties or maybe fifties opened the door, wearing a leopard-skin fez and an African cloth tied around his waist, over his pants.

He said, "You brothers come on in."

We walked in, following him, ducking under the beads hanging in the passageway, into the living room, where three brothers a few years older than me were sitting.

"You brothers have a seat," he said. "We were just discussing what to do about Whitey."

We introduced ourselves to the older brothers there. I recognized them from BSU and SNCC meetings. We sat down, glancing around at the candles and beads and African art scattered about the room.

"See, Whitey understands only one thing. You start spilling his blood and you get his attention. . . . We gonna have to call out the haints, call out the warriors. You understand me?"

We all nodded and sat and continued to listen to this older cat. He gestured with his long fingers as he continued to talk for hours about his ideas of rebellion. At one point he walked into the back room and came out with a .30-caliber US carbine, the kind I had seen in countless war movies, the same kind my father had carried into battle in the Philippines.

"Brothers, this is what y'all need, some guns."

We were surprised when a brunette white woman appeared from the kitchen and asked us if we wanted something to drink. After several hours of listening and talking, we left.

We didn't know who this cat was, nor did we care. We just wanted someone to point us in the right direction. We visited Voodoo Man often, and each time we saw more and more brothers and sisters over there from the SNCC and BSU circles we associated with. I think everyone was intrigued by his guns, and his talk was different from what we had been hearing at BSU and SNCC meetings. We didn't even care that he and his whole scene seemed a little weird. We just wanted to move, to act, to make some noise, to startle the white establishment, to let them know we were watching their every move.

One Friday night, Anthony and I accompanied Elmer and the Regents to the YMCA up on 23rd for a "Battle of the Bands" dance and contest. Elmer's band was doing battle with a band from the South End called the Noblemen. They were a group of brothers who were not terribly good musicians, but they were funky and their lead singer, George, knew how to work the audience. During the dance there was some gesturing back and forth between members of the two bands. Because they were from the South End, we did not really know these brothers, nor did they know us. While we were putting our equipment back in the van, Elmer and one of the Noblemen got into an argument, and soon we all squared off with each other and started fighting.

Within minutes the cops showed up and started pushing, shoving, beating us with their batons, and attempting to arrest us in their usual manner, and in a flash we united, turned on the cops, and attacked them. The crowd soon joined in. We chased the cops away and started throwing rocks and bottles at the white passersby, yelling obscenities. It was like an explosion of capped anger, like someone took a bottle of Coca-Cola, shook it up, and let off the cap. We erupted that night with Seattle's first little riot. Soon more cops came. We stood our ground, throwing whatever we could grab, but were slowly overtaken. I was on the corner cussing, throwing rocks, when I was grabbed by four cops and practically heaved onto the hood of a squad car. One cop grabbed my long Afro and pulled my head back by the hair, and out of nowhere came a white guy with a camera, wearing a trench coat. He snapped my picture and disappeared. I knew he was a cop.

Elmer, Anthony, I, and the Noblemen brothers were arrested and taken downtown. We were released a couple hours later without being charged.

The following evening, Reverend Lloyd, the most outspoken religious leader in the Central District, called a community meeting about the incident. His little church on Cherry Street was packed with older people from the community. Many of them were upset about the treatment of us young rebels. We were praised as innocent, brave warriors brutalized by the police. The meeting went on for hours and finally ended without resolution. That little riot at the Y was the first time most of us had an actual physical conflict with the cops. They did not have to come down on us the way they did. But through their actions, they brought us together, uniting us and politicizing us, all in one night. I remember the cop taking my picture, which could have meant only one thing: just as we were preparing ourselves for the inevitable, the authorities were doing the same thing—preparing, by identifying future enemies of the state.

9

The Death
of Martin Luther King Jr.

What's gonna happen now? In all of our cities?
My people are rising; they're living in lies.
Even if they have to die
Even if they have to die at the moment they know what life is
    —Nina Simone, "Why? (The King of Love Is Dead)," 1968

Not long after the incident at the Y, the BSU office received a
call from a distraught Black student at Franklin High School by the name
of Trollis Flavors. Trollis had gotten into a fight with a white student and
had been suspended, while the white student remained in school. That
was not uncommon. However, we had been observing dynamics at
Franklin prior to this episode, as it was a mostly Black and Asian school
yet had no Black or Asian teachers or administrators. The incident with
Trollis Flavors gave us an impetus for taking some type of larger action.

On a rainy Friday morning, twenty-five to thirty BSU members from
the UW, as well as Elmer, Anthony, and a handful of other Garfield High
School students, gathered outside the little sandwich shop across from
Franklin to demand that Trollis be reinstated, and that the school hire Black
and Asian teachers and staff. Led by Larry and Carl, we marched two
abreast as we crossed the street, chanting "Beep, beep! Bang, bang! Ungawa!

Black Power! Ungawa!" and headed into the school. Some of the Black students from Franklin joined us and we proceeded into the administrative office, drowning out the pleas of the little white secretary, who demanded we leave. We asked to meet with the principal, who refused, so we barged into his office, our chants growing louder as we began to feel more powerful. The principal ran out of his office in frustration, eventually canceling school for the rest of the day and sending home the staff, leaving the school in the hands of the students, who were too excited to leave.

Larry and Carl decided to hold a rally in the school auditorium and spoke to a packed house of excited Black, Asian, and white students. We felt overjoyed and victorious. Never before had we experienced this sensation of power. Our complaints and gripes had always been ignored and pushed aside, making us feel like victims without rights, without reasons for grievance. Well, that day we showed the racist school district that the youth were ready to challenge each and every unjust act until things were made right. That weekend we partied and reflected on our victory, eager for the next challenge.

My love for writing and the theater was being overshadowed by these social issues that kept popping up. My personal life was affected, too. My girlfriend, Brenda, gave me an ultimatum to let the militant stuff alone or she would leave me. She was my first love, and for a long time I thought there would be no other. But there was no decision to make. I seemed to be losing control over the events of my life, as though something were pulling me ever so slightly in an unfamiliar direction. It was like walking in one direction, only to have a strong wind overwhelm you, moving you in another direction, toward another place that in time becomes your rightful destination.

Several weeks later, while I was lying across the bed listening to Coltrane's "My Favorite Things," contemplating when to start my English assignment, the doorbell rang. I knew Mommy would answer it, but I figured it was for me, so I ran downstairs—only to find two police officers there, talking to Mommy.

"Mrs. Dixon," they said, "we have a warrant for your son's arrest."

"For what?" she shot back, a serious look on her face.

"For unlawful assembly at Franklin High School," replied one of the officers.

I was handcuffed and I left quietly with the police, telling Mommy not to worry. I was glad Poppy was not there—things might not have gone so peaceably. When I arrived at the police station, I saw Carl Miller and

Larry Gossett, the two BSU heads. I learned that Elmer and Anthony had been arrested right in the classroom and taken to the juvenile detention center, and Trollis Flavors had been arrested as well.

This was my first experience of going to jail. The King County Jail had been built at the turn of the century, and it showed. The place was a dark, archaic-looking dungeon, like something out of medieval times. The only comforting aspect was that I was placed in the same day cell as Larry and Carl. We were dismayed by our sudden arrest, having had no idea that warrants had been put out for us after the demonstration at Franklin. We sat in the dark, cold, gray day cell, exchanging small talk, wondering how we were going to get out. At times we glanced at the old black-and-white TV in the corner, sitting high up on a metal shelf.

The day was April 4, 1968. It had been one of those dreary Seattle days when the rain drizzles down constantly and passively. Then suddenly, Walter Cronkite came on the TV with a grave expression on his face. We weren't sure what we heard coming out of his mouth. Even as we stopped our conversation and listened closely, we were still uncertain.

"Today, in Memphis, Tennessee, Martin Luther King Jr. was assassinated."

The word *assassinated* reverberated inside my head, almost throwing me off balance. Carl and Larry gasped. "What? What? NO, man, no, man, this can't be real," said Larry.

We looked at each other in shock. Walter Cronkite continued the broadcast, talking about the assassination and the riots that were beginning to break out in Harlem, Chicago, and Detroit. Stokely came on in Washington, DC, holding a .22-caliber pistol, shouting, "It's now time to burn, burn, baby, burn!" as crowds of young people rampaged through the streets of DC.

Other broadcasts came through, showing similar scenes of riots and mayhem in city after city. It was looking like the revolution had come— and here we were, sitting in jail. The three of us retreated to some private, personal space to try to comprehend the moment. Tears welled up in Carl's eyes. My emotions were going wild. I kicked and banged the steel table, throwing whatever I could throw, wishing I were out there on the streets.

Martin had been heaven-sent, a modern-day saint, our Mahatma Gandhi, confronting America and its injustice as no other man had ever done, and doing all this with no malice, no anger, no hatred, just pure love and pure faith that someday we could all live in peace and harmony. Later that night those of us from the day cell were ushered farther back into darkness, down a dark corridor to our one-man cells. I was glad to be alone, glad to be away by myself where I could grieve in private. I thought back to when I was twelve and sat on the corner of that bandstand listening to Martin, looking out on the crowd, feeling somehow responsible for his well-being, looking at his smooth face, feeling his love. Despite becoming impatient with his nonviolent, nonthreatening approach, we young organizers still greatly admired his courage. He was our modern-day savior.

Anger filled me that night. There would be no more tears and no more dialogue. The war began that night all across America. I vowed to myself that Martin's death would not go unavenged. If a man of peace could be killed through violence, then violence it would be. For me, the picket sign would be replaced, and in its place would be the gun. It was now an eye for an eye and a tooth for a tooth. There would be no more unanswered murders. I finally dozed off to a painful sleep.

The next morning we were awakened for our bail hearing. We first met with two young ACLU attorneys, Mike Rosen, a Jewish man, and Chris Young, a white woman. They told us that the courtroom was packed with students and supporters and briefed us on how to respond to the questions presented by the judge. I was the last of the three of us to walk into the courtroom. Larry and Carl had already been released. Now it was my turn. I felt almost overwhelmed, looking at the sea of faces crowded into the courtroom. Some faces I recognized. Most I did not. They all seemed to melt together, and I tried to maintain my composure when the crowd gave a big cheer upon my release.

Mommy came over and hugged me. It was a relief to be out. But the pain of losing Martin was still immediate and very strong. At the same time there was an even stronger sense of certainty, a feeling that the time for major action was fast approaching, that our day of redemption was near.

The next day, the *Seattle Post-Intelligencer* ran a large photo on the front page of Larry, Carl, and me wearing my Stokely shades—putting me into the mind of every cop in the city. After that photo I could not go anywhere without being stopped and harassed by the Seattle police.

That night many of us met at Voodoo Man's house. America was burning over Martin's death, and we wanted Seattle to burn, too. So far Voodoo Man was the only one who seemed willing to meet our needs, to share our desire for revenge. He sent out three squads of brothers to throw firebombs and handed me and Dewayne Hall .30-caliber carbines, telling us he wanted us to stay there with him to protect the house. I remember squatting in the kitchen, guarding the back door in the candlelit den, the sounds of sirens all around, wondering what would happen that night and what the others were doing. Every now and then, a cop car with lights flashing would go by, streaking to some unknown destination.

Voodoo Man was walking around with his carbine, eyebrows arched with a crazy, far-off look in his eyes. "Man, tonight the blood is going to flow."

My thoughts wandered to images of armed Black guerrillas running across rooftops and through deserted, bloody streets. Suddenly, those thoughts were broken by the flashing of red and blue lights and unintelligible voices. There were four cop cars out front with their lights on.

"You and Dee wait here," said Voodoo Man as he stepped outside. Dewayne and I looked at each other, wondering what the cops were doing.

We heard Voodoo Man arguing with the police as they arrested four brothers from the firebomb squads. They had returned to Voodoo Man's house, followed by the cops. Dewayne and I thought for sure that Voodoo Man's bloodbath would start right then on that night, a night filled with conflicting emotions—whether to stay or leave, to live or die, to fight or surrender.

After several minutes, Voodoo Man came back in the house, the red and blue lights still flashing. "We goin' have to kill some of these cops. They arrested the brothers. The Man only understands one thing, and that's these things right here," he said, holding up his carbine. "You brothers get yourself ready 'cause I'm in need of you two warriors."

The cops eventually left. The night went on with the constant sound of sirens in the distance. Dewayne and I dozed off and on, clutching our carbines, hoping we would live to see the next day. He and I had played football and basketball together. Despite his diminutive size, Dewayne had become a phenomenon on both the football field and basketball court. And here we were, together on this ugly night, seeking to avenge the death of our fallen leader.

In the morning, Dewayne and I left Voodoo Man's house. Dewayne never went there again. I probably should have done the same, but I was in too deep now. For me there was no turning back, despite what seemed a dim, sometimes suicidal road ahead. As a show of his confidence in me, Voodoo Man gave me the carbine I had held all night. I sneaked it into the house and hid it in my bedroom closet.

10

The Panther Emerges

I left my home in Georgia
Headed for the Frisco bay
'Cause I've had nothing to live for
And look like nothin's gonna come my way
—Otis Redding, "(Sittin' on) The Dock of the Bay," 1967

Several days later, a group of fifteen to twenty of us—BSU and SNCC members—rented four or five cars through the BSU. Elmer disconnected the odometers so we would not be charged for the mileage we would be racking up. In a caravan, we headed down to San Francisco to attend the second annual West Coast BSU Conference. Anthony Ware had attended the first West Coast conference the previous year in Los Angeles and described a heated disagreement between two organizations that had almost led to bloodshed. One was a cultural nationalist organization led by Maulana Ron Karenga; the other was called the Black Panther Party for Self-Defense, led by two brothers named Huey Newton and Bobby Seale. They were the same group I had seen on the news a couple years before, leading an armed demonstration to the California capitol building in Sacramento.

This was the first time Elmer and I had traveled together without our parents. It was exciting to be in San Francisco, free of parental constraints. Young people from all over the country came to this city, searching for meaning, looking for their place in a conflicted society. Otis Redding's "(Sittin' On) The Dock of the Bay" had become a call of sorts for young people to come to the windswept hills and the beautiful bay of San Francisco. So it was no coincidence that we were here, too, searching, looking to the conference and elsewhere for direction in our quest for liberation.

After checking in at San Francisco State, where we registered and got our housing assignments, we were assigned a driver to show us around and take us to our sleeping quarters. Our driver was a smooth-skinned Black brother wearing a semi-short, neat, jet-black Afro. The car sped through the often narrow San Francisco streets, swishing past streetcars, old, colorful Victorian homes, and intermittent views of the Pacific Ocean. He took us through the Haight-Ashbury district, where throngs of long-haired white kids wandered through the streets wearing rainbow-colored clothing. Some were hugging each other, looking glassy-eyed. Within minutes we were on Fillmore Street, filled with proud Blacks and Black businesses, jazz clubs, blues clubs, barbeque joints, and corner liquor stores. Our driver pointed out significant landmarks, such as Marcus Books (named for Marcus Garvey) and the Black Muslim Mosque.

When we asked if he knew any Panthers, he began to open up. "Yeah, I know a lot of the Panthers. Matter a fac' we goin' to raid a Hell's Angels house tonight," he said, pulling some bullets out of his pocket along with a beret. He added, "They're havin' a funeral tomorrow over in Oakland for a Panther killed by the police."

Eventually, he dropped Anthony, Kathy Jones, Gary Owens, Elmer, and me off at the Black professor's house where we were staying, not far from the university campus.

The next day Elmer, Anthony, and I went around the conference and tried to find some workshops that interested us. We even sat in on a couple, but left disappointed. Not one was interesting to us. Or, at least, none seemed to fill our needs. We saw a flyer about the funeral the driver had mentioned, and decided to drive one of the rented cars to Oakland to check out the funeral of the slain Panther, a young man called Little Bobby Hutton. Larry Gossett, Gary Owens, and a few other BSU members went with us. On the way to Oakland, we stopped to buy some black berets to show our solidarity with the Panthers. After crossing the Bay Bridge into West Oakland, we spotted a small church in the distance. As we approached we could see a group of Black men in leather coats and black berets gathered in front. We pulled out our berets and put them on. As we got closer we saw Marlon Brando, my mother's favorite actor, dressed in a black leather coat and black beret, standing in front of the church, talking to a tall Black man—Bobby Seale, as we later learned, the chairman of the Black Panthers.

We got out of the car and walked quietly into the small, white church. Inside it was dark and packed full of mourners standing, and on both sides of the church were Black men dressed in black leather jackets, black pants, and powder-blue shirts, with black berets. They stood half at attention, their eyes focused toward the front, where a brown wooden casket held the body of the murdered young Panther. In the center front of the church, a group of older, heavyset Black women were bunched together, wailing uncontrollably, reaching out to the casket for the hand that could not reach back.

We stood there, listening to the preacher as he gave his eulogy over the soft cries that sometimes erupted into loud shrieks. The faces of the young men and women in black were unchanged, almost emotionless. We fell into the procession as it wound its way to the front, past the casket. I looked into the casket of the one known as Little Bobby. He was so young-looking, yet there was an oldness about him, his face uneven and somewhat swollen. The cries of Mrs. Hutton and the other women filled my ears, almost blocking out everything else. I don't think any of us had ever experienced anything as somber and as sad as the funeral of Little Bobby Hutton.

On the way back to our lodgings, I paged through the Panther paper handed out at the church and read the story of Little Bobby Hutton: how he had joined the organization at age sixteen and risen to the position of minister of finance, how he and Eldridge Cleaver, the minister of information, had been cornered by the police in an abandoned house and overcome with tear gas. Bobby Hutton had been shot numerous times, despite having come out of the house unarmed and with his hands up. He was killed just two days after Martin Luther King Jr., in the police crackdown on the riots following Martin's death. Seventeen Panthers had been arrested on charges of conspiracy to murder.

Later that evening we went back to San Francisco State to await the BSU conference keynote address by Bobby Seale. Those of us who had attended the funeral were in a solemn mood. Looking into the casket of Little Bobby Hutton had been almost like looking into the future and glimpsing what the movement might hold. It was not the glory and the victory we had romanticized.

It began to get dark outside. Bobby Seale was already an hour late. Elmer, Anthony, and I found a corner of the auditorium and stood quietly talking, waiting for the messenger. We were wondering if the Panthers were going to show up. Maybe something else had happened. Maybe the police had attacked the brothers again. Finally, the doors to the auditorium flung open, and in walked Bobby Seale, followed by a handful of brothers and sisters. I recognized the tall, light-brown sister with the big brown Afro as Kathleen Cleaver, the wife of Eldridge Cleaver. I had seen her picture in the Black Panther paper. She almost glided across the room. Next to her was a Panther walking with a limp. I would learn later that he was Warren Wells, one of the brothers wounded in the shootout. The entourage moved quietly, almost sullenly, occasionally whispering among themselves.

The Panthers spread out across the audience. Jimmy Johnson, the BSU president at San Francisco State, introduced Bobby Seale, who took center stage. Bobby Seale looked beleaguered as he began to address the crowd.

"All power to the people, brothers and sisters.

"We just came from burying our comrade, Little Bobby Hutton, who was murdered by a bunch of racist, fascist pigs. The pigs murdered Little Bobby despite the fact that he was unarmed, despite the fact that he had his hands up. The pigs also shot and wounded the minister of information, Comrade Eldridge Cleaver, who is locked up in the Alameda County Jail, along with seventeen other party members, including our national captain, David Hilliard.

"The comrades were transporting supplies in preparation for a rally for Huey P. Newton at DeFremery Park when they were ambushed by a bunch of low-life racist dog pigs.

"They killed Little Bobby because they knew Little Bobby was a revolutionary who wasn't afraid of confronting the pig power structure.

"Huey taught us that we have a right to defend ourselves, that we have a right to defend our community. Huey said the pigs occupy our community like a foreign troop occupies foreign territory. The pigs aren't there to protect us. They're there in our community to protect the interest of the pig power structure and the avaricious pig businessmen.

"Brother Malcolm didn't take no shit. Brother Malcolm was a revolutionary brother. He understood that racist white America would do whatever it has to do to maintain the power structure. Brother Malcolm also knew that we are in an international struggle for the rights of all people.

Whether you be black, brown, red, white, all oppressed people have a right to live decently. Brother Huey understood that. Brother Huey knew we had to go forth and organize the brothers on the block, the brothers that don't have any interest in this racist system.

"Black intellectuals always want to analyze, 'The hypothesis for this matter is. . . .' That's a bunch of bullshit. We don't need to analyze this shit. We don't need to intellectualize. We need to get serious. We need to organize. We need to pick up some guns."

I was standing in the middle of the crowd, separated from Anthony and Elmer. I looked around at the audience as the tall, rangy Bobby Seale continued, contorting his face, using his hands to punctuate his ideas and the philosophy of the Panthers. Some in the audience were becoming uncomfortable. Others were mesmerized, just as I was, listening to every word Mr. Seale had to say.

At one point, he stopped speaking. "Who got something to drink in here?" he asked, taking off his leather jacket and loosening his black tie. I remembered the vodka I had bought earlier in the day as a present for Mommy and Poppy. I went over to the corner where my belongings were, reached in the bag, pulled out a quart of vodka, and handed it to a Panther brother standing next to me. He handed it to Bobby Seale, who opened the bottle and took a long swig. Soon the bottle was traveling around the room. It came back to me, so I followed suit and took a swig of the tasteless alcohol and passed it on.

Bobby Seale was loosening up. He became more animated. His facial expression began to soften. He talked about being a drummer and a comedian and his stint in the air force. He talked about Martin Luther King and the Kennedy brothers, and for a few seconds he portrayed a Black man chained up, struggling to be free.

After nearly two hours, the speech was finally over, and the lights went on in the auditorium. Without thought or hesitation, I found myself making a beeline to where Bobby Seale was standing. Elmer and Anthony arrived in front of Bobby Seale at the same time.

"We want a Panther chapter in Seattle." The words came out of my mouth automatically. The four of us talked briefly, and we left our phone number with Bobby Seale.

I had seen Martin Luther King speak in person. I had listened to records of Adam Clayton Powell often, and to the taped speeches of Malcolm X.

All these had inspired me, but the speech I had just witnessed totally blew me away, pushing me off my safety perch, casting me out into the wind, my eyes wide open. I could not sleep that night. I only wanted time to move ahead; I wanted to speed up time, propelling me faster toward my fate.

At home in Seattle, a week after we returned from the BSU conference, I received a call from Bobby Seale. He and two other Panthers were coming in the following day at 1:30 p.m. I wrote down the flight information and told him someone would meet them at the airport. After the call, I immediately began to spread the word. By 1 p.m. the next day, about twenty-five people had appeared at our house. Chester Northington and John Eichelburger, whom I had met at Voodoo Man's, came carrying rifles. I sent Elmer and Anthony to the airport to pick up Bobby Seale and the others.

When they finally arrived, Bobby Seale looked tired yet energized, a man on a mission, ready to stir our hearts and emotions, ready to lay out the party's philosophy and platform to us young, eager listeners. He introduced his two companions. "This is George Murray, the minister of education, and Brother Reginald Denning, San Francisco State organizer," said Bobby Seale, scanning the faces of his young audience.

"All power to the people," replied Murray, a brother with uncombed hair and dark sunglasses.

The three Panthers sat down on the couch. Among our group were Kathy Halley, Kathy Jones, Larry Gossett, and a handful of other BSU members from the UW. Willie Brazier and some of his street buddies were there as well. It was quite a mix of young people. We sat or stood, huddled around these three men of experience, listening intently to every word.

"First off," Bobby started, "to be a member of the Black Panther Party, every member must have two weapons and a thousand rounds of ammunition. And you need to know how to clean your weapons and break them down and you need to know how to carry your weapons in a disciplined fashion—you dig?"

"Right on," we responded.

"The party isn't just about a bunch of niggas getting together with a bunch of guns. You gotta have some ideology. Brother Huey says the power of the people grows out of the barrel of a gun, but at the same time we have to study to understand how to unravel all the shit the oppressor has put down on the people. Right?"

"Right on," we answered, quietly.

"The minister of education, Brother George, is going to talk to you about political education classes."

"You know who Frantz Fanon is?" Brother George asked, as he pulled out several books from a large, overstuffed, black briefcase he was carrying. "This book, *Wretched of the Earth*, is essential for Panthers to read. Brother Frantz Fanon breaks it down about the psychology that develops between the oppressed and the oppressor. He talks about the Algerian people and the fight for liberation against the French colonizers. We, as oppressed people, have taken on a number of attributes that can be considered detrimental to our struggle for liberation.

"This is another book by Fanon." He pulled another book from the briefcase, *Black Skin, White Masks*. "Somebody here taking notes?" he asked.

Kathy Jones answered quickly, "I'll take notes," pulling out her high school notebook.

"Panthers must read at least two hours a day. Here is a list of books that you have to study. They got some righteous bookstores around here?"

"Yeah," someone bellowed out. "Mrs. Boyetta's bookstore."

"And the books you can't find, we will send you some."

The meeting went on all day and well into the night. People came, people left. My parents came in from work, prepared dinner as usual, not really saying much but sharing the sense of history we were all feeling. Many questions were asked, and the three visitors answered them all, including one Joyce Redman posed about the sisters in the party.

"We say that the woman is our better half. In the party, a sister is our equal. And we don't play that male chauvinism shit. You gotta respect a sister, just like you would a brother, you dig?"

"Right on," we answered.

Bobby spent considerable time talking about Huey Newton. "Brother Huey was a bad motherfucker when he ran the streets with his runnin' buddies. He was known as a fierce street fighter. But he also read a lot of books. He always studied a lot of shit. Huey understood what was goin' on with the masses of oppressed people. He realized that we have to organize the people against the racist pig power structure. We have to raise the consciousness of the people and educate them about the fact that they have a right to defend themselves, just as it says in the Second Amendment of the Constitution.

"Me and Huey and Little Bobby sat down and came up with the ten-point program and platform of the Black Panther Party. The ten-point program and platform speaks to the needs of Black people and all Panthers must memorize it, know it by heart. Number one, we want freedom, we want the power to determine the destiny of our Black community. Number two, we want decent housing fit for the shelter of human beings. . . ."

I sat and listened to the words of Bobby Seale as he continued detailing the Panthers' platform. The words eased from his lips. His face was unshaven, his hair uncombed. He wore an unbuttoned blue shirt and black slacks.

I felt privileged to have him and the others here in my house. I also felt uncertain. On one hand, I felt the pull of history. On the other hand, I felt afraid—afraid about the future, and scared that bit by bit my young freedom was now being committed to the struggle.

"Who's going to be the defense captain?" Seale asked.

I was caught by surprise, having slipped off into deep thought. Fingers were pointing my way. It was as if no one wanted the responsibility for leading what lay ahead. I felt a little like a trick had been played on me, and I fell for it because, as usual, my response was slow. Reluctantly, I accepted my new role.

"Okay, Dixon. You're the captain. I want you to come with me back to New York on an organizing tour through the East Coast. There's a lot of shit you have to learn," said Bobby Seale.

The title "defense captain" may have been placed on my head without my resistance, but I definitely was not ready to up and go with Bobby Seale and the others. I felt deeply about the movement that was rapidly gaining steam, coming over the horizon, but I was not yet a true, committed revolutionary. I was not ready to leave the comfort of my home, the love of my parents, or the tranquility of Madrona.

"Bobby, I can't leave right now. I have some stuff to take care of." I hoped my response didn't sound too weak, like a cop-out. I needed time to think, to adjust to everything that was happening.

The next morning, Bobby Seale and the others were gone, heading to their East Coast destination to appoint more captains, to arouse the hearts of hungry young men and women. A week later, I would be on my first plane ride—to Oakland and the beginning of a much different life.

11

7th and Wood—April 1968

Look over your shoulder
There will I be
Look over your shoulder
There I'll be waiting patiently
　　　　　—O'Jays, "Look Over Your Shoulder," 1968

Ever since my arrest for the Franklin sit-in, rebellious events had
been erupting in a quick, staccato manner. I was changing rapidly but also
had some inner resistance, creating a push-and-pull; it felt like a tug-of-
war, an exciting yet very dangerous game of tug-of-war. Yet, this rebellion
is what I was being prepared for. In some ways, this seemed to be what I
was born for—to add my voice to the chorus of dissent and the cry for
change. No matter the shyness, the inexperience, the doubts. Resistance
was my path and I was ready—even if reluctantly—to follow.

I, along with many others on the West Coast, was now a member of
the Black Panther Party, an organization born on the streets of Oakland,
born not out of desperation but out of an innate desire to be free—free
from the racism, poverty, and police brutality that seemed to engulf almost
every person of color in the United States. Fueled by anger, frustration,
and the Black Nationalism of the mid-sixties, the party began to unfold.
Two friends, Huey P. Newton and Bobby Seale, along with their young

protégé, sixteen-year-old Bobby Hutton, and later David Hilliard, Elbert "Big Man" Howard, and other schoolboy friends, formulated the organization. Ron Dellums, the inspiring radical whose words had so affected me when he spoke at our BSU lectures, also took part in the strategizing sessions. And in October 1966, the Black Panther Party for Self-Defense was born.

Based on Malcolm X's vision of a broad revolutionary movement, they began to piece together a militant, internationally minded organization, which Huey and Bobby infused with their knowledge of history and other, kindred liberation struggles in Africa and Latin America. Drawing on the US Constitution, Huey and Bobby based the party's ideology and strategy around particular Constitutional elements, the first being the right to bear arms. Dressed in the Panther uniform, armed with shotguns, .30-caliber carbines, and .45s, Huey and Bobby led their small group of young, Black, armed rebels into the streets on missions that ranged from providing security for Malcolm's widow, Betty Shabazz, to protesting the murder of young Denzil Dowell by a sheriff's deputy in Richmond, to patrolling the police on the streets of Oakland. And now I was about to enter into this world of tough Black revolutionaries.

I remember that first flight so clearly. It was late April 1968. This was not only my first trip to Oakland as a member of the Black Panther Party but also my first time ever flying in an airplane. My emotions were running wild—the exhilaration of my first flight combined with excitement, apprehension, and fear of what might await me at the other end. I could barely hold a single thought in my mind. In many ways I was leaving behind my childhood, all the games at Madrona Park, the innocence of youth, the protective comforts my parents had provided during the first nineteen years of my life. All those memories would soon be supplanted by defiance, anger, rage, uncertainty, fear, and pain—as well as dedication, hope, and occasionally victory.

When the pilot announced our approach to the San Francisco International Airport, I looked out the window at the glistening waters of the San Francisco Bay, almost lapping up against the runways dotted with airplanes, some landing and others taking off for faraway destinations. I wondered how this plane was going to land on that thin airstrip.

As we hit the ground, my thoughts quickly shifted to what lay ahead and who was waiting for me. I began questioning the decisions that had brought me to this point. Doubts rose in my mind and my palms began to sweat. Walking down the airport corridor in my Panther uniform, I realized it was too late to turn back, too late to change the circumstances that had led me to my destiny. The time was ripe for me to take my place in the movement.

My hands were clammy, my heart beat a little faster, and anticipation was building with each step. Yet I tried to stay cool, stay calm. In the distance, among the crowd of white faces, I could see a tall, slender Black man in a short black leather jacket. As I approached, he smiled confidently, exposing a missing tooth and several silver crowns. He was wearing thin black sunglasses, the kind we used to call "pimp shades."

"All power to the people, Comrade Eric," he said as he extended his hand. "All power to the people, Comrade."

"It's Aaron," I replied, as we exchanged the Black Power handshake. "I'm Tommy Jones."

With Tommy was a very stocky, brown-skinned brother with a neat Afro. He quickly introduced himself. "Hey, Comrade, I'm Robert Bay. Welcome to the Bay."

We walked out to the parking lot. Tommy threw my father's old suitcase in the trunk and we jumped in Robert Bay's blue '65 LeSabre, headed for Oakland.

I sat in the back, excited, exchanging small talk, listening to the sounds of the congas of Mongo Santa Maria blaring on the eight-track, looking at the small, white houses stacked like cards on the San Francisco hillside, the sun shining brightly.

The freeway took us through downtown San Francisco before reaching the San Francisco Bay Bridge. The gray, cold, steel bridge seemed to stretch for miles, yet it was only minutes before we took the exit into West Oakland and headed down Grove Street.

In the distance, on the right-hand side of the street, I could see a group of young Black men milling around, some dressed in the Panther uniform of black leather jackets and black berets. We pulled up in front of the group and got out, facing the National Headquarters of the Black Panther Party. The large storefront windows were plastered with posters. A large one of Huey hung in the middle—Huey was sitting in a wicker chair, a spear in one hand and a long, bolt-action shotgun in the other, looking boyish and pensive, distant, not quite real. This image of Huey with spear and shotgun would become the defining image of the party, a worldwide symbol of Black resistance to US imperialism.

There was also a poster of a young man. I recognized the young Panther's face—it was Bobby Hutton. The photograph must have been taken not long before he was brutally killed by the Oakland police. He was smiling infectiously, wearing a military-style hat with a military fatigue jacket draped over his shoulders. There was also a poster of Eldridge Cleaver, the minister of information, wearing dark shades and smoking a cigarette.

I was so warmly greeted by the brothers standing out front that I completely forgot my nervousness and apprehension. I met Jimmy Charley and Orleander Harrison, a sixteen-year-old who coolly introduced himself, a toothpick dangling from his lips.

In the office, behind a long counter separating the office from the waiting area, was a tall sister with a large, glistening Afro, who was very busy answering phones and organizing material. She stopped her work briefly and said, "You must be the brother from Seattle. I'm Betty, the national secretary. The chairman said for you to stay with Tommy and he would catch up with you tomorrow."

After mingling with some of the Panthers out front, Tommy and I split and headed to his pad about two blocks away on West Street. Tommy was much older than me, almost forty, but he looked to be in good physical condition. I was surprised when he told me he was originally from Tacoma, which instantly gave us a connection.

"I joined the navy when I was eighteen," Tommy said. "So after I got out, I just stayed right here in Oakland. I worked for a while as a cook." He had also become immersed in the Oakland street life, selling dope and hustling. Now he was a full-time revolutionary.

"The party is the best thing that ever happened to me," he said. "I was into all kinds of bullshit before I joined the party. After they killed Malcolm, a lot of brothers started gittin' involved in shit. Now they done killed Martin Luther King and Little Bobby. These pigs gone crazy, but we got somethin' for their ass. We don't take no shit from these pigs."

Tommy's apartment was a small, cramped studio full of the comforts for a single man.

"You got a piece, Comrade?"

I stuttered, not sure how to answer, thinking of the rifle from

Voodoo Man in my closet at home. "I—I have a .30-caliber carbine," I replied, "but . . ."

"Right on! Comrade, you need a handgun. You never know when the pigs are going to vamp. You gotta be ready 'cause they will try to kill us unless we can defend ourselves. I'll get you a piece."

I could tell that Tommy had taken a liking to me. Maybe it was our Northwest connection.

"This is what I carry," Tommy said, pulling out a snub-nosed .38 revolver. "You can conceal this piece real easy. I got some automatic weapons buried out in the woods. And check this out." He pulled out a picture of himself, bare-chested, holding a Thompson submachine gun. "We ain't going to let them kill Huey in the gas chamber."

Just then the phone rang. "That was Matilaba," Tommy reported after a brief exchange. "She's on her way over to do some studying out of the Red Book. You got a Red Book?" he asked.

"No, I don't," I responded.

"Here, take this one. We study Mao's Red Book. It gives us our ideology and revolutionary principles. We study this every day."

While I thumbed through the little pocket-sized book with the red plastic cover, there came a soft knock at the door. Tommy opened the door and in walked a beautiful, brown-skinned sister dressed in jeans and combat boots. She smiled ever so sweetly, yet seemed so serious.

"Aaron, this is Comrade Matilaba. This is Aaron, captain of the Seattle chapter."

"All power to the people," she said.

I responded, "All power to the people."

We sat down and Matilaba began to read aloud: "The revolutionary war is a war of the masses. It can be waged only by mobilizing the masses and relying on them."

I listened to Tommy and Matilaba discuss and break down each paragraph, applying each reading to the party and to America. I participated in the discussion whenever possible, even though I knew very little about Mao, let alone Marxist-Leninism.

After about twenty minutes, we concluded our study session, my first political education (PE) class. Matilaba departed like a fresh breeze disappearing into the midday sun. I later learned that she had joined the party at the age of seventeen, the first woman to join. An accomplished violinist and visual artist, she became one of the party's most important artists. I also learned she was part of a cadre with Tommy and Robert Bay. Cadres were small, informal groups within the party that studied, trained, and carried out missions together.

Tommy and I went over to Robert Bay's house. His place was on 45th Street, around the corner from National Headquarters. The house was in back of another home, as was common in Oakland. Sparsely furnished, with a chair and a small TV in the living room, it had two bedrooms in the rear and another bedroom adjacent to the living room. Robert shared these living quarters with two lanky brothers, Randy and Landon Williams, as well as a cute young sister named Ora Scott, who was relating with Landon. ("Relating with" was a Panther expression for being involved.) Randy and Landon had both spent time in Vietnam as Special Forces Rangers; now they were captains in the National Headquarters of the party. Robert Bay had also served in Vietnam.

The older of the two Williams brothers, Randy was very reserved, a man of few words. At times he seemed almost emotionless—a sharp contrast to the younger Landon, who was excited when Tommy introduced me as the captain of the Seattle chapter. The housemates showed me their artillery. Each kept a small arsenal in his room, including reloading equipment for making ammo. The weapons varied from AR-15s to carbines to Robert Bay's long, bolt-action shotgun, identical to the one held by Huey Newton in the famous poster. They also showed me their handguns. Randy carried a 9mm Astra and Robert Bay carried a snub-nosed .38 similar to Tommy's, a weapon common on the streets. Landon, in contrast, proudly showed off his big .44 Magnum.

Tommy left to attend to some party business that would extend well into the evening, so I ended up spending the night with Landon and Randy. They took me down to a juke joint in West Oakland near some railroad tracks. The place was full of Black folks drinking and talking loudly and listening to some down-home blues blaring from the jukebox. Landon and Randy, wearing green army fatigue jackets, moved freely through the crowd and appeared to know everybody. They talked to a number of people, with me following behind. Not long after we arrived, there was a loud crash. A fight had started, and someone got knocked through the big front window by a brother who looked really crazy.

Landon, Randy, and I quickly moved outside as the fight continued.

People were pouring out of the club, and sisters were screaming in panic. Landon and Randy separated themselves from the crowd by standing quite a distance away, observing the mayhem, and keeping their hands on their weapons. This juke joint was the kind of place where the poor and disenfranchised came to unwind, to release the week's tensions and frustrations. And things could turn deadly in the blink of an eye. We left to avoid the police, who would inevitably be arriving soon.

The next morning, Robert Bay took me around the corner to National Headquarters, where I waited for a ride to Bobby Seale's home. When my ride finally arrived, we sped wildly through the streets of North Oakland to arrive at a brown bungalow. Inside, I met Artie Seale, Bobby's wife, a gregarious, bright-eyed beauty, and their four-year-old son, Malik, who closely resembled Bobby. Little Malik was just as bright-eyed as his mother—full of energy, bouncing all over the place. Bobby Seale walked quickly out of his bedroom, buttoning his powder-blue shirt, dressed in black slacks and black shoes.

"All power to the people, Comrade," he said. "Did Tommy and the brothers break down for you what the party is about?" Bobby asked. "There is a lot of shit for you to learn, brother. We got a lot of work to do. We gotta keep these pigs from killing Brother Huey. I want you to go up to the jail and visit him before you leave. You dig?"

"Right on, Bobby," I answered.

"Since the April sixth shootout, the pigs have been vamping on Panthers, bustin' 'em on a bunch of trumped-up bullshit charges. I want you to stay with me today so you can understand how the party functions. I have to go up to Merritt College and meet with some brothers and sisters."

We left in a whirlwind, heading to the school, which was located down on Grove Street. Bobby talked to a class of students and met with BSU representatives. He introduced me to a young brother named Larry, the BSU president at McClymonds High School in West Oakland. Larry proved to be instrumental in organizing the BSU on high school campuses across Oakland. I would see him on many of my trips to the Bay Area, and we eventually became good friends.

I rode with Bobby Seale all day, racing from one meeting to the next. Toward the end of the day, we ended up heading across the Bay Bridge to a meeting of the party's Central Committee at the home of Don Cox, one of the party's three field marshals.

We drove up to a gray Victorian house. The entrance was a narrow hallway that led into a plush living room filled with books and tasteful furnishings. We were met warmly by a small, young Black woman with a short Afro. "Hi, I'm Barbara."

"Barbara, this is Aaron," said Bobby.

"Nice to meet you," I replied.

"Don will be with you in a minute."

Don Cox entered from one of the other rooms. He was a light-complexioned, very distinguished-looking man wearing a neat Afro, with touches of gray in his mustache. "All power to the people, Comrade. Welcome."

Others began to show up. Emory Douglas, the party's chief artist and one of its early members, introduced himself, then Captain Bill Brent, an older, steely-eyed brother, and Captain Crutch, another fortyish-looking brother, with a processed hairdo and a slight limp. He reminded me of some of the older brothers I knew who were involved in the street life in Seattle. He looked nothing like my image of a revolutionary. We were also joined by a tall, lanky brother named David Hilliard, the party's national captain, and, to my surprise, Stokely Carmichael, the one who had lit the flame of rebellion in my heart. I learned that he and the other leaders of SNCC had recently been recruited into the party.

The meeting began, and Chairman Bobby Seale introduced me. As the meeting progressed, members debated back and forth, mostly about the need for more rules and discipline in the party. I sat quietly, listening to these older men, these strong, brave leaders of the party.

After the meeting, Don Cox went into a back room and came out with several rifles.

"Hey, Chairman, I want to show you something. We got a big shipment of these in. They're called Santa Fe Troopers."

I marveled at the rifle. It looked almost exactly like an M-14 but shorter and more compact, and it used the same ammo: 7.62mm cartridges. This weapon was later dubbed "the Panther Special."

"Right on, brother," responded Bobby.

The next morning, a ride took me to the Alameda County Jail to visit our leader, Huey P. Newton, a requirement for all new chapter captains. I felt unprepared for this face-to-face meeting with the leader of the Black Panther Party. I tried to figure out what to say, how to present myself, and what he'd think of me. I signed in and waited for my turn to go up in the elevator to the twelfth floor of the jail. As I got off the elevator, I noticed how small and cramped it was up there in the visiting section. The place was jammed with Black people trying to visit family members and friends for a precious, limited time. The room was painted a dull, off-gray color, giving it a very dreary look.

Finally, my name was called and I made my way up to the window, which had a small metal piece that the visitor had to raise up in order to be able to speak into the cell. There, sitting in a tiny space on a metal stool, was a short, thin, light-skinned brother with responsive eyes.

It was Huey. "All power to the people, Comrade," he said, raising his clenched fist.

"All power to the people," I said as I awkwardly bent down and attempted to speak while giving the power salute.

"How are things going in Seattle, Comrade?" asked Huey.

"They're going good. The movement in Seattle is growing day by day," I responded, hoping my answer sounded revolutionary.

We exchanged small talk for a few minutes. I was nervous, not quite sure how to respond to this emerging hero of the movement. Huey offered up defiant words of encouragement. "Comrade, the pigs are going to intensify their attacks on the party, so you have to be vigilant, Comrade, and you have to work on the comrades' discipline, and remember to never turn your back on the pigs. They will not hesitate to shoot you in the back."

After that final statement, we both raised clenched fists.

I felt strange about leaving our leader behind—I had only just met him, yet I felt an almost paternal connection to this boyish-looking hero of the Oakland streets, the soon-to-be hero of the worldwide Black revolutionary movement.

We then both said, "All power to the people."

As I was departing, Huey added, "Stay strong, Comrade," again raising a clenched fist.

There really wasn't much else to say. After all, he didn't know me—I was just another brother joining the struggle for Black liberation. But the visit did give me an immediate connection with the leader of the party, which was quite different from seeing his picture on a poster at headquarters. It didn't seem right that the most important man in the movement was sitting in limbo in an Oakland jail. I would not see Huey again for another three years.

Later that day, I accompanied Bobby Seale and a bunch of other Panthers down to DeFremery Park, which the party had named the Bobby Hutton Memorial Park. At the park giving a speech was Bobby Kennedy, who was campaigning for president. Bobby Seale started his own spontaneous, small rally nearby, challenging the red-haired Kennedy to call for the release of Huey Newton, and protesting the murder of Little Bobby Hutton. We had no inkling that in three months, Bobby Kennedy would be the victim of yet another political assassination, the fifth in eight years, with more to follow.

The following day, while I was standing in front of the office talking with Jimmy Charley and Orleander Harrison, Tommy drove up, leaned over, and through the passenger window said, "Hey, Aaron, I got something for you."

I hopped into the passenger seat. Tommy reached beneath his seat and pulled out a semiautomatic weapon.

"Here, Comrade," he said, handing me the brown-handled pistol. It was a Spanish Llama 9mm. "You know how to put a bullet in the chamber?" Before I could respond, he took the gun, put in the clip, pulled back the slide, and let go. "This is the safety. Make sure you keep that on. Here's a shoulder holster."

I put on the holster and slid in the dark silver gun. Immediately, I felt different—more complete, more a part of this cadre of new friends. We walked around the corner to Robert Bay's house to show off my new piece. "Aaron, you drink?" asked Tommy.

"Heck yeah, man," I responded.

He turned to Robert Bay. "Hey, Robert, I'm going to run to the store and get some Bitter Dog." I wondered what the hell "Bitter Dog" was, but I was soon to find out.

Tommy returned within five minutes. "This is the Panther drink. We call it Panther Piss." He pulled out a tall bottle of dark port wine, poured out a little bit in the sink, opened a small can of lemon juice, and poured it into the port. He then put the cap on, shook up the contents, and passed the bottle around. When it came to me, I took a long swig. It was sour yet sweet, with an aromatic taste to it. We passed the bottle around while the O'Jays' "Look Over Your Shoulder" played in the background. Soon I could feel the effects—it was potent. We smoked some "Brother Roogie," the Panther codename for marijuana.

We continued talking and laughing, and I began to loosen up, losing my stiffness. I began to feel like I was in the company of close friends, like we had known each other long before the party, long before this time and place.

Meanwhile, Landon, who did not drink or smoke weed, sat in the living room in front of the TV watching a cowboys-and-Indians flick. Suddenly, there was a loud bang. We ran into the living room and there sat Landon, holding his smoking .44 Magnum. The TV was completely destroyed.

"What the fuck?" Robert Bay yelled.

"Fuck them cowboys," cussed Landon. "I get tired of the Indians getting killed by the fuckin'-ass cowboys. I'm tired of that bullshit."

We all laughed. It was funny to us at the time. Although I think we all related to his frustration, it was evident to me that this brother was capable of losing his cool when anger got the best of him. Our generation had grown up with that kind of stereotypical brainwashing shit on TV and in movies, especially when it came to Black folks and to Indians. It was always the same story: the Indians got wiped out. Landon's actions made clear that as far as the party was concerned, those days were over.

The next day, I was assigned to go out into the field to sell papers with two comrades, Sister Love and Jimmy Charley. Sister Love was a talkative, chocolate beauty, typical of Panther sisters: young, bold, brash, sweet, and tough. We were assigned to downtown Oakland. Being Friday, the stores and streets were busy with shoppers, mostly Black folks, spending their government checks or their hard-earned paychecks. Meanwhile, we stood on street corners in our leathers and berets, yelling out to prospective customers, urging them to buy the latest issue of *The Black Panther*. Unike any other paper I had seen, it was blunt, to the point, hardcore, addressing racism, police brutality, and the party's method of dealing with the police: basic armed self-defense. Pictures of M-16s and carbines were scattered throughout the text, which included the party's ten-point program and platform. On the back page was a drawing by Emory Douglas advocating armed self-defense.

Young people and, at times, middle-aged people were eager to buy the paper. Some older people seemed uninterested. It was energizing and exciting to be out on the streets in the sun with the comrades, educating the people. They knew we were standing up for them. We felt proud and special, representing the people's army. In our travels around downtown, we ended up at Housewife's Market, a large grocery store where many of the low-income Blacks shopped. There we sold all the remaining papers.

Afterward, Orleander and I ended up at Robert Bay's house, drinking Bitter Dog. Tommy, Landon, and Randy soon joined the group. Quietly, I observed each one. Orleander was the youngest of twelve children, a toothpick perpetually dangling from his lips. Having joined the party at age sixteen, the brash, fearless young revolutionary had participated in the protest on the Sacramento capitol, carrying a Riot 18 shotgun. Tommy was the oldest, a seasoned veteran of the streets and of life. Robert Bay— "Big Bay"—was a disciplined, stoic Vietnam vet who exhibited very little bravado. And Landon and Randy, also Vietnam vets, were opposites. Landon was powder keg, whereas Randy was cool, calm, and collected.

Later, the six of us found ourselves sitting in a soul food restaurant on 7th Street and Wood in West Oakland, eating black-eyed peas and fried chicken, trying to dull the effects of the Bitter Dog and the weed we'd smoked. After Orleander and I finished, we went outside and stood on the corner to light up a couple of Kools. Feeling full and feeling good, we watched the crowds of Black people on this warm spring Friday night. The clubs and restaurants were full of our people, wanting to get high, to drink, to gamble—anything to try to forget the racism and oppression of white America. We didn't register that we were standing at the very same intersection where Huey had stood on that fateful night the year before, with one pig dead and another wounded, as was Huey.

But we did notice the police cruiser slowly driving past. Orleander began yelling at the police. "You pigs better stop at that stop sign."

I joined in. We began yelling in unison, feeling both bold and foolish, as the young so often do. Then we began shouting epithets at the cops. "You mothafuckin' pigs better stop at that sign."

We were full of ourselves, in our uniforms, and on our own turf. I was armed but Orleander was not, as he was underage and not allowed to carry a concealed weapon. Soon Robert Bay, Tommy, Randy, and Landon came out of the restaurant to see what was going on.

The cruiser stopped and two cops got out, looking aloof. Orleander and I backed up off the curb, and the others moved away from the advancing officers. But Tommy, who earlier had taken a red devil or some other downer, was by this point what Panthers called "nonfunctional." He was standing by himself near the curb. One officer asked for his ID while the other returned to the car and called for backup. Within minutes, five police cars were on the scene. Suddenly, the streets began to turn chaotic.

People hurried past, whispering among themselves and yelling to others to get out of there. Amid the confusion, Tommy somehow slipped his small snub-nosed .38 to Orleander.

As the police poured out of their cars, hands on their guns, I heard Robert Bay say in his husky voice, "Spread out!"

I watched as the others formed a semicircle around Tommy and the cops. I followed suit, taking position next to Robert Bay. Shops and stores in the area closed their doors. People began running. I heard fearful cries and screams.

"There's going to be a shootout!"

"I'm getting outta here!"

I remember seeing a young brother, probably a year younger than me, wearing a McClymonds High School letter jacket, carrying two bags of groceries in his arms, probably heading for a quiet dinner at home. Our eyes met for a split second, his expression full of fear, my eyes pleading, *Stay. Help.* He must have read my mind.

He sputtered out, "Man, I would like to stay and help, but I gotta get home!"

In a second he was gone, leaving me, leaving us, just like all the other people fleeing, the same people for whom we had taken up the banner, the same people we had pledged to defend.

The comrades spread out with hands on their guns. In that brief second, fear engulfed my entire body; images of my childhood and my family flashed before me, yet I understood that here, on this corner with my new-found comrades on this fateful night, was where I belonged. I placed my hand on my gun in preparation for the worst.

Within minutes, the streets were empty except for a few prostitutes who refused to leave, proclaiming loudly, "We ain't going nowhere, we gonna stay out here with our brothers."

Tommy was arrested and the seven or eight pigs, now bunched together, turned their attention to the remaining five of us.

For a split second, time seemed to stand still. The Oakland night was deathly quiet. Orleander was standing to my right, legs spread apart, tooth-pick still dangling from his mouth, semi-smiling as he always was. Robert Bay, to my left, looked like an immovable object. Randy stood erect, emotionless, hand on his gun, almost daring the cops to make a move. Landon was out in front, his right hand on that big .44.

The pigs, on the other hand, were huddled together on the corner, hesitant, wondering what we were going to do. That is, all except for the hard-looking lieutenant out in front of his fellow officers. The lieutenant was almost face-to-face with Landon, hand on his service revolver. Like Landon, he, too, probably had been in Vietnam.

He blurted out, "I'm going to search you."

Landon defiantly snapped back, "You ain't gonna search me."

The lieutenant began moving toward Landon. In turn, Landon slowly, carefully, backed up. I thought about the TV blown to bits by Landon's .44.

The air was thick and heavy and eerily silent, the thoughts of blood and death lingering. The lieutenant repeated his demands to search, and Landon continued to resist. The five of us stood by, trying to maintain our defiant postures.

Suddenly, while stepping backward, Landon slipped and stumbled on the lid of a garbage can. The rattling sound reverberated, puncturing the tension and silence. Landon caught himself from falling and quickly bounced back up, maintaining his position, his hand still on his gun. Then, just when we thought the blood would surely spill and death would be upon us, the lieutenant and the rest of the cops quietly and slowly backed up, silently got into their cars, and drove off, making a U-turn beneath a transit construction project, and headed back downtown.

It was over. The pigs had decided that this warm spring night was not the time they wished to die. As for us, we had chosen this night as our time to stand our ground. Moments after the pigs left, some prostitute friends of Captain Crutch took our weapons for safekeeping in case the cops came back with reinforcements. We were not to about to give up our weapons to the cops, not after what had happened to Bobby Hutton just a few weeks earlier. We split the scene. That night I stayed at the house with Robert Bay, Landon, and Randy.

The tension had been so tight, the cops' fear of the combatants so heavy, that whatever rationale they might have given for backing out of this potential bloodbath was understandable. Simply put, we appeared to be more prepared to sacrifice our lives than they were. This was our street, our community. As Panthers, we had drawn the line in the sand. Although I was grateful to have escaped a potential gun battle, I felt proud of myself. I also felt this experience forever cemented my relationship with these four comrades.

The next day, Tommy was released and news of the standoff spread throughout the party. David Hilliard proclaimed that the incident on Friday night had served as my baptism into the party. Whereas I was relieved, the Oakland Panthers treated this as a normal occurrence. Ever since the shootout that killed Little Bobby Hutton, the police and the party were at war. This incident was a battle in that war, and there would be many more to come.

The following evening, Panthers from all over the Bay Area gathered in the basement of St. Augustine's Church. They came from Frisco, Marin County, Vallejo, Richmond, Palo Alto—most dressed in the Panther uniform—and warmly greeted each other, filling the room with energy and enthusiasm. There must have been two hundred Panthers. It was electrifying. I could hardly contain my excitement of being among these righteous brothers and sisters.

Bobby Seale brought the meeting to order, reminding the comrades of the importance of learning the ten-point program and platform by heart, and exhorting us to study the Red Book. He talked about the need to get out and sell the Black Panther paper, and took reports from captains from each area. As part of the meeting, I was introduced as the captain of the new Seattle chapter, the first Panther chapter outside California. Afterward, comrades welcomed me into the fold, asking questions about Seattle. I was able to meet Panthers from throughout the Bay Area, including Captain Dexter Woods from San Francisco, Captain Randy from Vallejo, Chico from Richmond, and Fred from Palo Alto. One brother in particular stood out, and I would later come to know him to be probably the most dedicated Panther of all—Sam Napier, a thin, disheveled-looking brother. I remember that while everyone else was standing and talking, he was in the street stopping cars, selling the Panther paper, moving as if powered by some secret energy source.

After the meeting I headed back with Robert Bay and Tommy. No sooner had we walked into the unlit house than the phone rang. Robert Bay answered in his usual, gruff voice: "Yeah."

He suddenly slammed down the phone, ran to his room, and came rushing out, carrying several rifles. He handed me a .44 Magnum carbine and a box of shells. "The pigs are vamping on some comrades at the church."

Tommy grabbed a rifle and we ran out, jumped into the LeSabre, and sped down Grove Street. "Hey, man, you know how to use one of these?" Robert Bay asked me.

Although I answered yes, I had actually never seen the weapon before. But I sat there in the middle of the back seat, loading short, stubby rounds into the .44 Magnum carbine, and awaited my fate.

When we arrived at the church, everyone was gone—the pigs, the Panthers, everyone. Either the caller had overreacted or the pigs knew that reinforcements would be coming and got the hell out of Dodge. I'm sure the pigs had heard about the standoff the night before down on Wood Street. They knew that since the murder of Bobby Hutton, the party was just waiting for an opportunity to take revenge.

In those days, Oakland was very much like a war zone. Wherever there was a party chapter and racist police, there would be confrontation and often bloodshed. I had the overwhelming feeling that there was a lot of work waiting for me back in Seattle in order to get the comrades organized into a disciplined force as had been done in Oakland.

The following day, I said my goodbyes to my new comrades. On the flight home, I did a lot of thinking. I pondered my immediate experiences in Oakland and reflected on the movement's growth from riots and demonstrations to armed resistance and grassroots organizing of the most downtrodden elements of the Black community.

It was clear that when Martin Luther King Jr. was killed in Memphis, a change had occurred in the political consciousness of young Black America. The door of the nonviolence movement had been slammed shut, but a window had been opened. Revolutionary thought was replacing the civil rights approach, manifesting with a seriousness, an intensity, that had not been in the earlier movement. The young would look to a new group of individuals, such as Huey Newton, Bobby Seale, and Eldridge Cleaver, and to organizations led by people like those I had just met in Oakland—Tommy Jones, Robert Bay, Captain Bill Brent, Landon, Randy, and Matilaba. I thought about my newfound friends, my comrades in arms, about the night at 7th and Wood and how I was embraced by them, encouraged and loved by them, unconditionally.

I visited Oakland many times during those early years, creating a lasting and unbreakable bond with these comrades.

July 1968, Seattle

Bobby Harding (left) and Lewis "LewJack" Jackson (right), Seattle, 1968.

12

The Panther Comes to Seattle

Move up a little higher
Some way, somehow
'Cause I've got my strength
And it don't make sense
Not to keep on pushin'
                    —The Impressions, "Keep On Pushing," 1964

This is what we all had been waiting for, whether we realized
it or not. Revolutions were unfolding all over the world. Liberators such as
Che Guevara, Ho Chi Minh, Kwame Nkrumah, and Patrice Lumumba were
international heroes, and Huey was poised to join that list. We were on the
cusp of making history and could feel its power and danger eerily creeping
up behind us.

Back home in Seattle after my week in Oakland, I felt more prepared.
I was now armed with a mission to organize the Seattle chapter into a disciplined wing of the Black Panther Party. Exactly how this would transpire,
I had not the faintest idea. I was merely a passenger on the train, and it
had just so happened that I was assigned to the front of this particular
car. I could only hope that with some wisdom, my eyes and instincts would
guide us in the right direction.

103

Our first and foremost task was to find a storefront office in a central location. We were fortunate to find one at 34th and Union in Madrona, only three blocks from my parents' house across from Madrona Park. The storefront was across the street from Miss Ruby's house. One of our big neighborhood supporters, from her large blue house Miss Ruby would operate as our eyes and ears, informing us when the police were snooping around. In front of Miss Ruby's house stood Mrs. Jackson's record store, where Mike Dean and I had spent a good portion of our high school years listening to Motown sounds and turning over our hard-earned money to buy the latest hits. Madrona was still the same quiet, working-class neighborhood it had been while I was growing up. But all that was about to change.

The storefront we had our eyes on was part of another connecting storefront, owned by Brill Realty. Mr. Brill, the building's owner, had never been particularly friendly to anyone in the neighborhood, especially not young people. When Willie Brazier, Chester Northington, Curtis Harris, and I approached the squat, bowlegged, pale Mr. Brill and asked him about renting the vacant office, he responded in an abrupt, dismissive manner, "No, I will not rent to you." We left quietly, though confidently. Later that night, a Molotov cocktail was thrown into the storefront, causing superficial damage. About a week later we approached Mr. Brill again, while he was repairing the building. This time he promptly agreed to rent to us.

Within days we opened our storefront office, getting several desks and chairs donated, as well as a mimeograph machine. Word spread like wildfire through the Central District and the Rainier Valley to the south, and we began taking applications from new recruits. In the first two months we received more than three hundred applications.

As I had seen in Oakland, the party attracted people from a wide spectrum of the Black community. Most were young Black high school kids. Others were in their twenties, and a few were older than thirty, like Ron Carson, a smooth-skinned brother who ran a local poverty program. He was known to carry several pistols, and was not one to bite his tongue. One cat was almost forty. This being Seattle, it was not unusual that a handful of the new recruits were Asian—like fifteen-year-old Guy Kurose, who was Japanese; seventeen-year-old Mike Gillespie, a Filipino trumpet player; and Mike Tagawa, a Japanese Vietnam vet. These guys had all grown up in our neighborhood and identified with young Blacks in many ways.

The new recruits signed up for a variety of reasons—some for the sense of belonging to something that instantly gave their life meaning and purpose; others because they had felt the sting of racism, the cuts of injustice, and felt this was their opportunity to strike back. A few were simply curious. A few others came with their own agenda and notions as to how the liberation struggle might be able to benefit them personally.

The array of characters was impressive. Chester Northington, John Eichelburger, and Vietnam vet Bruce Hayes were older cats who had been involved in other Black Nationalist organizations. I had met them previously at Voodoo Man's house. The Noble brothers brought two carloads of young recruits with them from the South End, including their two sisters. The Noble brothers earned the nickname "F-Troop," not so much for any resemblance to the bumbling idiots on the TV show *F-Troop* but due to their wild appearance and frequent lack of discipline.

Two seventeen-year-old students, Warren Myers, who went to Catholic school, and Steve Philips, later proved to be two of our bravest and best warriors. Also among the recruits were brothers who had been involved in street life and saw the party as their way of evening the score as well as redeeming themselves in the eyes of the community, like Willie Brazier and Jimmy Davis. And there was always a steady trickle of Vietnam vets.

Among the first Vietnam vets to join were three buddies who grew up together, went to war together, and were fortunate to return together—Bobby White, Bobby Harding, and Mike Tagawa. They brought invaluable experience and dedication to the chapter. Mike Tagawa and Bobby Harding drew on their military experience to instill discipline in the young Panther recruits. They started teaching classes on how to break down and clean weapons, how to aim and discharge weapons properly. They led close-quarter military drills with the Panther recruits three times a week. We needed a structured activity for all the new recruits. As the party considered itself a paramilitary organization, the chapters in Los Angeles and Oakland had adopted military-style drilling and marching, and now we did as well. All new Panther recruits were required to go through a six-week training program.

We gathered at Madrona Park, the scene of childhood memories of muddy football battles, wild baseball games, and occasional fights. Now in this same setting, dozens of Black young men, dressed in the Panther black, berets tilted to the side, were learning military formations, how to stand at attention and stand at ease—and, most important, how to follow orders. In Oakland and possibly in Los Angeles, Panther women also participated in the drills, but in Seattle they were not required to.

Bobby White, a slight brother who wore prescription sunglasses along with his beret, was one of the most dynamic writers in Seattle. He became lieutenant of information. He took charge of the community news bulletins that we put out every couple of weeks; he also decorated the office with posters and revolutionary slogans, and painted the Panther colors, baby blue and white, on the outer walls of the storefront, with "Black Panther Party" in the center. Bobby Harding was also a writer, a poet, and often the three of us shared our work and talked about someday getting published.

The new recruits were not only men. Many young sisters joined up, some of whom were tougher than the brothers. Joyce Redman had long been regarded as one of the baddest sisters in the neighborhood. No one wanted to mess with her because she was known to beat the hell out of her opponents, male or female. Maud Allen, articulate and hard-nosed about party rules, became the captain of the women. There were the two Kathys—Kathy Jones, still in high school, and tall, thin Kathy Halley, who had transferred to the UW from Wilberforce University, a Black college in the Midwest. She later changed her name to Nafasi, and became my close confidant, constantly worrying about my safety. I also met a little, cute, fiery sister named Tanya, a couple years older than me. She soon became my girlfriend and was the woman to whom I lost my virginity.

Buddy Yates and Curtis Harris were two brothers with similar personalities, and early on it was obvious they had an agenda that had very little to do with the liberation of Black America. Curtis, my brother-in-law, was two years older than me. He made up a title for himself, "assistant captain." It was a move that should have alerted me and others, but at the time we ignored it—a mistake for which we would pay plenty.

Of the many colorful individuals who signed up, none was as memorable or as committed in those early days as Lewis Jackson. "LewJack," as he was called, must have been about twenty-three years old. He had moved to Seattle from New Orleans, and used to tell many stories about growing up in the tough Ninth Ward of New Orleans. He had a tattoo of a football right between his eyes, thus his second nickname was "Football." His beady eyes lit up when he talked about the fights he had been in and what he wanted to do to the pigs, although sometimes his French Creole dialect made him hard to understand. One of the few recruits to come equipped with a weapon, a .45 that he carried everywhere, LewJack appointed himself as my personal bodyguard. He followed me around constantly, even sleeping out in front of the house in his car when there were threats against my life.

New recruits were given a packet of information, which included the party's national and local leadership structure, ten-point program and platform, twenty-six rules, and a "Pocket Lawyer of Legal First Aid," listing one's legal rights. Panthers were also given Mao's Little Red Book and a list of additional required reading, and were charged with memorizing Mao's Three Main Rules of Discipline.

Recruits were instructed to attend weekly meetings, which were not always held consistently in those early days of figuring things out. There seemed to always be something coming up to change the schedule. Sometimes I led the meetings and at other times Lieutenant of Political Education Willie Brazier led them. We formed a Central Staff, composed of officers appointed at the time of the initial meeting with Bobby Seale. In theory, the Central Staff was supposed to serve as the governing force of our chapter, similar to the Central Committee in Oakland. Of course, it never functioned as we had envisioned. There were just too many strong personalities, and at the time I did not quite have the confidence to command the necessary respect.

When Chairman Bobby was in Seattle, he had described an organizing tool created by James Forman, the former executive secretary of SNCC. Along with fellow SNCC leaders Stokely Carmichael and H. Rap Brown, Forman had recently been drafted into the Black Panther Party. The tool he developed, known as the "10-10-10," called for dividing the organizing area or community into ten sections, further dividing each section into subsections, and dividing subsections into blocks. Each section had a section leader, and each subsection had a subsection leader as well as block captains.

We attempted to use a variation of this tactic, as did other new chapters, dividing our organizing area into three sections and appointing section leaders. This was supposed to be a means of not only organizing the community but also engaging and coordinating the new recruits according to their assigned sections. During this time period, though, it was very difficult to make "10-10-10" work for us. Events were occurring at high speed.

Early on, because so many young people had signed up, discipline proved to be a problem. Elmer, who was rapidly becoming my solid right hand, organized a "goon squad" to administer some discipline to those young comrades who were not following orders or were conducting themselves in a rowdy, disorganized fashion.

The Oregon cities of Portland and Eugene also started Panther branches that came under the authority of the Seattle chapter. For me, this meant frequent trips to Portland to check with Captain Kent Ford, and to Eugene to see the Anderson brothers. A little older than myself, Kent Ford was a solid organizer with a low-key demeanor. The Anderson brothers were originally from Los Angeles. They had come to Eugene to play football at the University of Oregon, but they stopped playing football and instead dedicated their time to forming the Eugene branch.

It wasn't long before our little sleepy Madrona neighborhood had been transformed into a Black Panther fortress. On any given day, scores of young men and women in black berets and leather jackets congregated inside and outside our storefront office; sometimes they marched at the park, often carrying rifles and shotguns up the street. It wasn't uncommon for twelve or more Panthers to be sitting around the office, holding their weapons.

The Black community's response to us was mixed. There was fear and apprehension among many. Among others, there was a sense of pride and hope, particularly among the disenfranchised, the victimized, the hopeless. The Black Panther Party represented a proud, defiant presence in the community, something not seen since the likes of Marcus Garvey and Paul Robeson—a presence that would stand up and fight back against the racist cops and the racist institutions of the United States.

Many people felt a powerful sense of pride when viewing Panthers in action, and this was never more evident than one overcast Seattle Saturday afternoon, when more than a hundred Panthers attended the Saturday afternoon drills in full Panther uniform. Lieutenants Bobby Harding and Mike Tagawa had drilled the comrades for well over an hour, marching up and down the Madrona playfield. They looked superb and polished.

Like clockwork, the cops showed up and lined up in their cars on the side of the park. We decided we would give them something to look at. I instructed Bobby and Mike to lead the comrades onto the streets. They put on a display that day: marching out of the park, proceeding three blocks down 33rd Avenue, completely engulfing the streets, their eyes de-

termined, looking straight ahead as Bobby and Mike barked out the ca-
dences. They reached Cherry Street, one of the main streets coming up
to Madrona. Marching on Cherry, the comrades occupied the entire right
side of the street. The people in the neighborhood came out to watch, sitting on their porches, some cheering, others taking pictures, looking on
with a secret pride that many of them had never felt before.

Meanwhile, the cops had stationed squad cars at every intersection.
At one point the comrades marched directly toward one of the police
cruisers but at the last second veered to the left. It was as if they had been
marching together in formation for years. Finally, at the bottom of the
hill, they turned and marched back up and into the park. That was a very
proud day for the Black community. We showed that we were their pro-
tectors, their defenders.

Our phones at the office were constantly ringing with people calling
for help with landlord issues, spousal abuse, or problems with the police.
In one incident a single mother with a house full of kids called to report
that her landlord had removed her front door because she had fallen behind
in her rent. We dispatched a squad of Panthers to the landlord's house.
They secured the door, carried it down the street to the woman's house,
and put it back on its hinges. We got frequent calls from women complain-
ing about abuse from husbands or boyfriends. Usually, after a visit from a
contingent of armed party members, the abuse would stop, at least for the
time being. And we responded to constant calls about police harassment
by showing up with armed Panthers to confront surprised police.

During the last week in May, we received a call from a single Black
mother whose son attended Rainier Beach, a predominantly white school
located on the outer fringes of the Black community. She said her son had
been having trouble with the white kids at school. They had beaten him
up on several occasions and the principal refused to do anything about it.

Each week I mailed a chapter report to Chairman Bobby, and once
he'd received and reviewed it, we talked on the phone. The week prior to
this mother's call, the chairman had reminded me that we were not the
police, and our function was not to respond to every call, as we had learned
the community would often take advantage of our services. With this in
mind, I told the woman we could not respond to her request.

The mother continued to call our office nearly every day. We found out
that as the school year was drawing to an end, the white kids at Rainier Beach

stepped up the attacks on not only this particular Black kid, but also on the other Black kids at the school. Finally, early on a Friday afternoon, she called again, crying and sounding desperate, saying that the white kids had brought knives, chains, and bricks to school, threatening the lives of her son and the other Black students. We received at least four other calls from distraught Black mothers. When I hung up the phone after speaking with the last mother, I looked around at the comrades, who sat holding their rifles and shotguns. I could tell they were wondering if I was going to give the word.

"Let's go," I said, grabbing my carbine. We loaded up in three cars and headed south to Rainier Beach, taking back streets, past Lake Washington, past large, expensive homes and manicured lawns, finally arriving at the school. When we pulled in we spotted thirty cops lined up on the side of the building. As we got out and headed toward the school entrance, a fat sergeant, his belly hanging over his belt, met us. I recognized him— he and I had encountered each other on several occasions. He had once remarked snidely, "Oh, not the Panthers again," when we had responded to a community call.

"Dixon," he blurted, "you can't take those loaded weapons into the school."

I shot back, "They ain't loaded," rationalizing that if the carrier of the gun knew the bullet was not in the chamber, then according to the law the gun was technically considered unloaded.

We continued our way in and began looking for the principal. A man in a black suit hurried down the hallway—that was our man. Willie Brazier and several other comrades pursued him, escorting him back to an empty office where I confronted him.

"If you don't protect these Black kids, then we will do it, understand?" The words just seemed to shoot out of my mouth.

The poor guy was visibly shaken. "I promise I will make sure nothing happens again," he replied.

Satisfied with his response, the thirteen of us left the building. We backed our way across the street, keeping our eyes on the cops, just as Huey had instructed, hopped in our cars, and headed back to the office. The cops followed but did not stop us. That evening, I received a call from Mike Rosen of the ACLU, the same attorney who had represented me, Larry, and Carl after the Franklin High School demonstration. He said the district attorney was preparing an indictment against us, but it never came.

For us, this was what putting on the Panther uniform was all about—standing up strong, refusing to be brushed aside and marginalized. We were dead serious when it came to the rights of the people. One thing was certain: if we had to die in the process, most of us were ready for that, too. The Rainier Beach school incident was one of the most significant moves we made during that summer of 1968, and it would set the stage for upcoming battles with the police.

During those early days of the Seattle chapter, everything was happening so fast, and without a blueprint or methodology to guide us, we often had to learn how to operate on the fly, following our instincts. We had many recruits, yet we lacked a clear understanding or model of exactly what we were supposed to be doing on a daily basis and also in the long term. In response to the constant stream of requests from the community and beyond, we organized a speakers' bureau to give talks on the Black Panther Party and what it was all about. Gary Owens, a college student in his early twenties, along with Willie Brazier and others, took the bulk of the speaking assignments. Eventually, we started getting deliveries of *The Black Panther* newspaper from Oakland once Eldridge Cleaver got out on bail following the April 6 shootout. The paper had lain dormant until the return of the minister of information. *The Black Panther* was the most important and immediate mechanism the party had for educating people about what the party stood for and what was truly going on in the United States and the rest of the world. Sales of the paper also provided us with a much-needed source of revenue.

Since the death of Martin Luther King Jr., my life and the life of many other Black youth throughout America had taken on an overwhelming sense of urgency. The movement was accelerating and transforming. We were now consumed with the fight for justice and the right to determine our own destiny. For me, school took a backseat to the emerging struggle.

When I got back from Oakland after that first trip as a Panther, I immediately went through my closet, taking out all my suits and the Italian knit sweaters I had bought with my work money. I no longer had any need for those fine clothes. They would be replaced by green army fatigue pants, blue jeans, fatigue jackets, leather jackets, and combat boots. I gave my suits to Elmer, a futile decision on my part, because Elmer had no need for them either. We had both plunged in the lake of rebellion together.

Despite my plunge, I was still subject to the lure of spontaneous adventure. The Urban League program that had supported my entrance to the UW sponsored a summer internship program that kicked off with a five-day orientation trip to New York City, filled with workshops and field trips, all expenses paid. Going to New York is something many young people dream about, and it had certainly been my dream before the revolution took over my life. Mr. Page, the program director, called me on several occasions, attempting to convince me to go. I resisted until the last minute, when I caught a red-eye flight to New York City. I knew there was a lot going on in Seattle with our chapter, but I felt the other leading members would be able to handle things in my absence.

On the bus ride from the airport into the city, dressed in my Panther attire, I marveled at the forest of tall, concrete buildings as my nose burned from the coffee smell of big-city pollution. I finally arrived at my stop in Manhattan and made my way to the New Yorker Hotel, where Black students from around the country had converged, including several of my friends from Seattle. After an initial presentation we were assigned to our lodgings, with the men staying at the YMCA and the women at the New Yorker Hotel. The following day, when I called the office in Seattle, I was told that Chairman Bobby Seale had called for me. Upon hearing I was in New York, he left a message for me to meet him on Saturday morning at Brooklyn College in Flatbush, Room 104.

The next morning, I caught the subway to Flatbush. When I opened the door to Room 104, there were forty or fifty Black men and women dressed in Panther black with berets and leather jackets, directing their full attention to the front of the classroom. Chairman Bobby, along with David Hilliard, now the party's chief of staff, stood before the blackboard, giving a precise and thorough explanation of the theory behind the 10-10-10 organizing tool. The Panthers gathered in the classroom were the recruits of the new New York chapter of the Black Panther Party. After the session, I went with Chairman Bobby, David Hilliard, and Captain Ron Pennywell, who had been sent from Oakland to organize the New York chapter, to the pad where Ron Pennywell was staying. Chairman Bobby asked why I was in New York. He did not register any anger. But at the end of the conversation, he told me, "Get your ass back in Seattle!"

The next day at the Urban League conference, we received our assignments to cities throughout the United States, where participants would be doing community work for the summer. Even thought I had no intention of going, I was assigned to Houston, Texas, and given a plane ticket.

At the airport, I changed my flight from Houston to Seattle and flew back to Seattle. One of the brothers in the program, from North Carolina, was assigned to Seattle. Instead of working for the Urban League, though, he ended up working with the Seattle BPP chapter.

Amid all this activity, for a while I was still able to write a bit. Finding a little time and a quiet space in someone's empty apartment or my quiet room at home, with some heavy jazz and a bottle of cheap wine, I could forget my role as captain, and write about lost love or the difficulties of being Black in America. But that period lasted only a very brief time. There were just too many things happening too fast.

My draft card came in the mail. I was to report to the induction center. Just a few years earlier I had told Poppy I was going to join the Marines. The expression on his face had changed immediately to indignation. "No son of mine is going to Vietnam. Those people over there haven't called you a nigger," he responded, echoing Muhammad Ali. That was all he had said, and all he really needed to say. From the tone of his voice and the look on his face, it had not been a time to question or challenge him. I had mumbled to myself, feeling stupid, not quite sure what to make of Poppy's response.

I had grown up on American patriotism just like Poppy and the thousands upon thousands of other young men eager to go off to war and kill the enemy. Historically, going off to war was a rite of passage for a young man. Poppy had done it. He was more gung-ho and patriotic than I could ever be. But after the war was over, with its bloody battles and great loss of life, to face the rebuke by your own country, the slap in the face that says, "Yeah, nigger, you can fight for us, even die for us, but when it's over, you're still just a nigger"—Poppy was not going to let that happen to his sons.

Now, I had already been inducted into service, and it was not the US Army. It was a new kind of army, a righteous army that was going to fight for the betterment of everyone on this earth, starting with the Black people here at home.

I hopped in my '56 Buick, dressed in a black beret and a green army fatigue jacket, with my 9mm in my shoulder holster. By the time I arrived at the induction center my heart was pumping fast, my adrenaline moving rapidly. *The nerve of those bastards*, I thought to myself. *They think I'm going to fight and die in their army.* I walked through the door and was confronted by a sergeant sitting at a desk.

"Your induction card, please," he asked. Immediately, I pulled it out and tore it into little pieces as I blurted out a litany of words and profanities, ending with "I am not going to fight in your motherfucking army." I threw the pieces of the draft card in the sergeant's face and stormed out. I think we were both shocked at my actions. But under the circumstances, at the time, it was the only response I could give.

It did not take long before the chapter had amassed large amounts of weapons. My personal collection had expanded beyond the carbine given to me by Voodoo Man and the 9mm from Tommy to include a whole arsenal of weapons, including shotguns and rifles. One day Poppy approached me to discuss the guns stacking up in my closet. He was getting a little concerned. We often held weapons classes in the basement of the house or at the Hardings' next door, in their basement. Poppy had tried to ignore all the guns, but he had fought in one of the bloodiest wars in history and knew all too well the damage and destruction weapons could cause.

One night he issued an ultimatum: "Aaron," he said, "either those guns have to go or you have to go."

I recalled the confrontation three years earlier about my insubordination, his arms still big from all the morning pushups he had done over the years. He now had a few strands of gray in his hair, and a bald spot was beginning to spread on the back of his head. We both knew it was time for me to go. If I wanted to take on this role of a revolutionary, then I had to also take on the role of an independent adult. Late into the night I gathered my weapons and headed to my girlfriend Tanya's place, leaving the comfort of my parents' home behind.

My parents must have felt the tide of the growing movement. If they were afraid for me, they never showed it. They were more supportive than ever, their love stronger, and we were closer now than in the past. They felt the urgency and the significance of the hour just as we did. I did manage to finish out the year at the university; I felt I owed my parents that, at least.

Putting on the Black Panther uniform and committing our lives to the liberation struggle changed the purpose and meaning of our entire identities. It was a liberating experience. Societal restrictions and conformities dropped by the wayside, leaving a fearless, defiant, powerful human being. We no longer looked at ourselves in the same way, nor did we look at the system and its representatives in the same manner. We were the freest of the free.

13

Huey and the UN

Igqira lendlela nguqo ngqothwane
Sebeqabele gqi thapha bathi nguqo ngqothwane
(Diviner of the roadways—the knock-knock beetle
It just passed by here—the knock-knock beetle)
—Miriam Makeba, "Qongqothwane (The Click Song)," 1960

At National Headquarters in Oakland, the party was gearing up for the July trial of the minister of defense, Huey P. Newton, charged with murder in the death of an Oakland police officer. When Huey had entered the Alameda County jail in October 1967, he had left behind a core group of about twenty-five to thirty Panthers. Now the party membership had exploded to well over three thousand, scattered throughout the United States. "Free .Huey" posters were plastered all over buildings and walls from New York to Los Angeles. The party's refrain was "THE SKY IS THE LIMIT IF HUEY IS NOT SET FREE." Chairman Bobby traveled relentlessly throughout the States and Europe, organizing support committees and party chapters, attracting thousands of supporters all over the world. An alliance had been formed with SNCC, drafting its leaders onto the party's Central Committee. BPP Chief of Staff David Hilliard and Captain Landon Williams attempted to travel to Cuba to solicit support for Huey's trial but were detained in Mexico City by the FBI.

We wore our "Free Huey" buttons on our leather coats and fatigue jackets like medals of honor, hoping that someday Huey would come home. Huey P. Newton was our guiding force. He embodied everything a Black superhero could possibly be. It was Huey who'd had the courage to lead a band of armed and well-disciplined Black men to confront equally armed white, racist police officers, putting an almost immediate halt to the police brutality against and murder of the Black citizens of Oakland. And, as a result, he became a wanted, hunted man, eventually cornered and threatened with death.

Bobby Seale, knowing Huey's importance to the movement, dedicated himself to freeing the minister of defense. Right after departing Seattle back in April, Chairman Bobby immediately went on tour, organizing Black Panther chapters and branches all across the country, mainly for the purpose of expanding the movement to make sure the government understood we would not stand by and let Huey be unjustly convicted. There were "Free Huey" rallies throughout the world. The popular poster of Huey in the wicker chair turned up in far-flung places like the Philippines, India, Japan, and throughout Europe and South America. And, with Huey's trial starting in late July, the party wanted to leave nothing to chance.

One Friday evening Chairman Bobby called. He told me to fly to San Francisco on Saturday and call for further orders. The next morning, Lew-Jack and I were on the first flight to San Francisco. When we landed I called National Headquarters as the chairman had instructed. We were told to wait at the airport; Eldridge, Bobby, and others would meet us there.

About four hours later, Chairman Bobby arrived, along with Eldridge and Shermont Banks, captain of the Southern California chapter. Shermont came in place of Bunchy Carter, their chapter's deputy minister of defense, who had stayed in Los Angeles to drill and prepare the troops for Huey's upcoming trial.

Both of Huey's brothers, Walter and Melvin, came along, as well as Emory Douglas, the minister of culture. We all hopped on a red-eye flight to New York. On the flight Chairman Bobby explained to me that a delegation of Panthers was going to go to the UN to meet with representatives in an attempt to persuade them to intervene in Huey's trial, with the ultimate goal of addressing the general assembly. James Forman of SNCC, who had connections that could get us into the UN, would lead the dele-

gation. The plan was for Panthers in full uniform to hold "Fre
flags, one next to each flag of the UN member nations. The party n_
how to use the dramatic to its advantage. This display was intended to
symbolize for the world the importance of our leader's receiving a fair
trial, and also to bring attention to the larger human rights issue of the
plight of Black people throughout the ghettos of the United States.

Stokely Carmichael and several New York Panthers, including Chairman Brothers, a cat who had to be the oldest Panther in the party, met us
at the airport. After a fast, wild ride with Stokely behind the wheel, we arrived at his house, where we all sat down to talk. I was blown away when
his wife, Miriam Makeba, the famous South African singer living in exile,
was introduced to us. I wasn't expecting to meet Miriam Makeba on this
trip. I had grown up listening to her music and reading about the coura-
geous stand she had taken against apartheid and the South African government. She said very little, barely even looking us in the eyes as she
quietly served refreshments. The whole time we were at Stokely's house, I
was amazed to be in the same room as the beautiful, gifted Miriam
Makeba. I felt that we men should be paying homage to this true African
queen, not being humbly served by her.

Many years later, I learned about Stokely's abusive behavior toward
Miriam Makeba. The Black woman as subservient to the Black man was
a mentality that pervaded many Black Nationalist organizations, and it
would be something Stokely would have to change if he were to remain a
member of the Black Panther Party. The party's official position, set by
the Central Committee, was that women were equal to men and that a
woman had the power to do anything a man could do. However, in day-
to-day activity, things didn't always turn out that way. It was a constant
struggle to change the thinking of men in the party.

I had been inspired by Stokely as a student at Garfield, and then had
met him several times when we were both in Oakland. He had been one
of my heroes. The flame of struggle had been lit by his fiery words. But
he was different from Bobby, Eldridge, and other Panthers. In Oakland, I
had watched Stokely. He seemed uneasy, unsure of himself around the
hardcore Panther brothers, most of whom had not gone to college or even
entertained the idea of higher education, while Stokely was a graduate of
the very competitive Bronx Science High School and Howard University.
Those early California Panthers were some righteous, stomp-down broth-

ers, ex-thugs, hoodlums, pimps—as well as some serious college students. But they all had in common a real, honest, hard side. They were genuine, unpretentious; serious, yet easygoing. I guess Stokely could tell that those brothers and sisters were about as real as you would ever find.

' Emory Douglas, Walter Newton, Captain Banks, and I ended up in a cramped, stuffy apartment of the eighteen-year-old New York chapter captain, Judan Ford. Judan was a year younger than me, and I could see he had his hands full in keeping the newly formed New York chapter moving. I could relate, and I sympathized with him. In his nature he seemed even younger than eighteen, and I wondered how long he would last and how he would handle the older brothers and sisters. I'd noticed that Chairman Bobby seemed to like assigning young brothers at the helm. He probably liked the enthusiasm and fearlessness of young people, and I don't think he looked at youth as a limitation. After all, Little Bobby Hutton had been just sixteen when he became the party's first member.

That evening I called my parents to let them know I had arrived safely. My mother unfortunately had to give me some very bad news: Grandada, my grandfather on Poppy's side, had passed away from a massive stroke. I was stunned, unprepared to hear such devastating news. My first instinct was to run and hide, to find a closet somewhere to be alone. But for security reasons we were not allowed to leave the premises, so I went out onto a small balcony and looked up into the night sky, drifting off into memories of Grandada.

He had been such an important part of my life, as he was to all six of his grandkids. I thought about the summers in Chicago, sitting on his lap on the porch after supper, Grandada rubbing his whiskers against our faces. A giant of a man, he used to let all of us climb on his back and wrestle and tussle with him. He would sometimes tickle us until we cried from laughter. We caught lightning bugs while he played one of his many harmonicas. And we listened to his stories of our father as a young boy. We had never seen him angry, and had never seen him in despair. And I remembered how he loved his Limburger cheese and beer—Pabst Blue Ribbon—often adding a raw egg to his glass. He would be sorely missed. After some time alone, out in the muggy New York night, I finally went in and rejoined the others, trying to put aside my personal loss in order to prepare for the upcoming event, knowing that Grandada would always be with me.

The next day I found myself sitting on a hard wooden bench in a hot, stuffy outer office—the national headquarters of SNCC. Eldridge, Chairman Bobby, and Melvin Newton were inside James Forman's office along with Stokely, talking about the plans for the UN operation. In the outer room, I sat with Emory Douglas, Captain Banks, and Walter Newton in the sweltering heat, watching an old clock on the wall as we got to know each other and wondered how long this meeting was going to last. There were several SNCC field marshals in the building. One of them was Crutch from Los Angeles. I noticed they weren't very friendly toward us, but I didn't know why.

We could hear the voices in James Forman's office getting louder. It was obvious there was tension mounting behind that closed door. "Sonny Boy," as Huey called his brother Walter, was straight from the streets, and diplomacy was not one of his strong points. "What the fuck are they doing in there? They better not be bullshitting around. I'll hurt a mothafucka behind my brother." Emory and I tried to calm Sonny Boy down as he paced the floor, threatening to storm into the closed-door meeting. The voices were getting louder and sounding angrier. Suddenly there was a loud *BAM*, and we could hear Eldridge cursing, using a plethora of "motherfuckers."

Minutes later the three Panthers came storming out, followed by the short, stocky James Forman. Forman had been another hero of mine and probably of many others as well.

"Let's get the fuck out of here," Eldridge barked.

We left in a hurry, with Emory and me coaxing Sonny Boy out of the building. We hopped in our car and took off.

"That punk was trying to make a power play. The party don't play that shit," said Chairman Bobby. "You see, he brought his field marshals up here. Fuck it. He was supposed to get us into the UN. Fuck those jive-ass niggers."

I didn't know what had happened in the meeting with James Forman, but it was obvious things had not gone as planned. Apparently there were serious disagreements between the Panthers and Forman as to how the UN plan was going to work. An activist long before Bobby and Eldridge became revolutionaries, Forman evidently wanted to make sure the party understood who was in charge. He had even brought his field marshals up to New York, a move that, to us, seemed an effort to intimidate the party. The reality, however, was that no one intimidated the party—not the pigs, not the FBI, not SNCC field marshals, no one. Nevertheless, the plan to gain entrance to the UN and for Bobby and Eldridge to address the general assembly totally fell apart. The party was left trying to pull together something for the next day so the whole undertaking would not have been a total failure.

Eldridge said he knew someone else who might be able to help us— Mother Moore, whom he described as the mother of the Black Power Movement. It wasn't long before we made our way up to a high-rise in the Bronx, where we were introduced to a large Black woman in yellow-flowered African garb, including headdress. Although she didn't have the UN contacts James Forman had, she had one contact who was able to arrange a meeting at the UN with delegates from Tanzania and several other African nations, to be followed by a press conference. All week, the New York Panthers had been preparing the baby-blue flags with a silhouette of Huey, his tam tilted aside his head.

The next day, June 25, more than a hundred Panthers stood at attention, holding the Panther flags in front of the flags of each UN member nation. The Panther delegation went in and met with delegations from several African nations, including the Tanzanian UN representative. We all posed for a group picture and then left. Although we were not successful in our mission, we did get press coverage and generated more attention for Huey's upcoming trial.

Later we headed for Lenox Avenue, the famous street in Harlem where Marcus Garvey and Malcolm X had addressed great crowds of Black people. Someone said Chairman Bobby should get up on a box and give a speech. At that time not many people in New York knew who Bobby Seale was or anything about the Black Panther Party. Chairman Bobby immediately launched into an impromptu speech on a Lenox Avenue corner, talking about Huey and describing the party's ten-point program and platform. A few people stopped, but most people in New York had not gotten turned on to the party yet. Soon the New York chapter would be well-known, and it would make a dramatic impact on the ghettos of the city.

Emory and I spent the night in a run-down Puerto Rican hotel in Brownsville, Brooklyn. I went out several times to use a pay phone to call the office and Tanya. I had never seen anything like the poverty I saw in

Brownsville. It looked like a bombed-out, deserted hellhole. There were empty, glass-filled lots with weeds and grass growing unchecked, broken-down buildings, boarded-up windows, and liquor stores. Winos and junkies mingled on vacant street corners. This scene even surpassed what I had seen on Chicago's Southside. One thing was sure—places like this were fertile ground for the organizing the New York chapter would soon be doing.

We left New York just as we had come, determined that Huey P. Newton would someday be free, despite whatever obstacles appeared in our path.

14

July 1968, Seattle

The time to hesitate is through
No time to wallow in the mire
Try now we can only lose
. *And our love become a funeral pyre*
                                        —The Doors, "Light My Fire," 1967

As the Black Panther Party was exploding onto the scene all over
the country, unbeknownst to us, the US government and local law en-
forcement agencies were systematically plotting to destroy it. What we did
know is that they would try to kill us just as they had killed Little Bobby
Hutton. In South Central Los Angeles, three young Panthers—Tommy
Lewis, Robert Lawrence, and Steve Bartholomew—were shot and killed
at a gas station by the Los Angeles pigs as they were getting out of their
car. The Los Angeles Panthers were literally catching hell. And in every
city where the party opened an office, it would just be a matter of time
before the local authorities began to arrest the Panther leaders and sometimes shoot party members in cold blood.

In Oakland, National Headquarters was preparing intensely for
Huey's upcoming trial. Panthers from all over the West Coast as well as
supporters from around the world were converging on Oakland. The party
was adamant that we would not allow Huey to go to the gas chamber. In

122

the minds of party members, we were preparing for war. Trucks mounted with megaphones went through East Oakland, West Oakland, Hunters Point, and Fillmore in San Francisco, announcing the trial and calling for mass support. Panthers were dispatched throughout the area, putting up posters, handing out flyers, and talking to people in the community. "THE SKY IS THE LIMIT IF HUEY IS NOT SET FREE!" was our mantra, and no one knew what was going to happen.

Back in Seattle, early one July morning, I headed down to the office, hoping to get a head start on the day's activities. When I turned the corner to walk the final block, I was alarmed at the sight before me. Seven or eight police cars were parked in front of the office, and uniformed police officers were walking in and out. As some of the police exited, they were carrying items I could not quite make out. My first instinct was to flee and head back home. Instead, I decided to continue on and find out what the cops were doing. Just as I reached the office, Curtis Harris drove up and got out of his car.

I shouted at the cops, "Hey, what's going on? What are you doing in our office?"

"Are you Aaron Dixon?" one of them blurted.

"Yeah," I replied.

"You're under arrest for stolen property."

Curtis and I were immediately handcuffed, taken downtown, jailed, and booked for grand larceny. We were put in separate cells. Curtis was later released. After a while, several plainclothes cops took me upstairs to the detectives' office.

"Dixon, somebody said they saw you carrying a stolen typewriter into the office, and that's a felony punishable by five to seven years in prison. If you cooperate with us, we can work something out." The detective paused, apparently to see if I would take the bait.

Another detective interjected, "You know, Dixon, some of the older guys think you aren't doing a good job. Some of them think somebody else ought to be the leader."

Sitting in the sunlit office, listening to these cops, I was startled by this description of the state of affairs in our chapter. I was fully aware that there was some dissent among the ranks, but I was puzzled as to who was providing the cops with information. "I don't know what you are talking about," I answered.

As far as the charge of the stolen typewriter went, the accusation might not have been entirely untrue, I realized months later. An older brother who often hung around the office had told me that someone at Model Cities, a community support program, said we could have a typewriter, which we sorely needed. I had carried that very typewriter into the office, apparently an unwitting participant in a classic setup.

Eventually, the detectives took me back downstairs and put me in the high-security wing on another floor, isolating me from the main part of the jail. I was the only one on that floor, completely separated from everyone and everything, which in some ways was okay for me. This isolation gave me some time to reflect, some valuable time alone, which had been impossible since I had joined the party.

I was angered by the officers' allegations concerning my leadership. But I was more perturbed about who was giving the police information about the internal strife in our chapter.

I made several phone calls to the office and home to my parents. As word spread about my arrest, Elmer, Willie, and the other comrades called for a rally at Garfield Park, where I had listened to Martin Luther King years earlier. After the rally, they organized a march downtown to the jail, demanding my immediate release. Mike Rosen from the ACLU came down to visit me, and expressed concern that tensions were so high he feared a riot would break out. The party's position was that riots were futile and destructive. I wrote a note for Elmer to read at the rally, hoping it would quell the intense emotions and prevent the rally from breaking out into a full-scale riot. I could only sit, wait, and hope that the comrades would be able to keep the situation under control. I lay in my jail bunk, wondering where all this would lead, not realizing this was only the very beginning of a long, violent summer.

Later that evening I heard voices shouting in the distance. I could faintly make out the words, but as I listened closely, the chorus grew louder and the words came clearer—"Free Aaron, Free Aaron!"

It had only been a year since I had graduated from high school, just another obscure Black youth, unsure of my place or my role in this often contradictory, confused society. Now I had become the center of attention of Seattle's entire Black community. I desperately wanted to get out of jail so a confrontation could be avoided. I knew that dynamics in the community were at the point of explosion, and I did not want to be the cause of a riot that could lead to destruction and possibly death. Seattle had not yet had a big riot. Unfortunately, my arrest would be the spark that would put us on the list with Newark, Detroit, Philadelphia, Chicago, and many other cities throughout America.

I learned later that the marchers had headed back to Garfield Park, where the protest erupted into an explosion of youthful, pent-up anger, frustration, and mayhem. Police were attacked, cars with whites in them were stoned, windows of businesses were shattered, and police cars were overturned. Two news reporters were about to be attacked when Elmer intervened and rescued them from a ravaging crowd, escorting them to safety. A full-scale riot had erupted in Seattle. As I lay in my cell, I could hear continuous sounds of sirens blaring, as if the entire city were falling apart.

Around midnight, the guard came and opened my cell and said I was free to go. To my surprise, I had been released on personal recognizance. I guess they felt it was in their best interest to let me out onto the streets. It was too late. Once a riot has begun, it ends only when the rioters near exhaustion. As I walked out of the booking room, I was met by our lieutenant of information, Bobby White, and lieutenant of political education, Willie Brazier.

"Man, everything's gone crazy," Willie said. "They're fighting cops up on Cherry Street. Man, it's a full-scale riot."

We headed back to the Central District, taking side streets to avoid the barricades and the pitched battles between the young rioters and the police. As we headed to my parents' house, we could see throngs of young people rampaging through the streets, overturning cop cars and throwing rocks and Molotov cocktails. Scores of cops were grouped together, using batons to make attacks on the rock-throwing youth.

When we arrived at the house, there was a squad of armed Panthers waiting to get involved in the action down at Garfield Park. "Aaron, we gotta go down and help the young brothers," someone said.

I was in a precarious position. The party did not openly advocate attacks on the police. We were supposed to be organizing the masses, helping them to prepare for self-defense and eventually guerrilla warfare, if it came to that. We were in no way ready to engage the cops in warfare. Yet many of the young brothers and sisters rioting were friends and probably even relatives of those brothers gathered around, holding their shotguns and rifles. I, too, was caught up in the emotions and drama of the situation. I ιecided we should try to make our way down to Garfield Park on foot. What we were going to do when we got there remained unclear.

We headed out slowly, crouching along the way, carrying our weapons, unsure of what the hell we were doing. It wasn't long before a police helicopter spied us and shined its spotlight on us. A comrade aimed and took out the light with one shot. All of us knew that within seconds we would be surrounded by pigs.

Just then, we heard a voice. It was our comrade Ron Carson. "Hey, you guys, in here. Come in here." He was standing in the doorway of his enclosed back porch, beckoning. We ran over and streamed onto the dark, covered porch. Just as the last man entered, the entire area where we had stood only seconds before was swarming with police cars. The police stayed in their vehicles, shining their spotlights on bushes and behind parked cars. On the porch, we crouched in silence, hoping we would not be detected. Finally, the cops left. Recognizing it was foolish to think that, under these circumstances, we could possibly be successful in an attack on the police, we disbanded.

The following evening the rebellion resumed. Some older members on the Central Staff suggested that we divide into three groups and ambush the cops. I wanted to argue against such a move. Although the party often invoked guerrilla warfare in articles and pictures in the party paper and on posters depicting armed men and women, the chairman had never once informed me that I was to lead guerrilla attacks against police forces. At the time I did not realize that new chapters and branches all over the country were grappling with this same dilemma—to attack or not to attack.

As a generation, we were not far removed from slavery, and its remnants were with us constantly. Jim Crow had only recently subsided. We listened to our elders' stories about the rapes, lynchings, murders, and brutality committed against our ancestors. We had all experienced personal conflicts with the police and the daily bites of racism in all aspects of our lives. Additionally, the murders of Malcolm X, Medgar Evers, and, most recently, Martin Luther King Jr. were still fresh in our minds. At some point, we felt we had to stand up and fight. The party gave us that opportunity, and the present situation provided us with an excuse to exact our revenge for the evils of American racism.

Reluctantly, I agreed, feeling that my courage would otherwise come under question—that if I refused to go along, others would doubt my bravery and sincerity. We divided into three teams of four or five men to a team, and chose our operating locations. I ended up with three comrades with whom I was very close. Though I was a few years younger, they were loyal and willing to follow me into battle despite my greenness. Elmer went with another group, and I could only hope that he would be safe.

We initially headed to Washington Park Arboretum, a heavily wooded park not far from the office. Before we had taken our position, one of the comrades, high on speed, inadvertently fired at a passing police car. Luckily, he missed, but we decided we had better find a more suitable place for an ambush.

We finally located a ridge on a hill that faced a main street. Cars had to stop at the oncoming intersection below. Behind us was a densely wooded area that led down to Lake Washington. Trails crisscrossed each other, trails that Elmer, Michael, and I had hiked on overcast days, playing war, ducking in and out of bushes, hiding from invisible enemies behind trees. The comrades and I settled in on that ridge for several hours. Many times during that night I felt the urge to call off the operation. But there was no turning back. I knew I had to follow this through. We lay on that grassy spot for hours, swapping stories about experiences in Vietnam and the wild ghettos of New Orleans, about the fine women who got away and those we hoped to catch. For that time it seemed we were brothers, and our purpose a united one.

Looking down from our little knoll, we could see across the street. Out of nowhere, cutting through the silence of the night, it appeared—our enemy, our prey, the very bane of our existence—a lone police cruiser. No one said a thing. Almost simultaneously, we all took aim and fired. As I had the only semiautomatic, I tried to get off a second round, but my rifle jammed. We jumped up and hurried down the steep embankment to the narrow path below, running in the dark as fast as we could. I tripped over a rock, flew up in the air, and landed on my shoulder. I grabbed my carbine, and we continued toward a long, steel staircase separating the forest from a thick patch of blackberry bushes. We climbed over the staircase, unsure whether to go up or down, then we saw two cop cars pull up in the cul-de-sac below. We climbed over the other side of the steps, thrusting ourselves into the thick brush, trying to blend into the trees and bushes, all of us hoping we were black enough not to be seen. The cops got out of the car with shotguns and flashlights, sweeping the forest, trying to spot the raiders. The four of us stood motionless. Slowly LewJack lowered his .357 and cocked it, preparing to fire. I put my hand on his revolver and shook my head. We all thought for sure we were dead. But the cops, unable to detect our whereabouts, got into their cars and left.

We didn't know what to do, but we could not stand there in the bushes much longer. Suddenly, in the distance, I heard a familiar voice calling. We hurried up the steps toward the voice. It was Tanya with little Kathy Jones. Tanya lived nearby, and when she heard the gunshots she and Kathy came out to investigate. We ran quickly through several backyards to get to her place. A dog started barking wildly, and again I had to stop LewJack from discharging his weapon. Reaching Tanya's apartment, we ran up the stairs to safety. Throughout the night we heard sirens. We would learn later that hundreds of police, armed with machine guns, had marched through the woods looking for the attackers. Had it not been for Tanya and Kathy, we might not have made it to safety. Of the three units sent out that night, only ours had been able to engage the enemy.

The riot was over, leaving in its wake hundreds of thousands of dollars in damage and scores of young people arrested, many of whom would go to prison for years. The riot marked the beginning of a war in Seattle between the cops and the Black Panther Party. Across the country, that summer of '68 was seen by some as the beginning of the revolution. Elmer and I were named on the front page of the *Chicago Sun-Times*, along with a picture of Elmer addressing a crowd. Upon seeing this, Ma, my grandmother on my mother's side, who had dreams of Elmer becoming a doctor and my becoming a minister, claimed to want nothing more to do with Elmer or me.

That summer we sent out teams of firebombers and snipers with the purpose of closing down known racist establishments. One such establishment was the plush Seattle Tennis Club on Lake Washington, the same tennis club that had treated our Black and Jewish tennis team like pariahs during the summer of '65. Another was Lake Washington Realty, which over the years had refused to do business with Blacks and Asians. Each time they reopened, we firebombed them again until they moved to a different location and completely boarded up their windows. And there was Bluma's, the Jewish deli around the corner from Garfield High. For years, the two fat brothers there had cursed at Black students, talking to them in a very disrespectful manner; later, they took to selling drugs along with the maple and jelly bars and pastrami sandwiches. At first we proposed to picket them, positioning a ring of Panthers around the perimeter of the store. That proved too time-consuming, so we firebombed it.

Unfortunately, some establishments were hit that should have not been, like Brenner Brothers Bakery and the Chinese neighborhood grocery store on Yesler. They became innocent victims of payback rage. We also sniped at the fire station around the corner from the office to keep the fire trucks from going out to douse the blazes from the firebombs. We even used the brick fire station for target practice, and, oddly enough, at times the police did not respond. A block from our office was an empty, unkempt lot with bushes and trees that we used to ambush police cars.

That summer, *Time* and *Newsweek* published charts of the ten cities with the highest rates of firebombing and sniping. We were proud that Seattle was ranked number one in firebombing and number two in sniping. Detroit beat us out in sniping, but in the firebombing category we were unsurpassed, beating out New York, Chicago, Detroit, Philadelphia, and others. The Panthers had put Seattle on the map.

15

The Unromantic Revolution

Hang onto the world as it spins, around
Just don't let the spin get you down
Things are moving fast
Hold on tight and you will last
> —Donny Hathaway, "Someday We'll All Be Free," 1973

The revolution did not pause or slow down. There was no time for reflection or regrets. It was sometimes difficult to distinguish right from wrong, or truth from falsehood.

Tensions between the Seattle chapter and the police had reached dangerous levels. When darkness fell, Madrona Hill became a no-man's-land. The cops would only come up to the hill in three-car caravans, four cops deep, with shotguns protruding out of the windows. Madrona Hill was dubbed "Pork Chop Hill," after a famous Korean War battle.

One cloudy Saturday afternoon, party members had gathered at the office for the weekly political education classes. I was en route to the meeting in a car with Willie Brazier, Buddy Yates, and LewJack, when we found ourselves behind a police cruiser driven by a sergeant. He stopped in front of the office and peered in.

Suddenly Willie Brazier jumped out of our vehicle, ran up to the cop car, yanked open the door, and began tugging the shocked cop out of his car, yelling, "Pig, what are you doing here?"

The sergeant must have pushed an emergency button, because within seconds cop cars descended on the scene from every direction. Buddy, LewJack, and I had gotten out of our car. Willie let go of the cop and the four of us retreated across the street toward the office. The cops stayed in their cars, shotguns sticking out of their windows. Had they decided to start shooting, there was nowhere for us to go. For a few seconds we stood looking at the cops while they looked at us, all wondering what would be the next move.

The sergeant finally spoke. "This is a warning to you guys. We're ready for anything." After that the cops split.

Another afternoon, we were in the office, preparing for a meeting. There happened to be a bus stop right in front of the office. We had instructed the bus drivers to park about five feet back, so as not to block the front of the office. Most complied, but every now and then there would be a dissenter.

A dark-haired bus driver pulled in front of the office and sat there, blocking our entrance. Elmer and Steve Philips boarded the bus and commanded the driver to move.

"No, I'm not moving," he replied. Suddenly, Elmer and Steve pounced on the driver and grabbed his bus phone, ripped out the wires, and threw it onto the roof of the office building. The bus driver finally drove off.

Eventually, the transit company sent some managers over to negotiate on the bus stop issue. We still refused to allow them to fully block the front of our office. Meanwhile, a warrant was put out for my arrest for assault on the bus driver. The driver swore on the witness stand that I, not Elmer, had attacked him. Even though Elmer got on the witness stand and testified that he had done it, I was the one found guilty. Luckily, Judge Stokes was presiding over the proceedings. Judge Stokes was one of the few Black judges in town at that time, and I had gone to school with his daughter. Yet, even with the connections, I think we were all pleasantly surprised when he gave me probation and relieved me of jail time.

Plenty of people were supportive of our chapter. People dropped off money, office equipment, and supplies, sometimes even weapons. Thus, when Jack, a short, stocky, blond, Scandinavian-looking dude showed up, we were inquisitive, in spite of our skepticism. He was decked out in a three-quarter-length black leather coat and a black beret, and had on a button of Che Guevara. "Hey, my name's Jack," he said, extending his hand and giving me a firm handshake. "I belong to the Communist Party on Mercer Island."

We nodded and looked on, trying to size up this cat. He continued, "Yeah, I fought with Che and Fidel when they landed in Cuba."

After we had listened with interest to several of his stories, he left and promised to come back, which he did. He took us out to his house, where he lived with his two wives. He taught us revolutionary tactics, including how to make time bombs with a stick of dynamite and an alarm clock in a shoebox. Learning of his access to dynamite, we made arrangements for two cases of dynamite with nitroglycerine. The Molotov cocktails had served their purpose. Now it was time to move on to something more effective.

The plan was set: Jack would get the dynamite from his contact. Gary Owens and I would meet him near University of Washington campus. We picked him up without incident and headed to the office. When we got near, a cop car that had been tailing us for a while put on its flashing red lights and siren. We were all nervous, but Jack was sweating like a madman as he waited while the cop checked his ID. We were sure we would get busted. Luckily, a platoon of Panthers had seen us get stopped and ran down from the office to investigate, which spurred the cops to let us go. That was a close call.

We buried one of the cases of dynamite in a wooded area and took the other case to the basement of my apartment, where we left it in the care of two comrades who volunteered to stand watch until we decided what to do with it. When we came back to check on it several hours later, the two comrades informed us that the cops had come by and confiscated the case of dynamite—a very fishy story, but somehow we overlooked it at the time.

As a matter of fact, one night a week later these same comrades, along with Curtis Harris, decided they would escort me home from the office, which I found unusual. I usually walked by myself or was accompanied by LewJack. Besides, I knew these guys from high school, and they didn't have a political bone in their body—they pretty much hung out with the thug crowd. When we turned a corner, a slow-moving police cruiser appeared. Suddenly Curtis pulled out his .45 and fired in the direction of the cop car. A moment later, when I looked around, Curtis and the other two had disappeared and I was alone. Knowing full well the place would quickly be covered with cops, I ran up the stairs of the Melinsons' house nearby and into the backyard. Within minutes I could hear cars filling the streets, doors opening and closing, and the voices of desperate, angry white men getting closer. The backyard was completely enclosed by ten-foot-high, thick, green bushes. There was no escape, and I could hear the voices getting louder, quickly coming my way. I pulled out my 9mm and braced for the worst. Just then, the back door of the house opened, and out stepped Mr. Melinson. He silently motioned me inside. I ran in with my piece in my hand just as the cops were entering the yard with guns drawn. Mr. Melinson drew me into the living room, where we sat in the darkness with his family, watching the action out the windows. We could see the cops frantically searching for me, under cars, and behind buildings, but I was nowhere to be found.

Elmer, Michael, and I had grown up with the Melinsons. The family had seven kids. Their daughter, Wanda, had a strong crush on me in the sixth grade. My brothers and I had played football, basketball, and tennis with Wayne and Gary. However, when Elmer and I joined the party, Mr. Melinson ordered his children not to have anything to do with us, which was understandable. I had observed Mr. Melinson for many years. He was a very light-complexioned, conservative Texan who seldom smiled and was known for his strictness. He worked hard and sent all his kids to Catholic school. He was the last person I would have thought would risk his position and family to save a crazy young revolutionary, but he did, and he will forever remain in my heart. After the cops gave up, I ran home, thankful that I had been spared another day.

It was unsettling, to say the least, that Curtis and the other two would fire at the pigs without letting me know, and then disappear. I was still of the mind that if you were Black and down for the cause, you were un-questionable. But, in reality, there were far too many men and women who looked and acted the part who were willing to compromise themselves as human beings for a few dollars, for a shorter prison sentence, or just for the thrill of playing both sides. Informants had infiltrated just about every party chapter, quite heavily in some places, and Seattle was no exception. I heard later from sources on the streets that the cops had a price on my head. They thought that killing me would bring an end to all their worries.

The city had already tried to buy me out, sending a light-complex-ioned Black man, casually dressed, to the office a few months earlier. "Hello, Mr. Dixon," he began. His polite demeanor reminded me of my father. "The City of Seattle would like to offer you a position with the city at $35,000 a year," he said, providing no further details or information about the job. That was a large amount of money to offer anyone, let alone a nineteen-year-old, but I turned him down politely. He said with a smile, "Well, if you change your mind, give me a call," as he handed me his card and left.

That summer, for the first time, militant organizations in the Seattle Black community came together in a town meeting with the aim of form-ing a united front for greater organizing power. The groups included Con-gress of Racial Equality (CORE), the Black United Front, the *African American Journal*, the Black Panther Party, and a few others, as well as indi-vidual activists like Daisy Boyetta. That night it was a packed house at the YMCA on Madison, with mostly older members of the community. There were many impassioned speeches against the white man and the system, as well as against Uncle Toms, considered complicit with the man. Toward the end, I was nominated to head this united coalition of militants. I strolled to the front of the room, took the mic, and spouted some revo-lutionary rhetoric. They were looking to me for the answers to their dilem-mas, answers I did not have. I was just a nineteen-year-old idealist doing my best to run the Seattle chapter of the Black Panther Party. I was ill-prepared to take advantage of this brief moment of unity, and nothing ever came of the opportunity.

Toward the end of the summer, we lost a very dedicated, beloved comrade, but not at the hands of the police. Seventeen-year-old Henry Boyer came to the aid of his distraught mother, who was being attacked by her boyfriend. Henry was big and thick for his age, willing and able to give someone a good ass-kicking if he wanted to. The man grabbed Henry's shotgun and killed him. It was incredibly sad to lose Henry in this way. He had a lot of potential, not only as a revolutionary but also as a valuable asset to humanity.

Everybody loved Henry, and to honor our first fallen comrade, we wanted to send him away in splendid fashion. Nafasi, Maud Allen, and other sisters made beautiful baby-blue, African-inspired robes for the com-rade sisters, and all the comrade brothers wore full Panther uniform. We had a double line of nearly two hundred Panthers standing at attention, extending all the way down the block on either side of Angelus' Funeral Home. It was an inspiring, revolutionary farewell for our beloved comrade. The next day the *Seattle Post-Intelligencer* reported that it was the largest funeral in the history of Washington State.

A week after the funeral, Mr. Angelus, the funeral director, called and asked for Elmer and me to come over to the funeral home. When we arrived, he took us back into a side room full of caskets. It was dark and very eerie. He opened one of the caskets and inside were more than a dozen rifles.

"These are for you, brothers."

We couldn't believe our eyes—they were Argentine British .303 rifles. We thanked him and took them away. Though we never used these weapons, we were deeply appreciative of his gesture of support. There weren't any other professional Black people willing to risk their livelihood by giving us arms. We considered this a revolutionary act by Mr. Angelus.

Voodoo Man had moved to a house near the office. After I joined the party, I had never really trusted him anymore. He was definitely more than a little crazy, and even traveled to Oakland in an attempt to sow discord between the Seattle chapter and National Headquarters. He tried to speak with Bobby Seale about me, but the chairman sent him on his way. As the environment became increasingly dangerous, Voodoo Man, along with his white girlfriend, disappeared into the night, leaving behind everything in the house. We never heard from him again.

As summer drew to an end, I took a much-needed trip to Oakland to restore myself, reinforce my revolutionary direction, and gain some fortification against the struggles I was facing within the Seattle chapter. There had already been an assassination attempt by the police; the chapter had obviously been infiltrated. I was grappling with a general lack of discipline and insubordination among party members, as well as older comrades who questioned my authority. And the death of Henry Boyer had been difficult for everyone.

It was always good and invigorating to see Matilaba, Landon and Randy Williams, Tommy Jones, and Robert Bay. My timing was good; Tommy and Robert were going down to the Monterey Jazz Festival to set up a booth in the concession area to sell the party's posters, books, cards, and Black Panther papers. I was able to tag along. Being away from the stress of Seattle, in the sun of Monterey with Tommy and Big Bay was just what I needed. We were able to enjoy the silky voice of Carmen McRae and listen to the stellar sounds of the Modern Jazz Quartet. We even ran into Eldridge and Kathleen Cleaver and Bobby and Artie Seale.

A few tense incidents occurred, one while manning our booth. Some Los Angeles brothers wearing overalls, members of a gang known as The Farmers, came by our booth and made some provocative remarks, causing Tommy to go for his snub-nosed .38. At one point it looked like we were going to have to throw down with these apolitical jackasses. The Farmers had formed out of the ashes of the Watts riot. Apparently, due to their Black Nationalist stance, they had positioned themselves as adversaries of the party. But all in all, it was a peaceful trip. It would be the last time I would spend real time with Tommy, who had recently been appointed to the rank of captain and given his own office to run in West Oakland down on 7th Street. He still looked out for me, treating me like a little brother.

It had been a wild summer, the most rebellious in modern US history, and many of the new chapters were going through similar growing pains as we were in Seattle. We were all trying to understand what our role was to be as an organization, and trying to come to grips with our deep hatred toward the police and all they represented. The government was adjusting as well, and their tactics would soon become much more deadly for the Black Panther Party. We had no idea what lay ahead, no inkling of the undercover operation that was silently being launched against us.

16

Death in Winter

Sometimes in winter forgotten memories
remember you behind the trees
with leaves that cry.

—Blood, Sweat & Tears, "Sometimes in Winter," 1968

On September 8, 1968, Huey P. Newton was found guilty of voluntary manslaughter, which carried a two- to five-year sentence. Charles Garry, Huey's attorney and the legal counsel of the Black Panther Party, had developed a solid case for Huey's innocence. The prosecution's one eyewitness, an Oakland bus driver by the name of Grier, had told the police he had a clear view of the shooter. Grier had, in fact, stated on tape that he did not see the shooter. Charles Garry was able to get this evidence admitted in the court, but it was never disclosed to the jury. Huey had been railroaded. While we were angry about Huey being railroaded, we also breathed a collective sigh of relief that the charge against Huey had been knocked down to manslaughter, thus averting the death penalty. Huey gave orders that the party should fight the guilty verdict in the courts, not in the streets. An appeal was filed by Charles Garry and his longtime legal partner, Fay Stender, and we would have to wait for our leader to be vindicated in the courts.

For me, that winter began with another benchmark of manhood. Tanya became pregnant. She called my mother to tell her before telling me. I actually found out from my father. Poppy told me, "Aaron, you are going to have to marry her."

I replied, "No, I can't. I am too young."

Poppy's answer to me was, "If you don't marry her, I will disown you."

That was a heavy statement for him to make. I could not understand why Poppy was forcing me to do something for which I was ill-prepared. But this was the way of my parents' generation. Tanya's father, a nightclub owner known for his hot temper, called me over to talk to him regarding the situation. He toyed with his .38 as he asked me my intentions. Shortly thereafter, Tanya and I were married.

Elmer and I made a pact that he would interrupt the shotgun wedding. I remember standing at the altar in the church I had grown up in, my back to a sparse crowd, wearing a new, long, black leather coat Tanya had bought for me, occasionally looking over my shoulder, waiting for Elmer to interrupt this crazy proceeding. But he never showed. For me, this was yet another omen that it was time to leave behind my childish ways and brace myself for adulthood.

Up to that point our losses in the party had been minimal. Our only incarcerated leader was Huey, and there were only a few martyred comrades. However, destiny—in the form of the US government—was rapidly moving to change both of those statistics. Eldridge's departure from the party's leadership was imminent. Nicknamed "Papa Rage," he had taken a guest lecturer position at UC Berkeley, and used it as a stage from which to launch a continuous verbal assault against Richard Nixon, whom Eldridge called "Tricky Dick," and the then governor of California Ronald Reagan, whom he labeled "Mickey Mouse." Eldridge even came out with an album, *Dig*, a recording of a speech given at Syracuse University during his 1968 presidential run as a candidate for the Peace and Freedom Party.

Nationally, the Black Panther Party had formed a coalition with the white, liberal Peace and Freedom Party. The Peace and Freedom Party refused to recognize either the Democratic or Republican candidates, and instead nominated Panthers and other radicals to run for political office. For the 1968 national election, we collaborated with the Peace and Freedom Party to run Eldridge for president. In California, Bobby Seale, Kathleen Cleaver, and Huey Newton ran for local California political seats, while in Seattle, on the Peace and Freedom ticket, we ran two Panthers, Curtis Harris and E. J. Brisker, for legislative seats. We had a big campaign kickoff party on the top floor of the Sorrento Hotel, a classy place near downtown Seattle. Maud Allen, Nafasi (Kathy Halley), and the other sisters did a magnificent job of organizing this event. It was a festive occasion, with hundreds of Peace and Freedom Party members and Black Panther Party members and supporters. But despite all this successful momentum, a storm was brewing.

It had begun in October with the murder of seventeen-year-old Welton Armstead. Welton, like many young, Black, disenfranchised youth, had dropped out of high school, unable to see or find the value in a racist educational system. He turned to crime and eventually found his way into the party. He participated from the fringes, supplying us with weapons and sometimes money when we needed it. On a cold autumn morning, Welton watched from the window of his third-floor apartment as the Seattle police cornered his mother in the parking lot below, crudely questioning her about her son's whereabouts. Welton grabbed his Winchester and ran to his mother's aid. He was gunned down, shot in the back by Seattle police as he attempted to protect his mother. Welton was the first Seattle Panther killed by the police, arousing an angry, violent retaliation. That same evening, two pigs, while answering an emergency call, were ambushed by two seventeen-year-old Panthers. The pigs, despite being wounded, escaped death. Several days later, we buried Welton Armstead and attempted to console his grieving mother. The shooting left us bitter and angry, and Welton's death left a wound in his mother's heart that would never heal.

Here I was, nineteen years of age, at my third Panther funeral, presiding over the death of a seventeen-year-old man-child, Welton Armstead, in a little, dingy chapel, the family sitting and weeping, Panthers lining the walls. At that instant, standing in front of Welton's family, I felt an icy shield slowly cover my spirit. There would be no tears, no anguish, just a cold demeanor that slowly replaced the warm kindness I once carried. The Aaron my parents raised was now gone, for there would be many more dead comrades to bury, many more Panther funerals with stone-faced men and women, clenched fists thrust to the sky.

Shortly after my July 1968 arrest for the stolen typewriter, a young Jewish woman from the Young Socialist Alliance suggested that I organize a defense committee around the case. The chapter's Central Staff agreed and began organizing a Free Aaron Dixon Defense Committee. A pamphlet entitled "Hands Off Aaron Dixon" was created. Speaking engagements were set up around the Pacific Northwest as well as in Chicago.

In Oakland, during one of my frequent visits, I talked with Eldridge shortly before his exile, his long body sitting on the footsteps of St. Augustine's Church as he ate a plate of black-eyed peas, oxtails, and corn bread from the soul food restaurant across the street.

"Aaron," he stated, as he slowly ate, "you have to be careful of those Socialists. They like to use shit for their own purposes, you dig? I'm not saying the defense committee is a bad thing; it's a good idea. Just don't let them use you."

"Right on, right on, Eldridge," I assured him. That was my last conversation with Eldridge.

Eldridge was facing the possibility that his parole for the April 6 shootout might be revoked by the state, which would mean he would have to return to San Quentin. This was not something Eldridge was prepared to do. He had stated many times that he was not going back to prison. One cover headline of *The Black Panther* read "Damn Pigs and Prison." A vigil was set up at Eldridge's house in the Fillmore district of San Francisco. As the day drew near for him to report for his parole hearing in November, I was at his house with other Panthers, armed, waiting for the pigs to come. But Eldridge was long gone. He chose exile, in Cuba and later Algeria, rather than life in the dungeons of San Quentin. For those of us living in America—enduring in what Eldridge had coined as "the belly of the beast"—we would see our remaining leaders, one by one, killed off or imprisoned.

In December, without my knowledge or approval, Panther Sidney Miller, a Chicago transplant, was ordered by Curtis Harris to rob a West Seattle store for what Sidney had been told was Panther business. In the process, Sidney was shot in the head by the store owner, dying instantly. At the time, the circumstances leading to his death were unknown, but eventually the details would all come to the surface. It was a travesty that should not have happened. Sidney was a gregarious, happy-go-lucky comrade with an infectious smile. Everyone loved Sidney and his dedication, yet it was this same blind dedication that led to his death.

Not long after Sidney's killing, a young man named Larry Ward returned from Vietnam. A year older than me, during high school Larry Ward ran with the fast crowd. He was one of the sharp dressers and his hair was processed. I was surprised to learn that after returning from Vietnam he was interested in the revolution at home. Larry Ward reconnected with some of his old buddies who had joined the party and asked how he could join; unfortunately, a couple of those old buddies were suspected of being police informants.

Determined to put an end to the party's firebombing campaign, the Seattle Police Department had put out a $25,000 contract on my head, and since their attempts on my life had failed, they settled for setting up Larry Ward. Someone told Larry that if he firebombed Hardcastle Realty, he would be able to join the party. The people who set him up told him that the Molotov cocktails would be waiting for him in the bushes.

When Larry arrived, prepared to carry out his mission, the pigs came out of nowhere. A startled Larry raised his hands and the pigs opened up, shooting and killing him instantly. The pigs used one-inch deer slugs, solid pieces of lead used mainly for hunting large wild animals. Larry never had a chance to play the role of the revolutionary—instead he became a sacrificial victim.

To make things worse, LewJack was wounded accidentally by another party member, resulting in the paralysis of his left arm. It was becoming more evident to me that there were many things happening in the Seattle chapter of which I had no knowledge, and many of these were extremely serious, life-and-death matters. Around this time I began to feel a tremendous amount of pressure and to question the decisions I was making. I started drinking more often as I tried to sort out the problems in our chapter.

I took another trip to Oakland, which always seemed to give me the strength to carry on. While meeting with Chairman Bobby, I mentioned my upcoming speaking engagement in Chicago that the Socialists had set up.

"Aaron, when you go back there, I want you to check on some brothers who are starting a chapter," he said. "Their names are Fred Hampton and Bobby Rush. Betty will get you their number."

In early December, Bobby Harding, Jimmy Davis, and I were off to Chicago, where we stayed at my grandmother DeDe's house. Our first speaking engagement was at a high school near Cabrini-Green, a housing project in the southwest part of the city. The place was packed and there was a lot of excitement in the air about the party. The next day we spoke at a small college north of Chicago, and a few days later we found ourselves at the University of Chicago on a chilly Wednesday evening.

The auditorium was filled nearly to capacity with mostly Black students and others. I was pleasantly surprised to find I was sharing this speaking engagement with one of the brothers organizing the Chicago chapter, Fred Hampton. After I spoke, Fred Hampton, Bobby Rush, and about eight other very rough-looking brothers took the stage. One of the brothers, Chaka Walls, carried a large African walking stick. The brothers assumed positions around the stage and secured the doors as Fred Hampton, a large, husky brother with uncombed hair, wearing an army fatigue jacket, began to speak.

He began, "Ain't nobody leavin' this mothafucka until we finish."

Fred Hampton spoke for the next thirty minutes. It was a rough, sharp speech that expressed the end-of-the-road mentality that most young urban Blacks shared at that time. He said it was time to put the rhetoric and the analytical bullshit behind us, and be prepared to pick up guns and fight.

My speech paled in comparison to the powerful words of this young Black man, my same age. I had no idea—nor did any of us at the time—that we were witnessing the next Malcolm X, the next Martin Luther King. In essence Fred Hampton was poised to become the next great leader of Black America.

He and I talked briefly afterward and said we would try to hook up before I left, but a snowstorm prevented that from happening. We returned to Seattle to await my trial.

17

The Purge

People say believe half of what you see,
Son, and none of what you hear.
I can't help bein' confused
If it's true please tell me dear?
　　　—Marvin Gaye, "I Heard It through the Grapevine," 1968

After I returned from Chicago, I began preparing for the stolen type-writer trial. It was fortunate for me that a young, smart, dashing, white at-torney, a rising star in the legal community, came to my aid. William Dwyer was gaining a reputation as one of the smartest trial attorneys in the state. He came by the office in a dapper gray suit and offered his services to fight my case pro bono. He was not a political attorney like Mike Rosen, but he was very interested in making sure that justice prevailed. He invited Tanya and me over for dinner at his house. His beautiful Greek wife pre-pared many delicious meals to fuel our legal discussions.

　　I went to trial in December 1968. The prosecution in the case called two detectives who testified that they had observed me seven days a week, in the rain, the snow, the summer heat—and they were certain they had seen me, from almost a block away, carrying the typewriter into the office. Bill Dwyer brought in a weather expert from out of state who nullified their testimony. However, the prosecutor's case hinged on the testimony of a secret witness. We were all waiting for this secret witness to show up.

143

We knew there were some spies in the party, but we did not know who they were. The court took a two-hour recess to give the prosecution enough time to present the secret witness. I was facing seven years, and with Tanya nearly seven months pregnant and the movement facing mounting attacks, I was not prepared to leave the streets.

Well, the secret witness never materialized, and I was found not guilty. We were all relieved at the verdict. But the identity of the secret witness remained a question. Bill Dwyer had saved me from almost certain prison time. He would go on to prove himself as one of the most important individuals in the fight for human and environmental rights in the state of Washington, eventually rising to a federal judgeship.

On January 17, 1969, the Black Panther Party suffered one of its greatest losses. Alprentice "Bunchy" Carter, deputy minister of defense of the Southern California chapter, and John Huggins, the deputy minister of information, were murdered inside Campbell Hall on the UCLA campus, in a conflict over student leadership of the Black Studies Program at UCLA. The two party ministers were lending support to the BSU in its fight with Ron Karenga's United Slaves Organization (US) about the direction of the Black Studies Program. US was one of the organizations that had come about after the Watts Uprising. Its platform was based on Pan-African cultural nationalism and was opportunist in nature. Reportedly they had even received money from the mayor of Los Angeles. The US plan for the Black Studies Program had been voted down, but they continued to threaten the BSU, who asked the party for assistance.

Before joining the party, Bunchy Carter—"Mayor of the Ghetto," as he was known—was the leader of the five-thousand-strong Slausons, one of Los Angeles's biggest gangs. John Huggins was a bright and dedicated UCLA student who had moved with his wife, Ericka, from Connecticut. Bunchy and John, along with others, had built the first chapter outside the Bay Area into one of the most powerful in the party. With a cadre of former gang members and bright college students, the Southern California chapter was positioning itself to change the ratio and political balance of power in Los Angeles. The danger they presented to the status quo was immense. There was no way the bastion of right-wing conservatism that was the Los Angeles Police Department would allow this to happen. The stakes were too high. The tactics they had used for decades to keep the Black and Latino communities in check were in danger of being turned against them.

I had met Bunchy briefly at National Headquarters during the summer. An intense, sharply dressed sister named Elaine Brown had accompanied him. I remember how serious they both looked. I also remember how immaculately dressed Bunchy was, almost princely in his walk and mannerisms. Though I had never met John, his important contributions to the molding of the Southern California chapter were well known. Bunchy and John were allegedly gunned down by the Stiner brothers, who were (also allegedly) members of US. US and the Southern California chapter were rival forces, and we would later learn that the FBI had been using tools of provocation— forged death threats, degrading political cartoons, and more—to stoke the hostilities between the two groups, leading up to the murders of Bunchy and John. When, later that day, the Los Angeles comrades tried to regroup and retaliate, the pigs were there waiting for them in the alleyway of a comrade's home, arresting almost thirty Panthers and confiscating their weapons.

National Headquarters ordered West Coast chapters to bring as many comrades as we could down to Los Angeles for the funeral and to serve as reinforcements. We left in three cars, one of which was a station wagon borrowed from Dr. Bodemer, my advisor at the UW. I was traveling in the station wagon with five other Panthers, three of us in front and three in back, with no suitcases or bags. We drove straight through without stopping, except for gas and food, taking speed to stay awake. As we passed into Southern California, we ran into a massive rainstorm on a stretch of highway known as "the Grapevine" that goes through the Tehachapi Mountains. All of a sudden, one of the tires blew out. The car began to swerve and the driver lost control. We careened all the way to the other side of the freeway, into oncoming traffic. We covered our faces, certain we would be hit. Instead, the car continued sliding off the road and went backward over a cliff. About twenty yards down, the car got caught on a pipe sticking out from the rocks, and came to a halt. We all got out of the car without saying a word and climbed up the hill to the side of the freeway. In total shock and disbelief, we said very little if anything for a few minutes. It was another reprieve from certain death. Some Panthers driving from Denver to Los Angeles, whom we had passed earlier, picked us up.

We finally made it to the funeral. Many Panthers from the West Coast were in attendance. I remember that Panther Baby D from Marin County gave a eulogy for Bunchy. It was a very sad day, especially for those in the Southern California chapter, who knew Bunchy well and recognized his significance to the party. It rained for the next seven days, and some speculated that this was the gods' way of expressing their anger over the death of one of the most respected Black men on the streets of Southern California.

Bunchy wrote this prophetically haunting poem, dedicated to his mother, shortly before his assassination.

Black Mother

I must confess that I still breathe
Though you are not yet free
what could justify my crying start
forgive my coward's heart
But blame not the sheepish me
for I have just awakened from a deep deep sleep
and I be hazed and dazed and scared and vipers fester in my hair
Black Mother I curse your drudging years
the rapes and heartbreaks, sweat and tears
—but this cannot redeem the fact you cried in pain
I turned my back and ran into the mire's fog
and watched while you were dogged
and died a thousand deaths
but I swear I'll seize night's dark and gloom
a rose I'll wear to honor you,
and when I fall the rose in hand you'll be free
and I a man
for a slave of natural death who dies
can't balance out to two dead flies
I'd rather be without the shame
a bullet lodged within my brain
If I were not to reach my goal
let bleeding cancer torment my soul.

The Southern California chapter never recovered from this loss. There would never be another Bunchy or another John. Elmer "Geronimo" Pratt, a Vietnam vet, was named the new deputy minister of defense. And Elaine Brown was named the new deputy minister of information. Geronimo and Elaine continued to uphold the Southern California chapter as one of the most important in the party. After the funeral, the party arranged for the six of us to fly back to Seattle—as we had no car face whatever the state had in store for us.

In early spring of 1969, Washington State legislators had proposed a gun law aimed at preventing us from carrying our weapons out in the open. The legislation, largely a response to the Rainier Beach High School incident the year before, stated that it was illegal to carry a weapon capable of producing bodily harm in an intimidating manner. In protest, the Seattle chapter planned to send an armed delegation of Panthers to the capitol in Olympia. At the time, my youngest brother, Michael, was working in the capitol as a page for State Representative David Sprague, the father of our childhood friends Mark and Paul Sprague. In a phone conversation, Michael warned me, "Man, the highway patrol and National Guard have set up .50-caliber machine gun nests and bunkers, and troops have been deployed to wait for you guys." They thought it was going to be a Panther invasion.

We waited until the hysteria died down and then sent a reconnaissance scout to Olympia, who reported the coast was clear. There were only about nine of us—all under eighteen except Elmer and me. After the comrades got out of the cars with their rifles and shotguns, Elmer had them assume formation on the capitol steps, spread out in a line with their weapons pointed in the air. I entered the building with the aim of addressing the legislature, but was unable to do so. The piece of legislation passed, ending our phase of carrying our weapons out in the open.

Another major development occurred in the spring of 1969, this one with much deeper implications. Huey sent a directive from prison stating that any party member involved in or participating in any criminal activities was to be effectively expelled from the party. Thus began "the purge."

Since its inception, the Black Panther Party had attracted a rough breed of men and women into its ranks, particularly in the early days. Some were hustlers, ex-thieves, and crooks. These men had felt the direct effects of police brutality. They had seen up close the crookedness and corruption of the police authorities. Huey and the party not only provided them with a vehicle to address their just grievances but also allowed them to play a role in building an organization dedicated to confronting the oppressor and protecting the community. The party gave them pride and confidence, a sense of power and purpose—things most of them had never tasted.

Under Huey and Bobby, strict discipline and ideological correctness enabled many of these brothers to flourish. But with Huey's imprisonment and the party's explosive growth in the face of vicious attacks from the government, it was difficult to monitor and control all the new additions to the organization. The party asked total commitment and dedication of its members, but there was no way in those early days to provide comrades with money or the essentials needed to survive. In some cases, comrades resorted to old habits, infused with the power of the party. Some comrades took what they wanted when they wanted or needed it, robbing stores or banks.

In Seattle, the situation was worse. Willie Brazier, our lieutenant of education, was arrested for the robbery of a grocery store. When he asked me where the bail money was, the puzzle pieces began to fall into place. Curtis Harris, the one who had appointed himself "assistant captain," had secretly formed an outlaw posse of the most illegally minded comrades. Under Curtis's direction, they engaged in armed robberies of banks and businesses. He told his posse most of the loot from the robberies was for the party and that he was turning it over to me. When I learned about this I was totally thrown off guard; I had been utterly unaware of what was going on. These illegal activities went against what the party was all about.

Nationally, in response to illegal activities conducted by party members, Huey issued a decree calling for the expulsion of all members involved in criminal activity. Many people were expelled. Even Robert Bay had been involved in a holdup and was purged, to be later reinstated by Huey. In Oakland and elsewhere, the purge extended to comrades not involved in illegal activities, exiling many innocent party members due to paranoia and the uneven hand of Chief of Staff David Hilliard. Some of the decisions made by David and his brother, Assistant Chief of Staff June Hilliard, eliminated some of the best soldiers from the ranks. If you even had a close association with purged party members, you, in turn, could be purged and exiled.

One day while at the office, I received a call from Tanya that some people were waiting to speak with me in the front of the house. While approaching the house, I saw a group of former Panthers from Oakland. Three I considered my very close comrades—Matilaba, Orleander Harrison, and Tommy Jones.

We greeted each other and Tommy began to speak. "David and June and the chairman are doing some fucked-up shit. They assassinated one of our buddies who wasn't in the party, and when we spoke out about it we got expelled."

As I listened, I got a sick feeling in my stomach. I knew deep down inside these were some very good comrades, dedicated brothers and sisters. I also knew there was probably some truth to their accusations. Unfortunately for them, I had become hardened with the events of '68 behind me. I also was beginning to develop blindness to some things that did not quite seem right. I could not support their protest against the party. It was unclear to me exactly what they wanted me to do. But in the end, it was my commitment to the Black Panther Party that fueled my decision not to participate in their efforts to redress the expulsions.

This interaction was a sad moment for me. Tommy had been like a big brother to me, and Orleander, at sixteen, had accompanied Bobby and the other Panthers to the iconic demonstration in Sacramento. We had all been together that night in West Oakland less than a year earlier, backing down the cops at 7th and Wood. And Matilaba—the first woman to join the party—a sincere, soft, sweet, dedicated sister, fled Oakland, fearing for her life. She later joined the Nation of Islam in Chicago. The party would never be the same with these comrades and others dismissed from the ranks. I would never see Orleander Harrison again. Tommy and Matilaba I would see only many years later.

But I could not linger for long on these losses. I faced difficult decisions in Seattle, decisions I was reluctant to make. Section leader Buddy Yates, Curtis's right-hand man, had robbed a Safeway, jumping through a glass window in his escape, only to be captured. Curtis had even conspired with the president of Seattle's first Black-operated bank in a robbery scheme in which four Panthers robbed the bank and then split the money with the bank president. A week later they robbed another bank, which led to a wild chase and shootout, ending with the arrest of the renegades. All the participants were expelled from the party, including LewJack and Willie Brazier, at one time two of my closest friends and most trusted comrades. LewJack received twenty years and was sent away to a federal prison in Oklahoma, never to see freedom again; he died in a knife fight in prison. Willie also received a twenty-year sentence and was imprisoned at nearby McNeil Island. Oddly enough, Curtis went free, never doing a day in jail.

I sent Elmer and a goon squad to Curtis's house to administer a good ass-kicking to that fool. As they were leaving, Curtis ran out to his front porch with a pistol, ranting like a madman. A shot was fired back at him, barely missing Curtis's head. Death should have been his end. He did a tremendous amount of damage to the Seattle chapter, tarnishing our image forever in the minds of many people.

These were some of my most difficult times. Comrades I had counted on to assist me in building the Seattle chapter had either been expelled or left on their own, out of fear, or were disappointed and disillusioned. I had started drinking more, relying on the alcohol to pull me through, to give me some courage to face another day.

There was one bright light during those dismal times. On April 15, 1969, my first child, Aaron Patrice Lumumba Dixon, was born into the world.

Left: My maternal great-great grandmother, Emma, born in 1868. She is about eighty-two in this photo and lived to be ninety-four. Chicago, early 1950s.

Above left: My paternal grandparents, Elmer and Mildred Dixon (left), and two unidentified friends, dressed for swimming at the shores of Lake Michigan, Chicago, 1920s.

Above right: My maternal grandparents, Roy and Josephine Sledge, with infant Frances, Chicago, 1925.

Clockwise from top left: Poppy and his friend Madison Morrison shortly after the end of WWII, Chicago, 1945; Mommy with me as an infant, Chicago, early 1949; Grandada and I in our Seattle backyard. I've just caught my first fish, in nearby Lake Washington, 1963; Mommy and Poppy in downtown Chicago, 1945.

Press conference in front of the Panther office after the murder of Welton Armstead by the Seattle police. Front row, left to right: Earl Brooks, Bobby White, Curtis Harris, me. Back row, left to right: Michael Dixon, Artis Parker, Chester Northington, Browning, LewJack. Photo credit: Vic Condiotty, *Seattle Times*, October 1968.

Meeting with Washington State Governor Dan Evans at the Seattle Center, 1968. That's me in the foreground.

HANDS OFF
AARON DIXON
Captain, Seattle Black Panther Party

Pamphlet distributed after my arrest for the stolen typewriter. Photo credit: Gil Baker, 1968.

Elmer at my typewriter trial, Seattle, 1969.

Supporters at my trial regarding the stolen typewriter. Left to right: Michael Taylor (obscured, edge of photo), Jim Groves, my sister Joanne (Dixon) Harris, unknown, Willie Brazier, Kathy Jones, and attorney Mike Rosen, Seattle, 1969.

Valentine Hobbs (foreground) being arrested by the Seattle police at the airport for supporting Black contractors in a construction dispute, 1969.

Seattle Panthers on the steps of the capitol building in Olympia. Left to right: Anthony Ware, Clark Williamson, Wayne Jenkins, Elmer Dixon (front), Steve Phillips, Larry Tecino. Olympia, Washington, spring 1969.

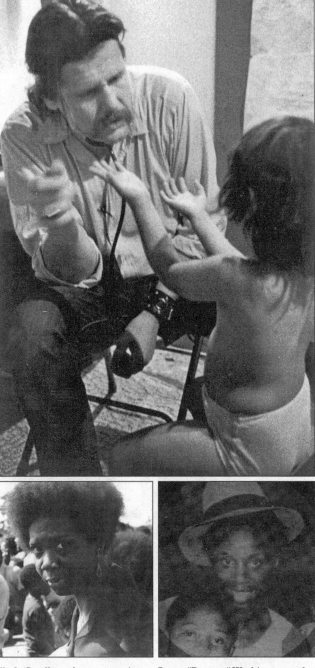

Dr. John Green and a patient at the Sidney Miller People's Free Medical Clinic, Seattle, 1969.

Cindy Smallwood at a campaign event, 1973. Photo courtesy of Bill Jennings.

Bruce "Deacon" Washington and his son at the Oakland Community School, 1974 or '75. Photo courtesy of Clarence "Stretch" Peterson.

The Seattle chapter's community center and free medical clinic, Seattle, mid-1971.

Serving breakfast to Madrona Elementary School students at the Madrona Presbyterian Church. Photo credit: Greg Gilbert, *Seattle Times*, 1969.

Poppy and I in our Seattle home, 1972.

Leslie Seale (left) and Valentine
Hobbs (right) at the LampPost, 1973

Me, Vanetta Molson, and Big
Malcolm at the LampPost, 1974.

Lola Wilson at the
LampPost, 1975.

With Lola's daughter, little
Natalie Wilson, 1976.

COINTELPRO Is Unleashed

Jake Fidler (left) and Nafasi Halley (right) carrying posters of Chairman Bobby Seale after his kidnapping by the FBI, Seattle, August 1969.

18

COINTELPRO Is Unleashed

The President, he's got his war
Folks don't know just what it's for
Nobody gives us rhyme or reason
Have one doubt, they call it treason
— Les McCann, "Compared to What?," 1969

In June 1969 President Richard Nixon, flanked by FBI Director J. Edgar Hoover and Attorney General John Mitchell, held a press conference. They announced that the Black Panther Party was "the greatest threat to the internal security of the country." COINTELPRO, the FBI counterintelligence program created in 1956 at the height of anticommunist hysteria, now geared up to focus almost solely on destroying the Black Panther Party and other radical groups. Although we didn't think the governmental repression could possibly get worse, it did.

Black Panther Party offices were raided from coast to coast. In Denver, Captain Landon Williams and Rory Hithe, two of the party's most important organizers, were wounded and arrested. In Nebraska, two Panther leaders were arrested, their office blown up, and the two leaders imprisoned for life. In New York, twenty-one of the leading members of the New York chapter were arrested and imprisoned on a variety of trumped-up charges. They became known as the "New York 21," and it took two years for them to be acquitted of the charges.

In mid-April 1969, the Frisco chapter had been organizing for a May Day "Free Huey" rally at the San Francisco federal courthouse. For weeks the comrades had been out in the community, passing out flyers, talking to people, and driving through the Fillmore, Hunters Point, Pattero Hill, Sunnydale, and Mission neighborhoods in a truck mounted with a loud-speaker, advertising the upcoming rally. The San Francisco pigs had been harassing the comrades for weeks, stopping the truck for petty reasons. Days before the rally, the pigs surrounded the truck in front of the Panther office on Fillmore and pulled their guns, sending the Panther comrades running into the office. They then fired tear gas through the office windows. Although the comrades were able to get out through a hole in the back wall, they were confronted there by armed pigs. When one sister began to collapse from the tear gas, Field Marshal Don Cox ("D. C.") ran to her aid. A pig known as Big Red yelled at D. C., "Didn't I tell you to put your hands up?" D. C. answered, "She's fainting!" Big Red responded by firing two rounds at D. C. The bullets passed through D. C.'s big Afro, just barely missing the head of the field marshal. All the comrades were arrested and released, except for D. C., who remained in custody, a marked man. And this was only the beginning of the repression.

The movement had expanded in many communities across the nation: the Brown Berets in Southern California; La Raza Unida Party (RUP) in the Southwest; the Red Guards and Los Siete de la Raza in Northern California; the American Indian Movement in the Midwest and on the West Coast; and white groups such as the Chicago-based Young Patriots and the Weatherman. Looking to the Black Panther Party as the vanguard of the movement, these organizations were determined to fight injustice in this country and US imperialism abroad, and in turn we all became targets of the US government. The antiwar movement also had spread to every college campus in the country. The government was determined to crush these radical leftist groups.

The party led the formation of a coalition with many of these groups, kicked off with the three-day National Conference for a United Front Against Fascism, held in Oakland in March 1969. I took a squad of Seattle Panthers down to help with security. People from all over the world were in attendance. There were speeches and rallies and an exclusive screening of *Z*, a film by Costa-Gavras about state control and a Greek assassin conspiracy. I was assigned to a security detachment of about eight people. We were given weapons and orders to mingle with the crowds, traveling in a van from event to event.

With us was a sixteen-year-old sister named Marsha Turner. Marsha was one of those rare persons with amazing beauty and the kind of enthusiasm and dedication that came along only every once in a while. She had a light, peach-colored complexion, a black, mid-high Afro, and high cheekbones. She had graduated from Berkeley High School at the top of her class and joined the party at age fifteen. In that short time she had risen to become national coordinator of the party's recently launched Free Breakfast for School Children Program. She could also outshoot most men in the party, which is why, at the conference, she was disguised as a prostitute, roaming the crowds with a big, snub-nosed .357 Magnum stuffed in her purse, keenly observing the crowd while Chairman Bobby and other well-known leaders spoke. And Basheer, a comrade from New York, led a goon squad on members of the Progressive Labor Party, who were foolishly attempting to disrupt the conference.

Out of this three-day conference came the establishment of an umbrella organization, the United Front Against Fascism, which opened community centers in white neighborhoods, led by white radicals, as well as new community centers in Black neighborhoods, led by the party. The Central Committee decided after the conference that there would be no more new Black Panther Party chapters; new offices would be identified as Communities to Combat Fascism centers. Existing chapters would remain as they were, with some exceptions.

A short while earlier, the party had launched the Free Breakfast for School Children Program, designed to provide a nutritious breakfast to hungry elementary schoolkids. Conceived by longtime Oakland Panther Glen Stafford, this program would also give party members something tangible and relevant to contribute to the community beside the focus on guns and self-defense. A number of brothers felt that such an activity was not revolutionary in nature and thus refused to participate. Most of those dissenters joined the ranks of the purged.

As part of organizing the Breakfast Program, Panthers were assigned to procure donations from businesses inside and outside of the community. One of the large stores we solicited was Safeway, but they refused to donate to the Breakfast Program. In response, the party ordered a national boycott of Safeway stores. The Seattle boycott of two Safeway stores in the Central District was so successful we ended up closing them down. Rather than donating to feed hungry kids, they decided to close their doors and move. There was not another Safeway store in the area for the next forty years. Their closing cleared the way for small, community-based stores to flourish instead, particularly Richland's Grocery, owned by Jack Richland, a Jewish man who not only donated regularly to the program but also became a long-time friend to the party.

Much of our attention that summer also focused on raising our distribution and sales of *The Black Panther*. We had discovered that the Northwest rock festivals were often good for selling up to a thousand papers in a matter of hours, so when a rock promoter, the husband of a good friend of Joanne's, asked if we would provide security for the Seattle Pop Festival at Woodinville, Elmer and I jumped at the opportunity. Not only would we be able to unload our weekly shipment of papers, but also Elmer and I would be paid fifteen dollars an hour for sixteen-hour days. For Elmer and me, it was a wonderful break from the intense year of being Black Panther Party members. Both of us had literally dropped every aspect of normal life as an eighteen- or nineteen-year old. We had been under constant stress from continuous battles not only with the police but also within the Seattle chapter itself. These three days at Woodinville would give us a little time, a little space, to breathe deeply, to mingle with the outside world and halfway detach ourselves from the constant battles on the revolutionary front.

On our first day, roaming through the tent city at Woodinville, Elmer and I strode through the grounds in our leather coats with our .357s tucked in our waistbands. Given that we were the only form of security for more than fifty thousand participants, it was amazing how orderly people were and how loving the atmosphere was. Throughout the whole three days, there was not one act of violence. After all, the hippie movement was based upon love, respect, communal sharing, and living freely. We also got to enjoy performances by the likes of Chuck Berry, Bo Diddley, Ike and Tina Turner, Chicago, Santana, and the Doors. As we strolled through the campgrounds the first day, people invited us into their tents, trailers, and campsites to share their wine, weed, and hash; they gave us mescaline and THC, which we deposited in our pockets. We even made some money on the side, selling tickets that a sister working the ticket booth had given us.

The last day, Elmer and I decided to enjoy ourselves, popping some acid, riding the roller coaster, and renting horses, which we rode through the throngs of concertgoers. Later that night, we manned the barricade separating the crowd from the stage in anticipation of the final act, Jim Morrison and the Doors. I had always been a fan of Jim Morrison, and to be so close to him as he performed "Light My Fire" was one of my best memories during this turbulent time. The crowd was going crazy, and only Elmer and I, a handful of ushers, and the wooden barricade stood between the band and the fifty thousand screaming fans.

It was the most fun we'd had together in a long time. The last year and a half had left me feeling cynical and unsure of myself. I had consumed more alcohol than was normal for me, trying to wash away the doubts, trying to bolster my courage, trying to fortify myself against the pain, the hurt, and the loss of good comrades. Yet there was never any doubt in my mind, never any second-guessing about the direction I had taken.

19

The Chairman Is Kidnapped

And if you had a choice of colors
Which one would you choose my brothers
If there was no day or night
Which would you prefer to be right
—Curtis Mayfield, "Choice of Colors," 1969

In August 1969 I was at the weekly party meeting at St. Augustine's Church in Oakland. Comrades from all over the country were in attendance, listening to Masai Hewitt, the minister of education. Masai had taken over for George Murray, who departed in the summer of 1968 to become a reverend in his father's church. Toward the end of the meeting, Chairman Bobby called on me to recite the ten-point program and platform, something often done at these meetings to make sure everyone was on their toes. I stumbled through the ten points, surprising even myself. Part of it was nervousness, the other part was indicative of the past year in Seattle, a year of turmoil and bad moves.

"Aaron, I want you to keep your ass down here for a couple of months," responded the chairman.

I had seen the chairman come down on a lot of people. He was pretty much a fair and compassionate person in his dealings with party members, but if someone was bullshitting or fucking up, he would come straight out and say it in no uncertain terms. I was stung by his rebuke, yet his words rang true.

In April 1968, I had jumped right into the fire. I had not been fully equipped for what was asked of me. More recently, National Headquarters had begun requesting that newly appointed chapter heads spend some extended time in Oakland. But I'd had only the one week in April 1968, along with the weekly meetings, for which I would stay only a few days. I desperately wanted some time away from Seattle. I needed to be around the seasoned comrades in the Bay, and hoped that some of their wisdom and experience would rub off on me. When I got home, I spoke with comrades and family about the prospect of an extended stay in Oakland. A few weeks later, Elmer drove Tanya, little Aaron Patrice, and me down to National Headquarters and headed back to Seattle.

Early in 1969, National Headquarters had relocated to a new office in Berkeley, which was quite an improvement over the old one on 45th and Grove in Oakland. This office was a spacious, two-story brick structure with a large glass window on either side of the entrance. The new office would be able to accommodate all the visiting officers from chapters around the country. Inside, toward the back of the office, was a big, comfortable chair where the officer of the day (OD) sat. The OD ran the daily operations of the office, among many other things. On the left side of the office was a long counter with posters and books and papers. There were several smaller offices in the back. On the second floor was a large room in which John Seale, the chairman's brother, had constructed two long drafting tables. This was where the layout for *The Black Panther* took place. In the back of the second floor were several more offices and a large kitchen.

On one of the office walls was a large map of the United States with scores of red pins indicating the locations of Black Panther Party chapters and branches. Chapters and branches, as well as the new Communities to Combat Fascism centers, were required to send people to National Headquarters for months at a time, and some stayed much longer. In contrast, with Seattle being the very first chapter to open outside of California, I had never spent more than a week at National Headquarters. There were many things to learn, things I'd had to learn on the fly. I was now prepared to stay and soak up all that was required of me in order to learn how to more effectively perform my job.

The first couple weeks I spent out in the field, selling papers, passing out leaflets, sometimes at designated spots, sometimes working with another person, going door to door, house to house, block to block, often talking with people, educating them, befriending them, connecting them to the party and its ideology. Wednesday nights, Panthers throughout the Bay gathered at the distribution office in Frisco at 7 p.m. to work on the folding, wrapping, counting, and boxing of the weekly newspapers, shipping them out to chapters throughout America and the world, and also sending out rolled individual orders to persons in England, Europe, Japan, and India, often in the most unlikely places. We worked through the night, finishing up early in the morning, taking breaks to smoke some Brother Roogie or drink some Bitter Dog, talking about the latest attack or what was happening on the political scene, or hooking up with a sleeping partner. Some days we were assigned to work at the Breakfast Programs, to leaflet union-organizing sites, or to attend rallies, selling papers and organizing people.

At the office, little Aaron Patrice sat in his bassinet in the middle of the floor, watching John Seale, Shelley Bursey, and the other newspaper staff as they laid out the paper. John Seale gave Aaron Patrice the nickname of "Moonbaby," because of his round head and the quiet, serious look on his face. Tanya sometimes stayed at the office to look after our son. Other times, she went out into the field with the others.

I met wonderful comrades like thirteen-year-old Madeline, mature and wise beyond her years, curly-haired Kathy Kimbrow, and a high-strung young brother named Poison, from New Orleans, one of the most energetic and compassionate brothers you could imagine. I befriended a brother named T. C., who did a lot of organizing at Laney and Grove Street Colleges. Sometimes I assisted the OD, a post that alternated between Robert Bay and Charles Bursey. In addition to running the daily operations of the office, the OD coordinated rides for Panther operations in the Bay Area as well as the pickup and drop-off runs to the airport, which seemed constant. The OD was also responsible for office security, not just from the police and agents but also from enemies in the community—those who didn't agree with the party, held a grudge, or had a bone to pick.

In one such instance, I was talking with Charles Bursey when a bearded brother began arguing with Robert Bay inside the office. Robert called for Bursey and me: "Aaron! Bursey!"

Bay nodded his bearded, chubby face toward the troublemaker. We escorted him outside to the side of the building. Robert Bay hauled off and hit the brother in the back of the head. Bursey and I joined in. We pummelled him to the ground and sent him on his way. "He was a pig," said Robert Bay afterward. I never knew whether that was true, but it was not my place to question my superiors.

The OD was also responsible for feeding the troops when they came in from the field. On certain days Chairman Bobby barbecued, spending hours preparing elaborate, delicious Southern dishes, talking party business as he cooked. Some evenings we had political education classes. Other evenings we just hung out drinking, smoking weed, talking with new comrades from faraway places. One night I had a long conversation with a brother from North Carolina about the meaning of the song "Choice of Colors" by Curtis Mayfield, as we tried to decipher the true meaning of the lyrics, coming to the conclusion that Curtis was trying to say some progressive political stuff in that song.

Tanya, little Aaron Patrice, and I were assigned to a big house in Berkeley on 10th Street, where Bobby and Artie Seale were also staying, along with Randy Williams and the woman he was relating to, Lauren Williams, who happened to share the same last name. Assigned drivers were responsible for picking up comrades scattered throughout the Bay to get them to headquarters by 8:30 a.m., then dropping them off at night, usually around midnight.

Cotton, one of the military experts from the Southern California chapter, had come up to National Headquarters to work on digging a tunnel beneath the office in the case of a police attack. We spent many long hours digging that tunnel, but there were just too many pipes in our way, so the project was eventually abandoned. Cotton spent much of his time traveling with Geronimo Pratt to chapters throughout the country, helping with the fortification of offices and the construction of tunnels.

One morning we received a copy of the *Berkeley Free Press*, a paper put out by hippies and white radicals. The front page revealed a detailed plan by the Berkeley Police Department to launch an attack on National Headquarters with assault squads, using Stoner rifles—weapons that could shoot through brick. When Chief of Staff David Hilliard was alerted, he immediately called a press conference, exposing the scheme before the pigs had time to carry out their assault. David also ordered increased nighttime security inside National Headquarters. For several weeks, there were about twenty armed comrades, alternating in two shifts, stationed around the office.

I remember a San Francisco Panther named Fred Knowland walking around the security perimeter, checking on the watch. He warned me, "Comrade, if I catch you fallin' asleep, I'm going to put this .357 upside your head."

When it came time for me to check the perimeter, I found Comrade Fred had fallen asleep. I did not hesitate in hitting him upside his head with my piece.

A few days later we began to prepare for a "Free Huey" rally in East Oakland at Arroyo Viejo Park. David Hilliard would be speaking and the Mad Lads were scheduled to perform. The Mad Lads had been on top of the charts before two of its main members were drafted to serve in Vietnam. The original group had not performed live in more than two years. It was good to see the Mad Lads back together, and it certainly was a joy for me and many others to be experiencing them live in a free concert in East Oakland.

Again, I was with a security detachment that formed a semicircle around the stage. It was another hot, muggy day in Oakland. There were many different types of people at the park that day. Some were political—some were not—and under these circumstances, you never knew what might happen. Of course, throw in a red devil epidemic and you automatically increase the likelihood of trouble. Red devils were little red pills that made you high as hell, but also made you crazy and ornery. It wasn't long before a fight broke out between some brothers with Doberman pinschers, the dog of choice of brothers in the streets. We moved in to break up the fight, unintentionally roughing up some of the combatants in the process. One brother separated himself from us and pulled out a gun. Randy Williams, who was in charge of security, told everyone, "FREEZE!" and began walking toward the brother. Slender, unemotional Randy looked the brother in the eye with that Clint Eastwood fearlessness and slowly walked toward him while everyone watched in silence. When Randy got five feet away, the brother turned and ran. From that day forward, Randy was known as "Cold Steel."

We had only been in Oakland three weeks, and each day had seen one event or another. You never knew what the next day would bring. One day in particular would impact not only the entire organization but also the movement as a whole.

With Huey in prison and Eldridge in exile, Chairman Bobby had become the heart and soul of the party. He was the force behind the "Free Huey" movement. Tireless and relentless, he was a fiery, persuasive speaker, and the party's spokesman. Within days he would be silenced.

It was a breezy Saturday morning. Most of the party officials were attending the wedding of the minister of culture, Emory Douglas. It wasn't often that a comrade got married. We went to far more funerals than weddings. With few celebrations, this was a moment to be joyous and happy for Emory, the youngest member of the Central Committee, and his bride. But after the short celebration, it was time to get back to business.

As Chairman Bobby, John Seale, and June Hilliard began to pull out of the church parking lot, five FBI vehicles cornered the car, drew their guns, pulled Chairman Bobby out of the car, placed him under arrest, and took off with him in one of their cars. I was at the house in Berkeley during the wedding. June called and informed me of the chairman's arrest.

"Aaron. The pigs just arrested the chairman. They might be coming to the house. I want you to secure the house and don't let the pigs in. Understand?"

"Right on," I answered.

I immediately grabbed Randy's CETME semiautomatic weapon, put a bandolier over my chest, and went to check the front and back windows of the house. Pig cars were circling the block, slowly driving by, casing the house. Suddenly, one stopped. I nervously ran downstairs and looked through the peephole. A sergeant had gotten out of his car and was walking up to the door. He knocked on the door and stood there for several minutes, looking around, knocking again. I remained silent, with my weapon ready. He eventually left.

Attorney Charles Garry, the party's legal counsel, learned that the pigs had executed a warrant for the chairman's arrest for a speech he had made at the 1968 Democratic National Convention in Chicago, where two hundred thousand people had gathered to protest the Vietnam War. The chairman was charged with conspiracy and intent to riot, along with seven others. They would be known as the Chicago Eight—later the Chicago Seven, when Chairman Bobby was bound and gagged and separated from the others during the trial.

The FBI took him immediately by car all the way to Chicago, subjecting him to horrendous conditions. On this maddening cross-country journey, the chairman was denied food, sometimes water, and access to the restroom. He was treated worse than a dog on this harrowing trip. He did not even have an opportunity to speak with his attorney or contact his family. Within days, the party released a large poster of the chairman with the caption, in large capital letters, "KIDNAPPED." It would be more than two years before the chairman would set foot back in Oakland.

With the chairman gone, David Hilliard assumed the main leadership role during a very difficult period for the party. Internal strife was on the rise. And David Hilliard's response would shape the future of the Black Panther Party.

Charles Bursey also went away to serve time for the April 6 shootout that had led to the death of Little Bobby Hutton. Besides David Hilliard, Bursey was the last of the seventeen brothers involved in that incident who remained in the party or on the streets, and even his days were numbered. Bursey was the epitome of a well-defined Panther: dedicated, intelligent, down-to-earth, tough. He had a rough-and-tumble look to him that was often softened with a gentle kind of smile. It had been a year and a half since the shootout, but I think Bursey suspected all along he would be going away to prison. He and a comrade sister named Shelly had just gotten married. Unfortunately, he never returned to the fold.

With the chairman gone, my function in Oakland was over. It was the chairman who had ordered me to Oakland, and it would have been his decision as to when I would return to Seattle. That decision now fell to David and June Hilliard. I was needed back in Seattle to begin the push to free the chairman and to prepare for what we knew would be a new wave of attacks.

20

The Resurrection
of the Seattle Chapter—
September 1969

But that's what makes the world go 'round
The up and down, the carousel
Changing people, they'll go around
Go underground, young man
—The Stylistics, "People Make the World Go 'Round," 1972

When I returned to the Seattle chapter in September 1969, only Elmer, Anthony Ware, Garry Owens, Nafasi Halley, Malcolm "Big Malcolm" Williams, and a few other comrades remained of the original members. Previously on the sidelines, Big Malcolm, whose wife, Jeri, worked with Tanya, was now a full-time member. Elmer had expelled those who had not shown much interest in doing the day-to-day, nitty-gritty work. Among that group were many who had become disillusioned and decided to move on. I can't say I blamed them. That first year and a half was wild at times, full of contradictions, and without real direction. I had not asserted my rank as captain as much as I should have. I was now determined to exert more control over the chapter. We put the past behind us, and, applying some of what I had learned during my weeks in Oakland, we began to rebuild the Seattle chapter.

177

Following the National Conference for a United Front Against Fascism, in the face of increasing repression, the party declared that storefront offices were too vulnerable to police attacks, as well as not effective for serious organizing of the people. Houses or duplex buildings in residential neighborhoods were safer and better suited for working with the community. At the same time, the party recognized that many people in communities of color were not prepared for the type of revolution we had envisioned. Many families were struggling just to make ends meet, as the Vietnam War had siphoned off funds for social programs. Thus, the party set its sights on winning over the people by providing them with services that their own government had failed to provide. We now devoted most of our attention to creating the innovative and groundbreaking Survival Programs. From Panther community centers, in the span of only a few years, the party launched twenty new Survival Programs nationwide.

The party also ordered all members to take off the leather jackets and berets in the interest of our dressing more like the people. By wearing a uniform, we had isolated ourselves from the very people we had pledged to uplift, and also made it easier for the police to identify, arrest, and kill us. We came to understand quite well that our very lives depended on our relationship with the people in the community.

In Seattle, we closed our storefront office in Madrona and moved into a two-story duplex on 20th and Spruce in the Central District, using the downstairs as our office and the upstairs as living quarters. The center was named the Welton Armstead Community Center, after the first Seattle Panther to be killed by the police. It was common practice in the party to name community centers and programs after fallen comrades. It was our way of keeping their memory alive.

Within a few months we had recruited twenty new members and opened up a branch in Tacoma. Elmer continued coordinating the Breakfast Program, expanding it to five locations, mostly in housing projects. Many mornings we would get up at 6 a.m. to head out to the Breakfast Program sites. Afterward, we would go down First Avenue to the Pike Street Cafe to eat our own breakfast of hash browns and sausage as we planned for the day. Eventually, we were able to get mothers in the community to take over the duties of cooking breakfast and feeding the kids, leaving us to make sure the food supplies were there.

Elmer handed distribution of *The Black Panther* over to a new rec
Jake Fidler, who increased the circulation of the newspaper to more than
three thousand copies a week in the Seattle-Tacoma area. On Friday nights,
five to eight of us would go down to 14th and Yesler or up to 23rd and
stand in the middle of the street, selling papers like hotcakes. The youngest
Dixon brother, Michael, began working on the Busing to Prisons Program
with new recruit Melvin Dickson. This program helped maintain the bond
between the incarcerated and their families by providing free transportation to prisons. Someone had donated a thirty-passenger bus, helping us
to expand our Busing Program to four prisons within the state. We also
organized local bands to perform at the prisons. Eventually, we started a
Panther chapter in Walla Walla Penitentiary, run by Clemen Blanchy, an
inmate who had been down for a number of years.

One of our most important new recruits was a brother from New
York named Valentine Hobbs. Valentine loved to fight. As a matter of
fact, we first encountered him at one of our political functions when he
tried to start an argument with a guest speaker, Preacherman, from the
Young Patriots, a white, working-class militant organization based in
Chicago. At the time, Valentine did not have the political understanding
as to why the Black Panther Party worked with white people, but in time
he came around. Valentine, who'd always had aspirations of becoming a
doctor, was assigned the task of working with Dr. John Green on the project of opening up a free medical clinic. By December 1969, we had opened
the Sidney Miller People's Free Medical Clinic out of our community center, eventually moving it to a separate location. It was the first free medical
clinic in the Pacific Northwest.

Asali Dickson, Melvin Dickson's wife, took on the party's administrative work and also facilitated art projects, such as assisting Deon Henderson, an art student at the UW and a volunteer from the community,
with painting a mural on the concrete retaining wall in front of our office.
Another new hometown recruit, Vanetta Molson, started preparing for
our summer Liberation School, procuring food donations in advance and
planning classes. A program for many of the kids who attended the Breakfast Program, the Liberation School was scheduled to open that summer
at two housing projects. Anthony Ware led a more consistent political education class for the chapter, something that had fallen by the wayside the
previous year. Anthony made sure we met at least an hour a week for PE,

sticking to required reading by Lenin, Stalin, Mao, Kim Il Sung, and others. We also required everyone to participate in weekly target practice and weapons classes. Using plastic caps, we were able to hold target practice in the basement of one of our three living quarters.

New recruit Tyrone Birdsong, originally from Pittsburgh, had found himself deposited in Seattle after being discharged from the military. He became the coordinator of our new Tacoma branch. Along with his Chicana wife, Rose, he recruited Larry Ulmer, a comrade named Marcus, and Teresa Britt. Another new Seattle recruit, Vietnam vet James Redman, brother of Joyce Redman, was a former Golden Gloves boxing champ and one of the baddest brothers in Seattle to join the ranks. We also had a cadre of Garfield High School student Panthers—Carolyn and Marilyn, who were twins, and young Tony. From Franklin High School we had Loretta Williams. Also recruited were Bob from Baltimore, Robert from the South, Bo Lang and Aaron Pierre from New Orleans, and Willy Ship from Arkansas. These rank-and-file comrades played a valuable role in reestablishing the Seattle chapter.

It wasn't long before the Seattle chapter was running smoothly. We launched seven Survival Programs in less than a year. With our guns put away, we became the champions and the voice of the people, working tirelessly day and night to respond to the most critical issues facing Black people, as well as the Asian, Latino, and Native American communities. The adage that a small, dedicated cadre was much more potent than a large army of undisciplined soldiers would prove the truest of words.

Sometime in October 1969, a man from the local justice department called and asked to speak with Elmer and me. Of course we refused. He called several more times, each time stating it was a matter of life and death. Finally, we decided to meet him on the corner of 5th and Madison, downtown, several blocks from the federal courthouse.

He was a distinguished-looking older Black gentleman. In fact, he reminded me of my maternal grandfather, Bop Bop, in the way he was so neatly dressed. He was very polite. He acted as if he knew us, and I'm sure he knew more about us than we realized at the time. What he told us was simply that the Bureau of Alcohol, Tobacco, and Firearms (ATF) and the FBI had plans to raid our office, with the purpose of killing us. We thanked him and departed, never to see or speak with him again.

Elmer and I had already been through so much in a short time. For us, this was just something else to prepare for. One thing was certain: if they wanted to come get us, we were going to make it as difficult as possible. Over the next two months, we shifted into high gear in preparation for the attack.

The first task was the fortification of our office. Thanks to Michael's organizing efforts at the UW, we got BSU members to volunteer time on our sandbag crew. Out at Alki Beach, they teamed up with the comrades on disciplinary duty—anyone who violated party rules was required to put in extra work—and filled sandbags all day for almost ten days. After a couple weeks, we had completely sandbagged our office upstairs and downstairs, with double the bags in the front part of the office. The inside of our office soon resembled a military bunker.

We put steel plates on the front and rear doors. We also sandwiched steel plates in between sheets of plywood, attached hinges to the plywood, and hung these over the upstairs windows. The hinges enabled us to raise and lower the protective steel over the windows. We also placed an intercom outside the front door. When it was left on, we could hear any sound outside within a twenty- to thirty-foot radius.

From the back pages of *Soldier of Fortune* magazine, we ordered bulletproof vests as well as a bunch of gas masks. An older white man from the Communist Party came by and built us a trap door with a ladder so we could get from upstairs to downstairs of the duplex without using the external staircase. We updated our list of supporters and kept it in the front desk in case we were attacked. We also put the office on "red alert," which essentially meant that on every shift, two people were on security duty.

It was around this time that Elmer and I received our final student aid checks from the UW, for $1,400 dollars apiece. We spent every cent on weapons and ammo. We also considered buying some automatic weapons from a dude Valentine and I had met during a brief jail stint as a result of a run-in with a pig. The dude said he belonged to a motorcycle gang, and they had some machine guns for sale. Valentine and I met him and some others out in a wooded area. Over the past year I had learned to trust my instincts more strongly, and things at that meeting did not feel right. I knew that a brother in the Chicago chapter, Olabatunda, had a similar meetup with some bikers for the same purpose, only to be tortured and murdered on some lonely railroad tracks. I found out later that the Hell's Angels had contracted with the ATF and the FBI to disrupt Black Panther Party networks and kill Panthers. "Sonny" Barger, the Hell's Angels leader, had a directive to kill Eldridge and "bring him home in a box." At the last minute, as badly as we needed some automatic weapons, I pulled out of the transaction. It had become more obvious this was likely a setup.

As the pigs were going crazy throughout the country, Panthers were catching hell as a result. But we moved forward as if nothing could stop us, opening up medical clinics, Busing to Prison Programs, ambulance services, Pest Control Programs, and more. All the while, Panthers were constantly being arrested, constantly going to jail, and sometimes being outright murdered. It was as if we were in a race against time, fate, and the US government. We were bound and determined that we would eventually be victorious, despite the deaths, despite the imprisonment of Huey and Bobby, despite Eldridge's exile, despite the threats of what lay ahead.

Our work ended only when sleep came late into the night.

21

The Murder of Fred Hampton

Mother, mother, there's too many of you crying
Brother, brother, brother, there's far too many of you dying
You know we've got to find a way
To bring some lovin' here today, yeah
  —Marvin Gaye, "What's Going On," 1971

December 4, 1969, was like most mornings—waking up with sand in our sleeping bags, rubbing sleepy eyes from the late night hours spent on security, and putting away the shotguns and handguns for the day. The comrades began preparing to go out and make breakfast for hungry ghetto kids. I stayed behind to hold down the fort, strapping on my shotgun bandolier and grabbing my new Riot 18 shotgun. I went up to the second floor to have a better view of the street so I could keep my eyes out for the pigs.

The phone rang. I answered, "Welton Armstead Community Center, may I help you?"

"Comrade Aaron, this is June. I am calling to inform you that Deputy Chairman Fred Hampton was killed by the pigs this morning in Chicago."

I hung up the phone. I did not want to believe the words I had just heard. It was without a doubt the most devastating piece of news I had heard since joining the party. My head began to reel. A great sadness rolled through my body. I could hardly stand. My body was shaken from the implications of this death. I felt a heavy anger and despair.

Fred Hampton was the most important member of the Black Panther Party still on the streets. Although only twenty-one, he was fast becoming the brightest star on the horizon. Those who knew Fred Hampton knew intuitively that he was the next great Black leader in the United States. He was the most unselfish, the most principled, most prolific Panther around. He was eloquent and powerful. When he spoke, you heard the Southern Baptist tone of Martin Luther King. You heard the profoundness of Malcolm X. He had the bravery of Huey P. Newton. It was Fred who got the two largest gangs in America—the Black Gangster Disciples and the Blackstone Rangers of Chicago—to call a truce, ending decades of gang warfare. It was Fred who reached out to the Puerto Rican communities and the poor white communities to create the Rainbow Coalition, which would last for decades. It was Fred who had the Chicago Panthers up at 6 a.m. doing calisthenics, shouting, "I am a revolutionary. I will die for the people!" It was Fred who disarmed a Chicago policeman, handcuffing him to a fire hydrant. It was Fred who awakened the poor people of Chicago to the point that the people came out with guns to defend the Chicago Panther office against police attacks. It was Fred who worked tirelessly, which prompted his comrades to tie him down in a chair just so he could rest.

On the evening of December 3, Fred met with his staff. The meeting ran into the night and everybody stayed over, which was not unusual for Panthers. As with others, the Chicago chapter had been infiltrated. Fred Hampton's security chief, William O'Neal, was an FBI informant. He had given the FBI a layout of Fred's home. He also put some seconal, the main compound in red devils and other downers, into Fred's drink on the night of December 3.

At 3 a.m. on the cold morning of December 4, a young captain, nineteen-year-old Mark Clark, the lone comrade on security duty, went to answer a knock on the door while Fred and his wife slept in their bedroom and twelve Panthers slept on the living room floor. When Mark, clutching his shotgun, asked, "Who is it?" several shots were fired through the door, killing young Mark instantly. The ATF and the Chicago pigs burst through the front and rear doors. The pigs charging through the front door lined up the Panthers who had been sleeping on the floor, machine-gunning several of the surprised comrades, including Panther Doc Satchel, who directed the Chicago Free Medical Clinic. The pigs coming through the back door ran directly to Fred's room, lowering their .45-caliber Thompson submachine guns as they entered. Fred's six-months-pregnant wife, seeing the barrels of the guns, attempted to wake Fred, then rolled off the mattress as the pigs began firing, killing Black America's last great leader, the next Black messiah, just as they had scripted.

I looked out onto the streets, clutching my shotgun, wishing a pig would show up so I could blast away. I began beating the wall with my fist, kicking over chairs and tables, crying without tears. For the remainder of that day, it was hard to function. It was as if a dark cloud had descended. The death of Fred Hampton would reverberate through Black American history for many years to come. We would make posters in honor of Fred just as we had done for Little Bobby and as we would do for our other fallen comrades, and as we had done for our imprisoned and exiled leaders, in the hope that the memory of their deeds would never be forgotten.

Two days later, early on the morning of December 6, the pigs attempted to raid the Los Angeles office of the Black Panther Party as well as several Panther houses. The pretext was the same as the murderous raid on Fred Hampton's home: a search for illegal weapons. But the Los Angeles comrades were prepared. They had built a sandbag bunker inside the office and stacked chairs and tables on either side of the entrance. The pigs, meanwhile, had cordoned off the entire area surrounding the building so no one could get in or out and there would be no witnesses to their attempt at mass murder. Residents near the office were kicked out of their homes so the buildings could be used as cover for the pigs.

When the SWAT team charged through the door, Cotton, one of the chapter's military leaders, let loose with a volley from his Thomson submachine gun. The other Los Angeles comrades followed suit, opening fire on the retreating SWAT team. The attack lasted five to six hours. The fighting was intense as the comrades defended themselves, battling in close quarters upstairs and on the roof of the office, where the comrades had a machine gun nest. The pigs used tear gas, helicopters, and armored personnel carriers, similar to tanks but without the cannon. They threw everything at their disposal at the Panther soldiers trapped inside. Finally, with the emergence of daylight, and the media and the people gathered out on the streets, the revolutionaries chose their time for surrender. They put up the white flag. Several comrades had been wounded, including a sister who had been shot in both legs. Eighteen comrades were beaten and arrested and charged with attempted murder.

The pigs also raided several Panther houses, including the house where Deputy Minister of Defense Geronimo Pratt, Elaine Brown, and others were staying. The pigs had machine-gunned the house. Luckily, nobody was standing up; they would have been shot dead. Thanks to the military expertise and foresight of Geronimo and Cotton, no one was killed. The Southern California chapter had lost at least six comrades since its inception. Right-wing elements had taken over the Los Angeles Police Department, bringing it as close to the Gestapo as you could get in America, which made the Los Angeles Panthers the toughest bunch of niggas in the country. Later, we would learn that Cotton, who had overseen the fortification of many offices around the country, had turned police informant after the raid.

Several days later, the ATF came to Seattle and met with the mayor in preparation for their final assault. However, they ran into a roadblock in the form of Mayor Wes Uhlman. The party was embedded in the psyche of not only the Black community but also Seattle as a whole. We were well known by everyone, and after the bloodletting in Chicago and Los Angeles, Mayor Uhlman could not politically afford to allow such an assault to go forward, nor did he want to have our deaths on his conscience.

He told the ATF his informant had reported that we did not have any illegal weapons in our office, contradicting the ATF's assertions that we possessed illegal weapons—the same pretext used in the Chicago and Los Angeles invasions. Uhlman went on to tell the ATF that if they attempted to raid our office, he would dispatch the local police in our defense.

It would be many years before we learned that J. Edgar Hoover had sent a memo to the offices of the Justice Department ordering the elimination of the Chicago, Los Angeles, and Seattle Panther chapters. The older Black gentleman from the Justice Department we met with had known of this memo, sharing with us only the information about the attack on Seattle.

Prior to the raids in Chicago and Los Angeles, the FBI had also raided the New Haven, Connecticut, office, arresting seven members of that chapter on charges of conspiracy to commit murder, including Captain Lonnie McLaine and Deputy Minister of Information Ericka Huggins, the wife of slain John Huggins. They also had the audacity to charge Chairman Bobby Seale with the same. Earlier in the year, an agent provocateur named George Sams had instigated and carried out the murder of Panther Alex

Rackley, who, according to Sams, was a police informant. At the time of the New Haven raid, the chairman had not even completed his trial in Chicago, where he had been bound and gagged, beaten, and held under deplorable conditions. In the courtroom, he was even chained to his chair. He was eventually exonerated in Chicago and then shipped to Connecticut, where he was held for almost two years.

It wasn't long before raids were carried out in Kansas City and warrants issued for the founder of the Kansas City chapter, Pete O'Neal. Fortunately, Pete and his wife, Charlotte, slipped away, eventually resurfacing in Algeria before moving on to Tanzania. A warrant was also issued for Field Marshal Don Cox in the murder of a police informant in Baltimore, where D. C. was assisting in the fortification of the office. As field marshal, D. C. traveled to chapters around the country. After the warrant was issued, he also went into exile in Algeria. D. C., Pete O'Neal, and many other exiled Panthers never returned to the United States.

With the raid on the Seattle office aborted, the FBI looked to other tactics of elimination. In the meantime, the Seattle Police Department hired Chief Gains from Oakland, who began to exert more pressure on the Seattle chapter, continuously attempting to provoke some type of incident they hoped would serve as a good reason to raid the community center. Two detectives were assigned to follow and harass Seattle Black Panther Party members. They followed us, harassed us, arrested us, and threatened us at every opportunity. Valentine and I had already experienced several altercations with these pigs.

One morning, Valentine headed down the street with a bundle of Panther papers under his arm and his trademark brown brim on his head. When he got about two blocks away from the office, the two officers pulled up.

"Hey, Valentine. Come here, we want to talk with you."

Valentine took one look at the pigs and knew there was going to be trouble. We had been in fights with these particular pigs on numerous occasions, and knew that when they were around some shit was going to jump off. Valentine had been a two-hundred-meter champion in high school. And today, he decided to see if he still had his old speed.

He turned around with his papers under one arm, the other hand on his brim, and took off running. The cops spun their car around and gave chase. Valentine, using every bit of his sprinter's speed, made it to the concrete retaining wall at the edge of the office property. Taking a giant leap up from the sidewalk, he landed on the grass and continued to the office door. The cops were right on his tail. One of the officers jumped out of the squad car and was running behind him. Once inside the office, Valentine went straight for the front desk, reached in the drawer, and pulled out the .357 we had named "Martin Luther King." He whirled around and took aim. The pursuing cop almost ran smack into the gun. When he looked down the barrel of that .357, he ran out of the office, back to the squad car, and called for backup.

Big Malcolm and I were just pulling up at this point. We rushed into the office. Within minutes the place was surrounded. Vanetta got on the phone and immediately began calling our emergency list of supporters. Elmer and Valentine broke out the weapons, bulletproof vests, and gas masks, and passed them out. Other comrades took up their assigned positions. Big Malcolm came up to me, a shotgun in his hand. He had squeezed his six foot four, 250-pound frame into one of the snug bulletproof vests, and sweat was pouring down his face, a bit of fear in his eyes.

"Aaron," he asked, "where do you want me stationed?"

Big Malcolm had more to lose than any of us. He had played professional football for the Buffalo Bills and a Canadian team; he had also earned a master's degree in urban planning, and used his position at a local poverty program to help us get the funding to put as many as fifteen comrades on the payroll. He could have done what some others had done at the first sign of a police attack—disappear, never to be seen or heard from again. But there he was, ready to defend the office.

As more cops showed up, throngs of supporters and people from the community began to gather, protesting the cops' presence. The Black contractors whom we had supported in their fight against the racist construction industry even showed up with their guns in their cars, as did former comrades Chester Northington and John Eichelburger. The popular local DJ from KJR, John L. Scott, arrived on the scene and somehow made his way into the office—and from there he began broadcasting live. The whole situation was beginning to take on a circus atmosphere.

The cops maintained they wanted Valentine for questioning in a purse snatching. We said they could not take him. Valentine and I went outside with flak jackets on, gas masks at our sides, and told the captain Valentine had nothing to do with the alleged purse snatching. The, cops, however, refused to disband, continuing their demands that we turn Valentine over.

June Hilliard called from National Headquarters. He had seen the standoff on the news and instructed us to surrender Valentine. We refused. Eventually, John Caughlan, a distinguished, white, longtime leftist attorney in Washington State, negotiated with the cops to let us bring Valentine down for a lineup. Elmer and John Caughlan took Valentine downtown to the lineup room, but the cops never showed.

Once again we were fortunate, but we were also well-prepared. The threat of an impending raid was always with us. Often we'd get a call saying, "We're coming to get you niggers tonight," and as we prepared for self-defense, some comrade would invariably disappear. The constant pressure and continuous fear took their toll in one form or another. At eighteen and nineteen, most of us thought little about our own deaths. As time passes, though, one slowly begins to acknowledge one's own mortality. Yet, I, as many others, was still far from the idea of surrender, of throwing in the towel. We were all convinced we would not stop until we were either victorious or in the grave. We felt very strongly about having the last laugh, the laugh of victory, and the last hurrah.

22

Day-to-Day Survival

You got no money, and you, you got no home
Spinning wheel all alone
Talking about your troubles and you, you never learn
Ride a painted pony, let the spinning wheel turn
— Blood, Sweat & Tears, "Spinning Wheel," 1969

In Seattle the summer of 1970, things were a lot quieter than the year before. With the passing of the gun ordinance in Washington State and the launching of the Survival Programs, we were no longer carrying our weapons out in the open.

The Vietnam War had created a weak economy at home. Unemployment was high, prices had increased, social service programs and school budgets had been cut, and, as a result, many families were having difficulty making ends meet. In response, the Black Panther Party had launched the Survival Programs, intended to support, uplift, and educate the downtrodden and the working poor. We were assisting them during their time of need with the hope that they would join in the struggle to create a new America, one that would provide free medical care, eliminate hunger, educate each child equally, and put an end to all forms of discrimination. We now focused our attention on organizing the community, feeding hungry kids breakfast, and implementing the other programs.

The Survival Programs—Free Breakfast for School Children, the fre medical clinics, Busing to Prisons, Free Food, Free Shoes and Clothing, and others to come—were simple, basic concepts that came mostly from rank-and-file members deeply embedded in the communities they had grown up in and now organized. These programs were the perfect vehicle for the party to address the concrete, immediate needs of the people. They were also a prime example of how the party put into practice our main philosophy, as described by Huey: Power is the ability to define a phenomenon and make that phenomenon act in a desired manner. In other words, we were able to define all the tools of oppression that besieged our communities, then transform those oppressions to the benefit of our communities. That's what the Survival Programs were about, as was just about everything we did—transforming a problem into a solution that we created and controlled.

Our community work continued to expand as we developed more programs, such as the Liberation School, the first summer program for children of the working poor. There was also an Ambulance Program that operated in New York and Winston-Salem, North Carolina, providing emergency transportation. We were now constantly working on behalf of the people.

In Seattle, we eventually moved the medical clinic out of the office to a separate building where we could serve more people. Under the leadership of Dr. John Green and Valentine, the Sidney Miller People's Free Medical Clinic was operating at a high level, focusing largely on community outreach and preventative medicine, which was not a mainstream medical practice at the time. Our first big project was the Well Baby Clinic. We wanted to address the needs of the most vulnerable members of the community, so we started with the babies and young children. Two nights a week, a pediatrician, Dr. Holzenburg, and two volunteer nurses checked babies for weight and general well-being, and the staff gave out vitamins, baby formula, diapers, and other necessities for ensuring a baby's health. Dr. Green and Dr. Holzenburg hustled up many of the supplies from the university hospital. We arranged for BSU members from the UW to give rides to patients without transportation, and the BSU members also did outreach to residents of Seattle's South End.

The second major project was sickle cell anemia testing. *The Black Panther* had reported an investigative story concerning sickle cell anemia, an inherited blood ailment predominantly affecting Black people. Most of us had never even heard of this disease. In sickle cell anemia, the body's red blood cells become malformed—shaped like a sickle instead of like a donut—and cannot deliver enough oxygen to the body's tissues. This can cause intense pain and fatigue, with severe complications, such as skin ulcerations, blindness, stroke, and, if left untreated, eventual organ failure and death. Through free clinics, the Black Panther Party began a nationwide campaign to test for sickle cell anemia and fundraise for a cure.

In Seattle, we undertook a massive testing operation at Walla Walla State Penitentiary. Valentine met with a friend and supporter of the party, a wealthy, prominent, Jewish attorney, and asked him if he could help us get into Walla Walla. This friend of the party had connections in the Washington State attorney general's office and had helped us on a number of occasions. He wrote a letter to the warden on behalf of the Sidney Miller People's Free Medical Clinic, and several weeks later, we were approved for mass testing for sickle cell anemia. The doctor who worked with us on the testing was a geneticist and Greek WWII freedom fighter by the name of George Stamatoyannopoulos. He trained Valentine in the use of an electrophoresis machine, which was able to determine from a blood sample if a person had the sickle cell disease or was a carrier. The electrophoresis technique allowed us to test many more patients than conventional blood testing equipment would have. We were fortunate that Beckman Medical Supplies donated two electrophoresis machines and an x-ray machine to the clinic.

In February 1971, we did our first mass testing at Walla Walla State Penitentiary. The warden was shocked to see that most members of the medical staff were not just Black but also Black Panther Party members. The trip to Walla Walla was a complete success: we ended up testing 278 Black prisoners and gave out two hundred copies of *The Black Panther*. Valentine was also able to take photos of inmates in the infirmary who had bedsores due to inadequate medical care, in order to advocate for improving conditions. Walla Walla State Penitentiary was the first site ever to conduct mass testing for sickle cell anemia.

Valentine also recruited a beautiful sister, Rosita Holland, to work in the medical cadre. She was a dead ringer for Angela Davis. Valentine and Rosita made a very good team, recruiting and training a cadre of medical workers who traveled to prisons throughout the state to test for sickle cell. Valentine later was able to share the electrophoresis technique with the party clinic in Berkeley.

Our prison work was a vital part of our Survival Programs. We viewed the prison population as a potential force in assisting us with the revolution. We saw promise in the inmate who was a victim of circumstances and American racism. No one fit that bill like Comrade George Jackson, arrested and sent to prison at seventeen as a result of a gas station robbery. Handed an indeterminate sentence, with dim prospects of release, he went on to become the premier political prisoner in America. Through his organizing of Black inmates and reaching out to Latino and white racist inmates as well, he soon posed a major threat to the prison system. In 1970, George Jackson and two other Black inmates were accused of murdering a security guard who had shot and killed three inmates. The accused became known as the Soledad Brothers, and their cause inspired support from activists around the world. George Jackson's book, *Soledad Brother*, a collection of letters to his younger brother, Jonathan, became an international sensation that catapulted George to the world stage and led to his being appointed by Huey to the office of field marshal in the Black Panther Party. George Jackson had a tremendous impact on the prison rights movement and helped build support for prison reform.

On a day-to-day basis in the community, we often received pleas for help from upset mothers concerning their teenaged daughters and the pimps in the area. The Seattle-Tacoma region boasted Fort Lewis, one of the largest military installations on the West Coast, two air force bases, and several naval bases, all of which contributed to the big business of prostitution. Elmer and I knew a number of the young girls who stood on the corners, soliciting. We had grown up with them, attended school with them. Whenever we saw any of the underage sisters down on the "Ho Stro," where the prostitutes strolled on Yesler Street, we sent them home. And, because our community center was near the Ho Stro, many of the prostitutes took refuge in our office when the police came down on them. Sometimes, at the request of mothers, we went out in search of their daughters on the streets of Seattle or at pimps' houses; on occasion pimps kidnapped young women and sent them to Utah to "break them in."

One day a couple of the comrade sisters came in from selling papers and told us they had been harassed by some pimps, so we sent a squad to the apartment where the pimps lived. The comrades broke down the door and administered some revolutionary justice. About a week later, we held a fundraising dance to benefit the medical clinic. Toward the end of the event, Elmer, Anthony, Jake Fidler, and Valentine were doing a security check of the perimeter when Valentine spotted a young girl sitting in a gold Cadillac, crying, while a pimp with a big floppy hat sat at the wheel. Valentine leaned in and asked the girl what was wrong. He got into the car as she scooted over.

"He won't let me leave," she said quietly.

"You want to leave, you can leave," responded Valentine. "He won't do nothing—watch," Valentine said, taking out his knife and beginning to slice up the leather interior of the car.

The pimp showed no reaction because Elmer, on the other side, had a 9mm pointed at his head. Valentine took the young girl home to her mother.

The next day, five Cadillacs of various colors pulled up to the community center. James Redman, Valentine, and I met them as they pulled up. We exchanged words as they voiced their anger at our interventions. I advised them to look up at the office windows, where they saw some heavy artillery looking down upon them. They took off. Shortly afterward, the troublesome pimps moved to Tacoma.

In addition to strengthening our ties with the community, we also worked to solidify our relationships with other organizations. The Communist Party in Seattle had helped us fortify the office, and our two organizations came together to develop a secret underground passage to Canada for revolutionaries or draft dodgers needing to get out of the country. It consisted of safe houses on both sides of the border, drivers to take the refugees to the designated location, and a contact to take them across the border. Using this passage, we managed to smuggle several draft dodgers into Canada. It was a great safety valve that we never had to use for BPP members.

Most of us in the party lived communally, pooling our resources and money from paper sales to pay for rent, feed ourselves, and meet other needs. After Elmer and I put our last university financial aid checks toward the fortification of the office, we also bought two .30-caliber assault carbines, which we spray-painted black, carving our initials into the stock along with the words "All Power to the People."

Securing the donations of food and funds for the Survival Programs was a full-time job. Elmer and I were able to solicit donations from a wide variety of sources. One of our favorite fundraising activities was attending the concerts of big-name entertainers like Archie Bell and the Drell, Hugh Masekela, and James Brown, afterward meeting with the performers, who were often very generous and supportive. James Brown invited us out to his hotel suite on several occasions, each time writing us a $500 check. Our last encounter with him, however, was a lot different from the previous three visits. He had us meet him upstairs of the concert hall. He was flanked by several bodyguards as he spoke. This time, James Brown didn't give us a contribution and was anything but cordial. I later heard that he'd had some problems with Panthers in another city. Lou Rawls was one of the few entertainers who refused to meet with us, let alone make a contribution. As he was escorted to his waiting limo he told us, "Man, I know how it is. I've been there. I'm from the Southside of Chicago," and disappeared out of sight.

One morning, Chief of Staff David Hilliard called and ordered me to raise $2,000 within two days. This was an unusual demand from National Headquarters. Funds were hard to come by in most chapters and we were no exception, pretty much living day to day. Nevertheless, we immediately sprang into action, calling our white supporters, meeting with wealthy people who lived by Lake Washington and in affluent Bellevue. We had heard of Mr. Smith, a wealthy, eccentric old Communist living in isolation on one of the islands up north. We had no way of contacting him because he had no phone. All we had was a detailed set of directions to his house. Elmer, Anthony, and I set out early in the morning and drove three hours, catching several ferries and then driving on remote dirt roads until finally coming across a run-down shack.

An old, bearded, white-haired gruff of a man came out to meet us. He invited us into the very sparsely furnished shack. For two hours we listened to Mr. Smith talk about the old days of his participation in the Communist Party and his disdain for his two sisters, who he swore would never get any of his money. During the conversation he asked one of us to go to the cabinet and get him a Lipton teabag. Other than the tea, there must have been twenty bottles of Tabasco sauce in the cabinet. At last, he was through talking and handed us a check for $500, the remainder of the money we needed to fulfill the chief of staff's request.

The next day, I was on a flight to National Headquarters with the $2,000—and in 1970, $2,000 was a lot of money, especially for those small chapters, like ours, that lived off of newspaper sales, donations, and outright hustling. At headquarters, there seemed to be a lot of tension. Granted, David Hilliard was practically the only leader of the party not in prison or in exile, and the constant pressure exerted by the government on all aspects of the party was immense. I sensed an atmosphere of uncertainty and mistrust. In *The Black Panther*, members were being identified as agents provocateurs and summarily expelled.

I sat in the hallway for hours, waiting to be summoned to meet with David. Finally, late that evening, David appeared with Geronimo Pratt. I gave David the $2,000.

He said, "Right on, Comrade."

The three of us left in a car along with Brenda Presley, who was on the newspaper staff, and headed to Frisco to drop her off. As "Crystal Blue Persuasion," a favorite of David's, played on the radio, I sat in the back, quietly unsure of what might happen on this sudden, short trip.

David was under a tremendous amount of stress, which had caused him to develop ulcers, as did a number of comrades. Only a few days earlier, Randy Williams and Melvin Holloway had been transporting weapons late at night in the party's van and ended up in a shootout with the pigs, which would send Randy and Melvin to prison for at least a decade. Losing Randy Williams was a serious blow in terms of the party's military capacities. In that tense atmosphere, I was relieved to be on a plane home the following morning. I never found out what the emergency $2,000 was for; it had been an order from the chief, so that was that.

In Seattle, we had taken up the practice of throwing our unwanted LP records at a wall in the upstairs barracks with as much force as we could summon. Shards of vinyl were embedded in the wall, which we called the Wall of Frustration. It was a way for us to release some of our pent-up anger and frustration, especially after a death or arrest or attempted raid. I had developed a nervous condition in my stomach area, prompting my physician to prescribe me Valium, which I took on only a few occasions. Enemies were constantly at our door; at times it seemed there were enemies inside the door. Mistrust ran high, and for those of us still standing and willing to fight, we had only two options: to leave or stay. At times I fell into pockets of deep depression, sometimes staying upstairs in the barracks after making sure everyone had his or her assignment for the day. Sometimes I just wanted to be left alone. Fortunately, these bouts did not last long. There was simply no time for such moments of despair.

There was a ray of light during these dark days. It was the birth of my daughter Nisaa, despite the circumstances of her conception. Her mother was a young community worker who had run away from home and was living at the center. Tanya was not happy about this new development. Soon after her birth, Nisaa's mother joined the Nation of Islam and moved to Chicago. I did not lay eyes on Nisaa again for many years.

23

Huey Is Set Free

Find the cost of freedom
Buried in the ground
Mother Earth will swallow you
Lay your body down

—Crosby, Stills, Nash & Young,
"Find the Cost of Freedom," 1970

Through all the turmoil and chaos, it was difficult to focus on the quiet victories. However, in May 1970, we had great occasion to celebrate. Huey P. Newton's appeal was successful. The California Court of Appeals reversed the conviction, and the minister of defense was released from prison.

We had expanded the party throughout the country, organized hundreds of "Free Huey" rallies worldwide, and attempted to petition the United Nations. We had formed numerous coalitions with some unlikely allies. Our leaders had traveled the globe to raise support, and we had even threatened violence. All this so our leader would be set free.

Oddly, it was almost anticlimactic. So much time had passed. So much had occurred since his arrest in 1967. The party had gone from a small group of revolutionaries in Oakland and Los Angeles to an international organization. By 1971, the number of martyred comrades would total more than twenty-five. Black Panther offices throughout the country had been raided, bombed, destroyed. The paper had gone from a circulation of 500 to 350,000. Many of the party's leaders had been imprisoned, exiled, or killed. The Black Panther Party was a far different organization than it had been at its inception, and Huey's release gave us new hope that the party would become stronger and more focused for the next phase of our struggle. However, we could not pause to celebrate.

On August 7, 1970, seventeen-year-old Panther Jonathan Jackson, the younger brother of field marshal and prison organizer George Jackson, entered a Marin County courtroom with a satchel of weapons and disarmed the county sheriff. Jonathan then armed three Black San Quentin inmates—defendant James McClain and witnesses William Christmas and Ruchell Magee; he took the judge and prosecutor as hostages, and demanded the release of his big brother, George, along with the other two Soledad Brothers, and a plane to take them all to Cuba. The group made their way through the courthouse, disarming bewildered sheriffs along the way. In the parking lot, Jonathan let off a burst of gunfire to put the pigs on notice.

The San Quentin prison guards and California Highway Patrol, having learned about the plan from a source, were waiting. They flooded the area, aiming their weapons on the group, who were loading themselves into a van. As the van began to pull forward, a shot was fired by a Marin County sheriff, instantly killing young Jonathan Jackson. The pigs were determined that no Black revolutionaries were going to escape with any hostages. The enemy showed its true nature: without any regard for the innocent hostages, the pigs opened fire, killing the judge and two of the inmates. Only Ruchell Magee and the prosecutor remained alive; the latter was wounded and became paralyzed for life.

Watching this on the news was painful and heart-wrenching. It was a drastic, desperate move by a brave young man longing to see his brother free. It was the boldest revolutionary mission in the war between the government and the party. Young Jonathan marked his place in history and would not be forgotten. Implicated in providing one of the weapons to Jonathan Jackson was Angela Davis, the Communist Party organizer and Black Panther Party associate. A national manhunt was put out for her. She was eventually arrested in New York and put on trial in California, but she was acquitted of the charges. The Marin County incident was henceforth known as "Black August."

In September 1970, the party, along with a coalition of leftist and radical organizations and the United Front Against Fascism, conceived of the People's Revolutionary Constitutional Convention, to be held in Washington, DC, in November. The first stage was a three-day plenary session at Temple University in Philadelphia, birthplace of the Constitution. The plenary session was slated to be a huge event, a profound statement to the American people concerning the need to reconceive and rewrite the US Constitution in a manner that would speak directly and truly to creating a more humane and just society. We expected people from all over the world to descend on Philadelphia, where Huey was to give the keynote address.

During the weeks leading up to the September plenary session, the Philadelphia chapter had several run-ins with the Philadelphia Police Department and its Chief Rizzo, the epitome of everything we detested about the pigs. He was a racist dog, fat and repugnant, bent on not only destroying and humiliating the Philadelphia chapter but also keeping the plenary session from happening. His threats culminated in a raid on several of the party's community centers, eventually forcing the comrades to surrender, stripped to their underwear. All this went down just days before the plenary session.

Big Malcolm, Valentine, James Redman, and I arrived in Philly the first night of the plenary session. A huge demonstration was in progress, with thousands of people protesting the repressive police tactics. When we arrived at Temple University, the scene looked explosive. On one side of the street was a battalion of Philadelphia pigs with riot gear and large batons, waiting to unleash their fury and hatred. On the other side was a mass of radical demonstrators of all colors, yelling, chanting, fists pumping, egging on the pigs. The four of us were thrust into the middle, along with a squad of other Panthers, forming a long line between the amped-up demonstrators and the robotic riot squads of police. It seemed the lid was going to blow any minute. We tried to push back the demonstrators, all the while keeping our eyes on the crazed-looking cops. One demonstrator threw a Coke bottle at the cops, only to have it plucked out of the air by Comrade Valentine.

The line of Panthers was able to keep the two sides apart, bringing calm to the streets so the conference could begin. As the event got under way, the four of us were pulled away by June Hilliard, and we next found ourselves with several other Panthers forming a semicircle at the front of the stage as Huey began to speak. I kept wanting to turn around to marvel at our leader, who had spent two and a half years in solitary confinement, who had issued important declarations and strategic positions from his cell, enabling the party to withstand the most violent attacks by the US government. But I kept my eyes straight ahead, looking out into the sea of people, only occasionally glancing at Big Malcolm to my right and Valentine to my left.

Several hours later, we were given our housing assignment. We eventually found the place, a small, reddish church on Susquehanna Road in a run-down neighborhood. Inside, we discovered there was no running water and no blankets or other bedding. Some of us ended up knocking on neighbors' doors. They provided a few blankets and let us use their bathrooms to wash up in the morning. Big Malcolm, always the one with creative initiative, met a young sister from the North Carolina chapter to sleep with for the night. They ended up in one of the church pews, wrapped in an American flag that Malcolm had borrowed from the front of the church.

The next day, dozens of planning workshops began, and we were all put on several work details. The remainder of our time was spent working, unable to witness or participate in any of the sessions or workshops. For one assignment I taught a Red Book class to more than a hundred East Coast rank-and-file comrades, all dressed in the Panther black uniform, which was reserved for special events. These were the young warriors we hoped would be the impetus for the revolution. I wondered how long these young brothers would last in the party, and how many would withstand the various assaults against us. How many would become disillusioned and drop by the wayside?

On our way back to Seattle, the flight stopped in Chicago. Four FBI agents boarded the plane and detained James Redman. James had worked in intelligence during his tour in Vietnam. They let him go after a few hours of questioning.

The plenary session proved a major success, laying the foundation for the larger event. The People's Revolutionary Constitutional Convention was held November 27–29, 1970, in Washington, DC. The Seattle chapter put in a lot of time organizing and fundraising to send twelve party members and a handful of community members to the convention. Those of us who had attended the plenary session in September stayed behind. The People's Revolutionary Constitutional Convention had been conceived by

Eldridge, initially. It wasn't something Huey fully embraced; as a result, nothing specific or substantive came of it.

Following the conference, Huey made a move to establish an Ideological Institute for the party leadership, including captains, who by this time were to be called coordinators. Once a week, selected coordinators from around the country would go to Oakland in order to develop a broader, more philosophical approach to thinking. At the institute, we were introduced to the ideas of British Marxist philosopher Maurice Cornforth and his works on dialectical materialism. We learned to look at matter, history, and all other phenomena in dialectical terms. This was an attempt to expand the minds in the party to become deeper, more analytical thinkers and thus better leaders and organizers. We discussed change: the fact that nothing in the universe is permanent except for change, and how, when two contradictory forces collide, a transformation takes place.

A number of comrades were not ready for such heady dialogue. People grumbled, surprised by this development and unsure of their ability to adapt to this new way of thinking. As a matter of fact, it was the party's adaptability that allowed us to grow stronger rather than weaker under the constant government assaults. It was this philosophical approach that would allow us to continue to grow and change and adapt, yet many remained skeptical.

It wasn't long before the old and new began to clash. We all carried a tremendous amount of paranoia. We were always on alert, aware of phones being tapped, of close comrades being fingered as informants and snitches—people we never would have thought of as collaborating with the police. This left lingering doubts and questions.

When Huey came out of prison in May 1970, few original members were left in Oakland. Even his right hand, Chairman Bobby Seale, was locked away in Connecticut. For an introverted personality such as Huey, the paranoia and distrust must have been immense. The party had grown from a small band of friends and neighborhood buddies to a bicoastal organization with thousands of new faces, personalities, and egos. Even before Huey was released, tensions were brewing between the New York chapter and the West Coast leadership. Without Bobby Seale on the scene as Huey's voice of reason, the party was headed for monumental internal struggle. The work of COINTELPRO had further undermined the relationships between party leaders and created distance and suspicion between East and West Coast party leadership. On top of that, the party was slowly dividing into opposite strategies: all-out guerrilla warfare versus a focus on the Survival Programs. The New York chapter leadership was advocating for armed struggle, along with working with the Weatherman (also known as Weather Underground). The official policy of the party was that the people were not ready for guerrilla warfare; they were in need of Survival Programs, and we would use these as tools to organize, educate, and politicize the people.

Over the next several months, these factors and more led to ongoing disputes involving members of the New York chapter and David and June Hilliard. The disputes eventually resulted in the expulsion of the New York 21 while their trial was still under way. Later, Geronimo Pratt, along with twenty members of the party's underground who had been traveling with Geronimo in Texas, were also expelled by the Central Committee.

Hearing of the expulsion of the New York 21 was a blow to morale, as was the loss of any leading party member. But you could not publicly show any sympathy or feelings about the loss, nor would you dare question why someone had been expelled, for fear that your own loyalty to the party could be called into question. Some of the best comrades on the East Coast were among the New York 21, very bright minds and very creative comrades such as Joan Bird, Afeni Shakur, and Michael Tabor, to name just a few. Even knowing about the conflicts, it always felt to me that we had cut off a part of ourselves. Geronimo was also a great loss. When I first met him he was brash and arrogant, without a sense of humility or correctness. After taking the helm of the Southern California chapter, he eventually centered himself and was able to develop a strong defensive strategy for the chapter, as well as directing the fortification of other chapters around the country.

To make matters worse, an issue of the party paper declared Huey "Supreme Commander." Upon reading that, I got a sick feeling in my gut. This was not the way things were supposed to happen. Huey seemed to be moving to change his image from that of a selfless revolutionary to an all-powerful leader. I fought these feelings and thoughts, putting them away, trying to maintain my belief that the party and Huey knew best, and trying to hold on to my commitment to the struggle. I could only hope that these things would pass.

24

Seattle: Riot 18

Beware, beware of the handshake
That hides the snake
I'm telling you beware
—The Temptations, "Smiling Faces Sometimes," 1971

It was one of those perfect early fall Saturday afternoons in Seattle. All the comrades were out in the field, trying to unload the last stack of Panther papers. Poppy had called to say he was making me some barbeque and Mommy was making my favorite apple pie.

Big Malcolm and I had some special work to do that day. We had to take the weapons out for testing, to make sure all the technical equipment was in proper working condition. As we drove Big Malcolm's big green step van through the sunlit woods, we puffed on some hash, marveling at the tall evergreen trees. When we reached our destination, a secluded area with a dirt hill, we climbed out and unloaded the weapons from the van, one by one. We fired ten to twenty rounds from each rifle, taking turns as we went along. Finally, we were left with the Riot 18, a beautiful weapon I had bought in an El Cerrito gun shop near Oakland, the same weapon Big Malcolm had clutched as we prepared for the aborted raid during Valentine's run from the pigs.

"Here, it's yours," said Malcolm in his deep, gruff voice. He sat down on a stump. I glanced down at my wrist at an expensive, gold-and-jade watch given to me by Beverly, one of the young prostitutes we had befriended. She had taken it from her pimp and given it to me to show her appreciation for our trying to help her get off the streets. For a moment, I marveled at the glistening gold, jade, and the intricate jewelry work.

As I put the shotgun up to my shoulder, a slight voice whispered on the wind, *Don't fire it from your shoulder.*

I had learned to listen to my inner voice in these uncertain times. Lowering the shotgun to my side, I pulled the trigger. As the firing pin hit the primer in the middle of the shell, a tremendous explosion occurred. Malcolm would say later that the blast had lifted me off the ground as it blew my left arm almost in two. I stood there in unbearable pain, screaming in shock, as I attempted to hold my damaged arm together, blood shooting everywhere, my arm a tangled mess. I looked down. Blood was bubbling and veins, arteries, and bones were sticking up. It was a gory sight and we knew we had to get to a hospital fast.

Two white teenage boys in a white '69 Ford Mustang had just pulled up to see what was going on. Malcolm commandeered their car, knowing his van would have been too slow and too bumpy on the uneven country road. We hopped in and desperately tried to find a hospital. At one point, we pulled up to a park, where a group of elderly white women were gathered, all dressed in white.

"Do you know where a hospital is?" Big Malcolm frantically asked.

As they looked inside the car at my badly mangled arm, they shrieked in horror, eventually giving us directions to the nearest hospital. We arrived at the one-story, small country hospital, running inside only to find out there was no doctor on duty. My brown corduroy jeans were covered in blood. I immediately demanded the nurse give me a shot of morphine.

"I'm sorry, I can't give you any morphine," said the black-haired nurse.

"You better give me some fucking morphine now!" I shouted.

Patients and staff poured out into the hallway to see what all the commotion was about. I must have looked pretty crazy with my big Afro, holding my badly injured arm, and blood all over the place. The nurse eventually gave me the morphine and prepared me for the doctor's arrival.

I was taken by ambulance to the University of Washington Medical Center, where I was admitted to surgery. I remember lying there late that night, sedated, trying to figure out what had happened. I could vaguely make out Poppy in the background. As a soldier in many bloody battles in World War II, he had witnessed much worse, but I imagine seeing his son wounded was extremely difficult for him.

I heard the doctor talking to Mommy, telling her he might have to amputate my arm, and my mother saying angrily, "No, you're not going to amputate his arm!" They finally gave me some sodium pentathol, a pain drug used by the Nazis during World War II and CIA in later years. It was called the "truth serum" because it made you want to talk. As the drug's effects began to take hold, I became relaxed and very talkative, finally slipping into unconsciousness. The next morning I woke up, and as I tried to fight the pain, I reluctantly looked over at my bandaged arm, blood seeping through the gauze. The doctor said that had I not smoked the hash beforehand, I probably would have bled to death. The hash had lowered my blood pressure and heart rate, so the heart was pumping less forcefully than usual.

The bones in my left arm had been shattered, and the nerves and arteries almost destroyed. They put a steel rod in my arm and two plates on the wrist to hold it together. The comrades came in with posters of Fred Hampton, Chairman Bobby, and Little Bobby Hutton, turning the room into a Panther den. Later that day, Poppy and Elmer came by. They had taken the shells from my bandolier to a lab to have them tested. The shells had been tampered with. The gunpowder had been taken out and replaced with a high explosive. Similar tactics had been used by the Vietcong against American soldiers who carried shotguns into battle, even though it was against the Geneva Convention to use shotguns in war.

That night I lay in bed in pain, trying to put my finger on who had set me up. Who was the informant? Who was the agent? Who was the pig that participated in this scheme that could have led to my death? When I kept thinking about Big Malcolm and others, I knew it was best to try to put this behind me, not to waste time thinking about who had done this awful deed. There was too much work to do. If anything, this near-tragedy only strengthened my resolve. This was not something I had expected, but in war the unexpected always happens. I could only hope that my arm would someday be okay. After three days in the hospital, I was back at the office with my arm in a cast past my elbow and a sling with some rubber-band gadgets that attempted to keep my fingers straightened. Despite the constant, piercing pain, I could not afford to be away from duty.

Over the next six months, I underwent four operations in an attempt to repair my badly damaged arm—skin grafts, a bone graft, and a nerve graft. They took skin from both my thighs to replace the skin of my arm. For the bone graft, which was extremely painful, they took bone from my hip and used it to reconstruct my shattered radius bone. After the surgery any movement or even a slight cough sent immense pain emanating from my hip. I even had to walk with a cane until my hip healed.

The strangest and most terrifying experience was in preparation for the nerve graft. I remember slipping into my hospital bed late that night after going out and drinking with my old friend Mike Dean. The next morning the nurse gave me a shot of something to "relax" me for the procedure. The orderly came up and wheeled me down to the operating room, placing my gurney in a corner until they were ready for me. It seemed that I lay there waiting for a long time. When I decided to ask a question regarding the start of the procedure, to my shock and horror, I realized I could not speak or move. It was unbelievably frightening. I was totally defenseless, and for an enemy of the state, it was about the last situation you wanted to be in. After I had lain there, watching scores of nurses and doctors passing by without acknowledging my existence, and struggling mightily to say something or to catch someone's attention, the orderly reappeared and took me into the operating room. The anaesthesiologist held up a gigantic needle-like contraption and told me he was going to stick the needle into a bundle of nerves in my neck in an attempt to deaden the main nerve leading to my left arm. He must have stuck me four or five times until he gave up on finding the nerve. They wheeled me back up to my room. My face was completely numb but they had been unable to find the nerve to my left arm. Later they made another attempt and succeeded in stitching the nerves back together. The chief physician was a short, bespectacled Austrian man with an accent. He was one of the best orthopedic doctors in the country. I have him to thank for saving my left arm through his innovative surgery.

In the spring, we were contacted by a congressional committee member regarding a hearing that the House Un-American Activities Committee (HUAC) was conducting on the Black Panther Party. I sent Elmer to meet with him, and from that meeting, the congressman surmised that Elmer would be a cooperative witness. As a result, Elmer was subpoenaed to Washington, DC.

We contacted National Headquarters to inform them of Elmer's subpoena. John Seale connected Elmer with a party attorney in DC. Elmer flew to DC and spent the night at Panther headquarters. The following day, after meeting with the party attorney, Elmer appeared before Strom Thurmond and the other members of HUAC. After giving his name, Elmer took the Fifth Amendment fifty times, frustrating and angering Strom Thurmond, who banged his fist and yelled after Elmer's every reply according to the attorney's instructions. The hearing went on for months as they investigated other chapters around the country, trying to find reasons to proclaim the Black Panther Party a dangerous and un-American organization.

That same year, Elmer had also been sentenced to five years in the Oregon State Penitentiary and was waiting to turn himself in. Back in the winter of 1969 I had sent Elmer to Eugene, Oregon, to troubleshoot some problems the comrades were having down there. As he was about to return, he was arrested by the Eugene pigs for armed robbery, accused of trying to take someone's leather coat at gunpoint, even though Elmer himself was wearing a full-length leather coat at the time.

Before Elmer left for prison, I found myself in the middle of a fight between Elmer and Valentine that nearly tore up the office. Valentine did not like a particular disciplinary measure that Elmer had given to a sister Valentine was involved with. Both of them were hot-tempered—I remember Valentine leaping from a ladder onto Elmer as they fought from room to room, from desk to tables to chairs, and with me, recently out of the hospital, still in pain, trying to call a truce between the two best comrades in our chapter. Finally, I was able to separate the two of them. Shortly after that fight, Elmer was gone, exiled to the middle of nowhere in central Oregon.

It was difficult to lose a comrade who played such an integral role in the day-to-day operations, let alone my brother. However, we always had to be prepared. Valentine assumed the next-in-command role, and Jake Fidler, Elmer's assistant, stepped in to take over some of Elmer's duties. As part of the reconfiguration, we closed the Tacoma branch and brought Tee, the coordinator, and three other comrades to Seattle. In Eugene, the Anderson brothers decided that the continuous attacks by the sheriffs and local vigilantes were too dangerous, so they closed down the chapter and headed back to Los Angeles. We brought two of the Eugene comrades, Bill and Alice Green, up to Seattle to help us mount a campaign to win Elmer's freedom. We had "Free Elmer" buttons and posters printed up and began a petition drive.

A year later, Poppy, myself, and several of our attorneys met with the Oregon governor in an effort to get an early release for Elmer. After several months, we received word that the governor had agreed to a full pardon for Elmer. It was a great triumph and probably represented the only pardon given to a Panther during those very turbulent times. In a sea of continuous battles and internal conflicts, it was only one small victory, but these small victories seemed to provide us with a little more optimism to face the upcoming battles. Still, Elmer would not be released for another year.

A Party Divided: The Split

Aaron Patrice, age three, at the Oakland Community School, 1972.

25

A Party Divided: The Split

Staring down reality don't do me no good
'Cause our misunderstanding is too well understood
. . . I've really got to use my imagination
To think of good reasons to keep on keepin' on

—Gladys Knight and the Pips,
"I've Got to Use My Imagination," 1973

With so many strong personalities in the party, it's a wonder there weren't more physical confrontations between members. There was the fight between Elmer and Valentine, and I remember an altercation between June Hilliard and Willie Dawkins. Party rules and principles as well as the sense of duty and camaraderie kept most disputes in check, but we were about to experience a different kind of clash that would have an irreversibly damaging effect on the party.

Eldridge had been living in Algeria with Kathleen and their two children. He and the party had been granted diplomatic status by the Algerian authorities, who provided him with a villa and gave him travel privileges to North Korea and other socialist nations to garner support for the party. Even Yasser Arafat of the Palestinian Liberation Organization visited Eldridge in Algeria, bringing along a case of AK-47s. Other party members eventually joined Eldridge in Algeria, including Field Marshal Don Cox, who had chosen to go into exile with his wife, Barbara, rather than face

urder charges leveled against him by the Baltimore police. Pete
̲ ̲ ̲al, the deputy minister of defense of the Kansas City chapter, also
chose exile over a four-year prison sentence for a bogus gun-smuggling
charge. He was joined by his wife, Charlotte. Another couple who found
their way to Algeria were Michael "Cetewayo" Tabor, from the New York
chapter, and Connie Mathews, originally from Jamaica, who had lived in
Copenhagen and worked as the party's international coordinator. Together,
these comrades in Algeria comprised the International Section of the
Black Panther Party. Their objective was to develop contacts outside the
United States to help forward the party's agenda.

Many African liberation organizations were offered headquarters and
support from the Algerian government, including organizations from An-
gola, Mozambique, and Zimbabwe. But none of their offices compared
to the compound provided for the Black Panther Party. At the party's
compound, the International Section entertained revolutionary fighters
from all over Africa and the Middle East. Don Cox even attended PLO
training camps.

Like most of the party's prominent leaders, Eldridge had his own disciples. Many comrades respected and admired Eldridge. He possessed great
oratorical skills and was one of the fieriest writers in America. He often
romanticized about the revolution, and was the chief proponent of guerrilla warfare as the main tool for destroying the rotten, imperialist US government. However, Bobby, Huey, and the Central Committee understood
that, in reality, Black Americans—let alone the American people as a
whole—were not prepared to engage in guerrilla warfare themselves, and
were also not politicized to the level necessary for supporting a guerrilla
fighting force, which requires the strong backing of the people to survive.

Bobby, Huey, and the party made it very clear that the Survival Programs would be the tool for deepening the party's close relationship with
the community. The programs would help the people meet their day-to-
day needs, and through these programs, we could educate the people as
to why it was necessary to challenge and change the status quo.

These two divergent ways of thinking had always been present in the
party, and were not uncommon to other grassroots struggles. This same
clash of ideas had led to Little Bobby Hutton's death, because Eldridge
and others had wanted to attack the police after Martin Luther King's
assassination. We experienced the same conflict in Seattle, when some

comrades had unrealistically wanted to attack the police. Had Huey not been in jail at the time, maybe these incidents could have been avoided.

Unknown to us at the time, as part of COINTELPRO the FBI had initiated a campaign of sowing dissent among Black Panther Party leader ship, taking advantage of the ideological differences within the party. These covert actions had been under way for some time already, but accelerated now that Huey was out of prison. The FBI forged derogatory commu niqués to Eldridge, supposedly from Huey, and sent inflammatory letters to Huey, supposedly from Eldridge. With Eldridge and Don Cox thousands of miles away, Huey was surrounded by California Panthers, and was very distrustful of many of the new faces in the party, especially some of the New York Panther leadership.

The Jim Dunbar talk show in the Bay Area arranged a live satellite interview with Eldridge and Huey on March 4, 1971. Their exchange soon turned contentious, leading to an argument and charges being leveled on the air by both Huey and Eldridge. Eldridge demanded that the Hilliard brothers be expelled, mainly because of the heavy hand they had used in expelling and disciplining members of the party, including the New York 21. He made other accusations against the Hilliards as well. Huey refused to expel the Hilliard brothers and, instead, expelled Eldridge on the talk show right on the air.

This division between Huey and Eldridge became known as "the split." The next issue of *The Black Panther* listed all the chapters that aligned with Huey. Not on that list were three: Berkeley, San Francisco, and New York. This came as another huge shock in the middle of our day-to-day struggle for survival. We lost many good comrades, who now became our enemies.

Valentine and I were called down to Oakland to Central Headquarters, as it was now called. Valentine had a patch on his eye as a result of having gone through the windshield of a car, and I had a cast on my arm in a sling. We looked like two disabled war veterans. The headquarters were now on Peralta Street, in a Victorian house in the middle of a block in West Oakland. Many comrades were present from around the country. A great amount of tension and uncertainty was in the air, much more than before. The comrades were surprised and confused about the recent events, even though no one displayed any outward signs of discontent. Zayd Shakur, the deputy minister of defense of the New York chapter, was there, as was John Brown from Frisco; however, the following day ad disappeared, eventually resurfacing in New York, having defected to Eldridge's side. Most of the New York Panthers and many of the Frisco Panthers, as well as the Berkeley Panthers, headed by John Turner, sided with Eldridge, and the remainder of the chapters, including Seattle, stayed faithful to Huey. When a revolutionary, paramilitary force splits into ideological factions, one of the results will almost always be violence. People were killed on both sides of this crazy intra-party war.

Robert Webb, a longtime Panther from San Francisco, had been sent by the Hilliard brothers to organize on the East Coast. He was a very dedicated member of the party and one of its key organizers. Comrades loyal to Huey gunned down Robert Webb on the streets of San Francisco.

The greatest loss for our side was the torture and murder of Sam Napier. Sam was the skinny little dude I had seen in the summer of '68, standing out in the street selling Panther papers while others stood around and socialized. He had risen to circulation manager, increasing the sales of the paper to 350,000 and finding ingenious methods to thwart the FBI's attempts to stop its distribution. Sam was probably one of the most dedicated party members, a very gentle and serious person. For him to die the way he did, in the Corona office in Queens, was unforgivable. He had been bound and tortured before he was killed and the office set ablaze. Although there was retaliation for these acts, it did not come close to making up for the loss of one of the most beloved Panthers.

Before the argument between Huey and Eldridge, the party had planned a large rally at the Oakland Auditorium as a fundraiser for Chairman Bobby Seale and Ericka Huggins, who were on trial in Connecticut. Kathleen Cleaver was returning from Algeria—unlike Eldridge, she was able to travel—and was scheduled to be the featured speaker. Posters and flyers had been put up all over the Bay Area and an announcement featured in *The Black Panther*. Despite the split, the event was still scheduled to happen.

Many comrades from other chapters were summoned to Oakland to fortify the offices and strengthen the party in the Bay Area in case of reprisals, as well as to assist at the fundraiser. I was assigned to the West Oakland Center to work with Sam Castle, known as "Center Sam," a young brother from New Orleans. Valentine stayed at Central Headquarters and worked in some of the other facilities. Center Sam and I built up the West Oakland Center, starting Free Clothing and Free Food Programs, and sponsoring an open house with free barbeque, which gave me the opportunity to use my grandfather's Kentucky recipe. Center Sam and I made a good team. I really enjoyed working with this true New Orleans brother.

About fifteen comrades from around the country were assigned to the West Oakland Center, including John L. Scott, who had recently been released from prison for his participation in the shootout on April 6, 1968. John, who had joined the party at seventeen, had been away for three years and had missed out on a lot. I could tell he was unsure about all the changes rapidly taking place. We often sat up at night while on security, listening to Freddie Hubbard's *Red Clay* and talking about many things. John didn't stay long, and soon left the party.

Not long after John departed, I met an older cat named Mojo, who wore a long black overcoat and a big black brim, which gave him the appearance of an old-fashioned undertaker. He was a real street nigga with that "old mother wit"—a Black Southern term for wisdom that comes not from formal education but from life experience, with a natural knack for understanding life's many complexities. Everyone loved Mojo. He was in charge of security at Central Headquarters, responsible for making sure the office was properly fortified, securing the weapons, and giving out security assignments. I also developed a close relationship with one of the brothers from Washington, DC, named Jacobi. Jacobi had a distinctive look due to his Black and Portuguese ancestry. We sat together on guard duty and talked about missing our wives, wondering when we would be sent back home.

The night of the fundraiser, several Panthers, including Valentine and me, went down to the Oakland Auditorium to provide security. I was stationed in the rear. Valentine was up front with Big Man, one of the few Panthers left of the original group from 1966. There was security at all the entrances. Just as expected, a group of Eldridge defectors showed up in an attempt to disrupt the event. Fights broke out at several entrance points but were quickly contained.

Shortly after the event, Jacobi's marching orders came in: Jacobi, James Young, Tim Thomson, "BillyO" Overton from New Haven, and a bunch of other comrades, including Chief of Staff David Hilliard, left for the East Coast for the Connecticut chapter, which had become the new East Coast headquarters. I never saw Jacobi again. I heard later that he died of appendicitis while in the underground. He was out on bail, waiting to go to trial with Charles Bronson for transporting weapons across state lines. Rather than go to trial, he went underground. In the party's underground, you could not go to a hospital. A trusted physician had to come to you. Being underground required a lot of resources.

A couple of days after the comrades left for Connecticut, Valentine was allowed to return to Seattle, but I was ordered to stay in the Bay Area. I had OD duties to perform at Central Headquarters, along with security detail. On many occasions I pulled security with the four brothers of the party's singing group, the Lumpen. On our watch, late into the night they would harmonize along with the Carpenters, singing "Close to You." True revolutionary artists, they had traveled the country, performing revolutionary songs at fundraisers and concerts. The Lumpen even came out with an album. I enjoyed being with the four of them—James Mott, Michael Torrance, Clark Bailey (aka Santa Rita), and Bill Calhoun. They helped make things light rather than heavy.

In this tense atmosphere, the only comfort came at night, sometimes, if there were no duties to perform or security to pull. If you got lucky, you could go home with one of the comrade sisters and be comforted and held and make love, putting away the pain, the fears, and the sadness. One night I was asked by a beautiful sister, Gwen Fontaine, if I wanted to go home with her. We ended up in the Berkeley Hills in a quiet little white stucco apartment. She treated me like a king, soothing my fears and mental pains. When I finally got my orders to return to Seattle, Gwen Fontaine drove me to the airport. I said goodbye and kissed her for the last time.

The split had a major impact on the Black Panther Party and the movement as a whole. The party was the vanguard of the whole left revolutionary movement, and Eldridge was its most powerful and prolific voice. The movement now was at an impasse: it had become an ideological question of guerrilla warfare or organizing the people. A collision had been inevitable. Yet the split was more than ideological; it also had much to do with the way that valuable, longstanding members were being dismissed, pushed aside, and degraded. It was also a war of egos. For some comrades, the split meant death. For others, it was a fate perhaps even worse—exile from the party into oblivion.

One result of the split was the creation of the Black Liberation Army (BLA), made up of former Panthers, mostly on the East Coast. In its effort to push guerrilla warfare, the BLA, united with the Weather Underground, would suffer heavy casualties by the police. With the party split in two, we were like a dog with three legs and missing a few teeth. How we would survive, how we would adapt was very unclear.

It was ironic that all this unfolded just as we had begun to focus on philosophy, particularly the concept of change and how it is the only constant in the universe. A gradual change was taking place in the United States itself. In the late '60s, alongside Black Power, there was the "Black Is Beautiful" movement—the Afros, the dashikis, the clenched fist at every greeting between brothers and sisters, the undeniable feeling that we were in this together, the closeness, the unity, the strong identification with rebellion. I remember the last concert by Jimi Hendrix. He had asked us to provide security for him at the old Seattle Sicks' Stadium. Before the show, Elmer had been backstage blowing some weed with Jimi. I stood in the rain, watching Jimi in his final performance, burning up guitars, playing like a man possessed.

The '60s era seemed to be coming to an end, the closing of one chapter and the beginning of a new one. Only about six months later, Jimi would be dead. A new genre of Black films had began to appear, the first being the most revolutionary—Melvin van Peebles's *Sweet Sweetback's Baadasssss Song,* portraying the Black man in a more defiant way, an outlaw to be championed, which was a new development in American film. After that came a cavalcade of Black movies with Blacks dressed in long coats and floppy hats, with processed hair, touting new images of drug kingpins, Black gangsters, and "Superfly" pimps—missing the revolutionary message of van Peebles's film. It was as if people, Black people in particular, were assuming the fight for justice was over and there was no need to fight anymore. Ever so slowly, helped along by integration, this shift in attitude continued. And just as Huey had taught us that everything in the universe is subject to change, the party was affected in many ways by the changes around us. Yet most of us were still dedicated to the mission of the party, and to changing America into a place where all its people could have the opportunity to grow into healthy, loving human beings.

In August 1971, George Jackson was assassinated by prison guards in San Quentin during a foiled escape attempt, a year after the death of his brother Jonathan. I believe that George wanted to be free, even if it meant freedom through death. The field marshal of the prisons, the dragon, the Black guerrilla, the prison genius—George, who was bigger than life itself, was gone from our midst, depriving us of the opportunity to see him bloom into a true leader of the people.

George Jackson's death was very much a part of the era that was rapidly drawing to a close, that period in the United States when the revolution seemed inevitable. At George's funeral, Huey gave the eulogy as Panthers stood at attention, holding shotguns. The legion of mourners spilled out of St. Augustine's Church into the streets of West Oakland. I stood there, watching a grieving Mrs. Jackson. I wondered if the people would ever get revenge.

And they did. Police stations were attacked and police were ambushed throughout the country. But the biggest response came three thousand miles away at Attica Correctional Facility in upstate New York. The day after George Jackson was murdered, an estimated seven hundred Attica inmates responded with a powerful silent protest, wearing black armbands or other makeshift signs of solidarity. Tensions had been brewing at the prison for a long time, and Jackson's death brought them to a boiling point. About two weeks later, more than a thousand inmates rose up and took over the prison, taking hostages along the way. They elected officers and presented a list of demands, including improved living conditions and an end to the attacks by racist prison guards. They came up with a list of outside observers and negotiators. On that list was Bobby Seale, who had been recently released from prison along with Ericka Huggins. When the negotiations at Attica broke down, New York governor Nelson Rockefeller ordered an all-out assault, employing helicopters and snipers. The highway patrol and prison officers turned the Attica prison yard into a bloodbath and torture chamber. In the chaos, the ten hostages and twenty inmates were murdered, and more than eighty inmates were seriously wounded. It was the bloodiest day in American prison history. The government, in a little less than two weeks, had eliminated the most important figure in the fight against the unjust American prison system and had overwhelmingly wiped out the largest and most organized prison rebellion to date.

By March 1972, Huey, Bobby, and the Central Committee had decided to centralize the party in Oakland. The stated purpose was to build a strong, solid base in Oakland, with the eventual goal of taking control of all aspects of the city, from the politics to the streets. But I'm sure there was an additional underlying reason that Huey made such a drastic decision. Chapters and branches throughout the country began sending most of their members to Oakland, leaving only skeleton crews in their place. In many instances, chapters closed down altogether.

It was difficult leaving Seattle. We had established ourselves so firmly in the community and in the hearts and minds of the people of Seattle. In four short years, we had challenged the power structure, putting them on notice that they would have constant opposition when it came to making racist policies or committing brutal acts against Black people. We had established one of the city's first free medical clinics, opened up five Free Breakfast Programs, and developed the first Free Food Program in Seattle, which became the forerunner of the city's food bank operation.

Our summer Liberation School was a major success, as was our Busing to Prisons Program and our community organizing. Before the orders came down regarding the centralization, we had just begun a campaign to defeat the Seattle school district's proposal for forced busing integration. We had organized the community to turn out to the school district. We held meetings to oppose this ill-conceived plan that would take Black kids out of their community, leaving them without a support network. Unfortunately, our departure gave the green light to this failed policy, which would eventually wreak havoc on Black schoolchildren and their families. We had also begun looking for a larger facility for the Sidney Miller People's Free Medical Clinic. Valentine had found a building, a former nursing home, that was perfect. It had everything we needed. It was equipped with a leaded x-ray room, a nursing station, a room for minor surgeries, a small in-house pharmacy, a dental room, a small cafeteria with a picturesque view of Lake Washington, and a number of rooms that could be used for overnight stays. With great regret, we would be forced to abandon this project.

Big Malcolm decided to head down to Santa Barbara to take a break from the movement and spend time with his parents, traveling with a group of former comrades who had called it quits or been expelled. I would miss that gentle giant, but I would see him again.

Rosita Holland, Valentine's assistant and lover, reluctantly stayed in Seattle to keep the chapter going until Elmer got out of prison. She would rather have not parted from Valentine. A handful of community workers also stayed in Seattle. We left and headed to Oakland for the new centralization campaign, leaving behind many memories, many friends and loved ones, as well as unfinished business.

26

Centralization—March 1972

Now is the time to come together
And show our force
Now is the time for all the people
To speak in one voice
I'm talking about unity

—O'Jays, "Unity," 1975

The key component of the takeover of Oakland was gaining control of the political seats of power. Our main targets were the mayor's office and city council. We were coming to understand that political power was no longer just in the bullet, but also in the ballot.

When Shirley Chisholm, the first African American woman elected to Congress, announced her bid for the Democratic presidential nomination in 1972, the Black Panther Party was the only entity on the political left that rushed to support her, even though we knew it was far-fetched that a Black woman who fought so tirelessly for the downtrodden could be elected US president. But we saw her candidacy as a step in the right direction. We understood that those seeking seats of power in the name of the people needed to have a true desire to create change for the better. In Oakland, we aimed to set the example. The main focus of the party's centralization became running the campaigns of Bobby Seale for mayor and Elaine Brown for city council.

Change is never easy. There is almost always a sense of apprehension, and the notion that maybe the decision made was not the best one. The idea of something new, something unfamiliar, often evokes mixed feelings: excitement combined with fear of the unknown. In the party there was very little time to think things over. Either you did or you didn't; either you stayed or you went. If this new move would further our cause, bring us to the brink of victory, there was no reason for debate. And despite the controversy around the split and the loss of many very good people, including entire chapters, I still had faith in the party and in the belief that victory would eventually be ours.

Central Headquarters had moved, once again, from the Victorian house on Peralta to a large, two-story storefront on the corner of 85th Avenue and East 14th Street. Connected to the main section was another large, one-level storefront that became the newspaper's distribution headquarters. The main office was a large reception area with two desks, one on either side of the room where the OD operated, and in the back were two smaller offices, one for finance and the other for special projects. The large office to the right was used for the prison and legal programs. In the far back was the printing department. Upstairs on the right side was a large area that became the layout and editing department, and across the hall was the photo department. In the back was a sleeping room and a large kitchen area.

At least twenty other party facilities and houses were scattered through the East Bay, including the LampPost, a restaurant and bar that became a hip Bay Area destination. The LampPost often served as Huey's meeting place. The party was also looking to purchase a large building downtown for a clothing factory, as well as a smaller building for a shoe factory. The idea was to manufacture affordable items while providing jobs for the community, but these projects never got off the ground.

The party even leased the Fox Oakland Theater from the Mafia, employing comrades to do renovations on the historic movie palace before hosting a grand opening, featuring the premiere of a film called *Black Girl*, a Black family drama directed by Ossie Davis. Other films, concerts, and events promoted by the party would follow.

Gracious donors purchased a large church in East Oakland that took up almost an entire city block. This building housed the party's new venture, the Oakland Community School and Community Center, which started as a school for Panther children. It grew to become a full-fledged private school with a large cafeteria and a large auditorium, a venue for talent shows, concerts, and fundraisers. On Sundays, the auditorium was the site of the Son of Man Temple services, a sort of revolutionary worship service with guest political speakers, community leaders, party officials, and a choir made up of party members and the Charles Moffett Band. A great jazz artist who had collaborated with the likes of Ornette Coleman, David Izenzon, and Pharoah Sanders, Charles Moffett had taught his four kids to play the various instruments that made up the band. He was also the school's music teacher.

The party's centralization was a huge, bold undertaking and it slowly became apparent that the new direction would move us closer to creating a liberated territory. Comrades were arriving almost daily from all parts of the country: New Haven, New York, Boston, Pittsburgh, Philadelphia, DC, Detroit, Toledo, Cleveland, Indianapolis, Baltimore, Winston-Salem, New Orleans, Atlanta, Miami, Dallas, Houston, Los Angeles, Seattle. They came by plane, car, bus, and truck. The Chicago chapter drove their own Greyhound bus. Big Malcolm moved to East Oakland from Santa Barbara. Upon arriving, people were assigned to living quarters and job assignments prior to having a physical and an eye exam at the party's medical clinic in Berkeley.

I was assigned to the Legal Aid Program, working specifically with the prisons, and I would also be alternating as OD with James "Bubba" Young from New York. As for others from the Seattle chapter, Anthony Ware and Larry Ulmer were assigned to the school and the child development center, the party's day care. Melvin Dickson was assigned to the LampPost as a cook. And Tyrone Birdsong, his wife Rose, and Marcus were assigned to Central Headquarters.

Four comrades were assigned to the photo department, led by Lauren Williams. Each had his or her own camera equipment and would be engaged to follow every move of Bobby Seale and Elaine Brown in their electoral campaigns. They also covered stories for the party newspaper and all Panther events. They had their own darkroom, where they spent many late hours developing photos for the paper or brochures. The comrades working with Lauren were D. C. from Boston, Bunchy from Houston, and Melanie from Los Angeles. No one looked more out of place in the revolutionary atmosphere of organized chaos than Melanie. She was always well-dressed and perfectly manicured. Whereas most comrades fell asleep in their underwear or clothing from the day, Melanie put on pajamas. She was a really sweet sister, but also no pigeon or pushover. We had a special friendship, and many times I wished it were more than that. But Robert Bay was her sweetheart.

Many East Coast writers were assigned to the paper, including Sherry Brown from Baltimore, Jonina Abra from Detroit, and Daryl Hopkins from North Carolina. Michael "Tapps" Rhyms from Chicago, a quintessential temperamental journalist, and a brother named Michael Fultz, one of the brainier comrades from Boston, would have looked right at home in the pressroom of the *New York Times*. Fultz constantly smoked and twisted his beard, drinking cup after cup of coffee, his eyes darting around. As assistant editor, Fultz spent almost all his time in the newspaper room. Asali Dickson was assigned to work with Emory Douglas on the paper's artwork. And no one was as distinctive as Benny, a light-brown brother with curly hair, thick glasses, and perfect diction. A printer, he ran the party's printing press, which always seemed to be in use. Benny printed all the flyers and brochures, as well as outside printing jobs. I can still hear the clickety-clack of Benny's press in the back of Central Headquarters.

Worldwide distribution and local circulation of the Panther paper was handled by the distribution and circulation department. James Pharms and Sherman Wilson from Los Angeles along with Naomi Williams and Cindy Smallwood from Frisco made up the staff of this vital department.

I ended up working with a chain of different ODs, but the one who impressed me most was Bubba Young. He dealt with comrades and problems better than anyone. Although a year younger than me, he carried himself like a wise old man, and sometimes looked like one in the body of a twenty-one-year-old. Bubba had skills in other areas that were far more valuable than what he was called upon to do as OD. It wasn't long before he was assigned, along with his friend Omar from New York, to run one of the campaign offices.

Comrade assignments also included the free medical clinic in Berkeley, the LampPost restaurant, the school, the child development center, and the community center, among others. The medical clinic, in addition to many other services, provided outreach testing for sickle cell anemia on a regular basis. Monday through Saturday, when not working other assignments, comrades were sent out into the field to sell the Panther paper or collect donations for sickle cell anemia research. Comrades received 25 percent of the proceeds of their paper sales and collections. Many carried a three-inch Buck knife for protection.

And there was the weekly garbage run. Huey disliked the Mafia, who controlled the sanitation industry in Oakland, so rather than paying them to pick up our garbage, he initiated a garbage service. Using the big black truck owned by the party, we would start at 5 a.m., picking up garbage at each of the many Panther houses scattered throughout Oakland and Berkeley. We would finish around 9 a.m., shower, and go to our next assignment.

When not working as OD, I spent most of my time in the Legal Aid Program, coordinating and revitalizing the Busing to Prisons Program, and corresponding with inmates in the Panther cadres scattered throughout the California prison system. We also prepared gift boxes for the inmates at Christmas, one of the most important and challenging times for prisoners. The party was committed to supporting inmates during the holidays as well as the rest of the year.

Tanya and I had been estranged ever since she learned of the birth of my daughter, Nisaa. Now, Tanya had revenge on her mind. Not long after our relocation to Oakland, she began a relationship with John Seale. It was torturous for me to see her moving on, but I had brought it on myself. What made the situation even more difficult was that Tanya became assistant coordinator of the Legal Aid Program, and thus my supervisor. With our relationship already strained, this only made matters worse. For four years I had been Captain Dixon of the Seattle chapter, one of the party's strongest chapters—at least in J. Edgar Hoover's eyes. Now I was a line worker, a rank-and-file member. I agonized over this demotion, but had to put it behind me, put my ego aside, and do what was right for the movement and for the party. Even Gwen Fontaine, who had consoled and comforted me a month earlier, was now living with Huey. She and I would never hold each other again. We could only smile ever so politely.

One beautiful aspect of the centralization was meeting and getting to know the comrades from other parts of the country. Each chapter seemed to have its own distinct culture, a specific way of relating—the way they talked, acted, joked, responded. The Philadelphia comrades were outgoing, sometimes comical. The Chicago comrades were often quiet, kind, and almost introverted. Detroit, Connecticut, New York, North Carolina, Boston, Ohio, and Southern California chapters were all distinct. Yet we were bound by our determination and dedication to true justice. The New Orleans comrades, in particular, stood out from the other chapters. They were as close as a family, with good organizers and a very easygoing manner of getting things done. In contrast, the Los Angeles comrades were serious, hard, and occasionally dogmatic.

All the different faces and personalities together brought a warm feeling to the sometimes tense atmosphere. Yet, despite all the new comrades and the excitement about the move, the atmosphere was not as compassionate, close, or unified as it had been in April 1968, when I first came to Oakland. There also was a lingering air of fear, not of the pigs and raids as earlier, but a fear from within.

In this tense and dynamic environment, many friendships blossomed from the geographical mixes. I became close to many comrades, including Allen Lewis from Philly, later called "House Man," and Tapps from Chicago, but I became closest to Louis "Tex" Johnson, who was from Detroit. I remember the day Tex arrived in Oakland, grinning from ear to ear, showing his gold tooth, his big applejack hat covering almost his entire head. He proclaimed that he felt like he had just landed in paradise—Oakland.

The Boston chapter was the brainiest in the country, with a few comrades recruited from the halls of MIT and Harvard; it was probably also the most efficient and organized of the chapters. The chapter coordinator was Audrea Jones, a short, serious, dynamic sister, who would be appointed to the Central Committee. Another Boston comrade was Robert "Big Bob" Heard, a former football player who stood six foot seven and weighed 350 pounds. He was as tough as they come, and was soon assigned as one of the bodyguards for Huey P. Newton. One of the best organizers from the East Coast was the effervescent Doug Miranda, also from Boston, with the perfect Afro and movie-star looks. He hit Oakland like a lightning flash—he was a potent organizer with the gift of gab. He managed to organize the Laney and Grove Street College campuses in a matter of weeks. On top of that, he had the student sisters from the colleges following him around like the Pied Piper. But Doug Miranda's stay in Oakland was short-lived; within months he left the party and went back to Boston.

Another of the dynamic organizers also came from the East Coast, "Big Herm" from Philadelphia. He was a heavy-looking brother, but he was the only person I ever met who had more energy than Sam Napier. Big Herm became Bobby Seale's campaign manager as well as the coordinator of the LampPost. With his knack for business, he turned the Lamp-Post into a money-making machine. Big Herm developed plans for an entire array of potentially lucrative businesses for the party, but many of his suggestions fell on deaf ears.

I often chatted with Billy "Che" Brooks, one of the brothers from Chicago. He had been onstage with Fred Hampton back in December 1968, when Fred and I spoke on the same program. Che had been through jailings, beatings, and the deaths of six Chicago comrades. He found himself assigned to the newly formed security squad of the party and sometimes worked as bodyguard to Bobby Seale.

While working at Central Headquarters, I developed a friendship with Ericka Huggins. She and Chairman Bobby had been released from a Connecticut jail three or four months earlier. Ericka had endured a tremendous amount of suffering since the death of her husband, John Huggins, in Los Angeles. After his death, she had gone back to Connecticut to organize the New Haven chapter, and not long after was arrested and imprisoned on murder conspiracy charges, forcing her to leave her daughter, Mia, with her parents. Ill in health yet strong in spirit, she had endured a long confinement. When I first met Ericka, she seemed so soft and fragile. But slowly she became a nurturer for many comrades in need of comfort and consolation. She and I started making birthday cards for comrades, together providing a little compassion for overworked, emotionally spent party members. She sauntered around Central with her long, curly hair, looking mystical and writing poetry.

One day Ericka sized me up and said, "Aaron, why are you walking around holding your arm like it's still broken? You need to stop!"

I was surprised by her comment. I thought about it that night and realized she was absolutely right. I tended to unconsciously hold my damaged left arm, clutching it to my body. I had been walking around like a wounded puppy, looking for sympathy. From that day forward, I stopped holding my left arm. I started writing left-handed and driving with just my left hand, using it more than my right, slowly letting the memories of the shotgun explosion subside. The pain remained constant and the nightmares vivid, but Ericka was right. I had to put it behind me. Ericka and I definitely felt some kind of connection. Maybe it had to do with our both being Capricorns and needing a lot of quiet, introspective time alone. She and I never got involved in a physical relationship, though. She only related to one brother, James Mott.

The party had an open sexual relationship policy, meaning that brothers or sisters could have sexual relationships with as many partners as they wanted to. This policy seemed to work mainly because there was so much uncertainty from day to day. On any given day you could suddenly be on your way to prison, or to another party assignment across the country, with no guarantee of returning. You might be sent underground, or, worse, you might be killed. Life for us was so uncertain that we wanted to enjoy love when the opportunity came. Of course, there were some comrades—mainly men, and mainly in leadership positions—who abused this policy.

Because so many comrades were congregated in close quarters, it was necessary to implement a "sexual freeze" whenever a sexually transmitted infection was diagnosed in the party clinic. A freeze order meant no sexual relations until the infection was stamped out.

One morning I was lying in bed in my living quarters at the Fulton Street house, one of several Panther houses. I had been on guard duty most of the night, so I was allowed to sleep in. Most of the other comrades were gone for the day, except for a very attractive comrade sister named Brenda. Before I knew it, we were in her bed kissing, caressing, our passions heating up. Since first laying eyes on this comrade sister, I had wanted to make love to her. She was relating to one of the leading members of the party, so thus far I had kept my distance, but now we were in each other's arms. As I gently got on top of her to consummate our desire, she whispered in my ear, with that Eartha Kitt voice of hers, "Aaron . . . don't forget the freeze." With those words, my passions cooled and I slowly moved off. We got dressed and left for our assignments. I was not always the most principled comrade, but on this occasion I decided I should be.

Another freeze had to do with the increasing number of babies in the party. During and shortly after the most heated periods of attacks against the party, pregnancies would rise. This phenomenon has repeated throughout history—during times of war and great stress, humans have sought comfort and release through sex. The big house in Berkeley, where

Tanya and I had stayed along with Chairman Bobby and Landon Williams back in August '69, now served as the party's child development center. Eight to twelve party members were assigned to look after the babies and toddlers, who required round-the-clock care, because their parents were all working in various other party capacities. It took a lot of people and resources to care for all the babies born in the party over the previous two years.

The freeze order stated that no party members could have any more children until further notice. So, if a sister became pregnant, she was required to have an abortion from a private doctor. The Panther clinic tested for sexually transmitted diseases and provided birth control but did not perform abortions. Some people also got birth control through private doctors. This freeze lasted almost six years, from 1972–1978, with only one exception: Ericka Huggins and James Mott were granted a special exemption and allowed to have a baby.

The older children, three years and up, were housed in dormitories. There were two large houses in Berkeley around the corner from each other, and another large house on Santa Rosa Street, where some Central Committee members also stayed along with the school staff. The staff cooked, cleaned, washed clothes, took kids on field trips, helped with homework—everything a parent would provide and more. There was also a huge house on 29th Street, where some children stayed along with their parents. In the morning, vans picked up the kids for school. On weekends, the kids in the dorms went home to their parents. Aaron Patrice, who was now four, stayed with me on weekends and occasionally during the week. It was an extremely difficult arrangement for both parent and child, but it worked to some degree.

The party's paper, renamed *The Black Panther Intercommunal News Service*, was gradually becoming one of the finest alternative newspapers in the land. The centralization had brought the party's best writers, photographers, and editors from around the country to Oakland. The party even hired the talented journalist David Du Bois, stepson of W. E. B. Du Bois, as editor in chief. Under Huey's orders, the party also hired a top-flight typist to work with the newspaper staff. Roderick also happened to be an out-of-the-closet, flamboyant homosexual.

Huey was a proponent of freedom of choice and expression, and he wanted the sometimes macho men of the party to embrace those concepts. It was interesting to see how the male comrades of Central Headquarters responded to Roderick, who stood over six feet tall and was well-built, with a long, brown perm, earrings, and makeup to boot. Some of the comrades were intimidated by his presence. However, in the party, accepting change was not only important to accomplishing our goals, it was also an integral part of being a Panther, and accepting change went hand in hand with accepting others. Save for a few rough moments, before long Roderick had become a part of our family.

Huey and the Black Panther Party helped pave the way for the emergence of the gay liberation movement. As the vanguard, the party influenced and gave direction to many emerging movements in the United States—the white radical movement, the Latino revolutionary movement, the Gray Panthers, the women's movement, and eventually the gay rights movement, which had been in the shadows, waiting to raise its voice. The historic Stonewall Uprising in New York City in the summer of 1969, when dozens of gay men and women resisted arrest and fought back against the police, put the gay rights movement on the scene. Shortly afterward, in 1970, Huey wrote an article from prison on the importance of gay people having the same right to freedom as all Americans, advocating that the party have a working coalition with the gay rights movement and other revolutionary movements. Soon after that article, with the support of the party and the momentum from Stonewall, the gay rights movement in New York became a revolutionary force to reckon with.

At its core, the party was made up of lovers. We loved life, we loved each other, we loved the people, and we embraced our mission and our responsibilities, so it was easy for us to embrace others, particularly if they were not embraced by society as a whole. However, there was still an undercurrent of fear I sensed in a very subtle way, and I was about to find out more about it firsthand.

With David Hilliard on his way to prison for his participation in the shootout on April 6, 1968, June Hilliard assumed the responsibilities of chief of staff and John Seale became assistant chief of staff. Under Huey's direction, the party also created the "security squad," composed of party members from around the country who were considered the toughest and most vicious, most of whom had been handpicked for the squad by Huey himself. The security squad's main function was to protect Central Committee members and provide overall security for the party and its facilities. They also were involved in enforcing whatever the party wanted to enforce, whether on the streets or within the party. This included physical discipline of party members, which was new to me as well as many other comrades.

Valentine had been recruited to this newly formed wing of the party. Squad members, including John Seale, had lobbied for me to be recruited, but for some reason Huey denied this request. John Seale often strode through the office with his black leather coat draped over his shoulders, sometimes followed by one or two members of the security squad.

One day John Seale and his comrades asked me to come into the photo department, and closed the door behind them. Calmly, John said, "Tanya told me that you had disrespected her."

As I was sitting on the corner of a desk, explaining to him why I had cursed at my estranged wife and supervisor during a disagreement over some procedures, I was blindsided and knocked to the floor. Darren "The Duke" Perkins and Carl Colar pounced on me and began pummeling me. It was over within minutes. For the first time as a party member, I had been physically disciplined. They did not really hurt me physically, not because they couldn't; they were probably ordered not to. But my ego and my pride were bruised. That night I left Central Headquarters angry and uncertain as to whether I would ever return.

I took a long ride on the 43 bus line to Berkeley and spent the night with a friend, a Berkeley student from the Bahamas. She comforted me, tended to my mental and emotional wounds, while I tried to understand my feelings of hurt and betrayal. I could not share with her my larger dilemma. That was something I dared not divulge. After a few drinks of rum, I finally went to sleep.

The next day I headed back to Central Headquarters. I had been through many trials and tribulations since joining the party. I had witnessed the many successes of our Seattle chapter, and I had felt the pain of losing comrades and the sting of humiliation, arrest, and harassment by the pigs. I did not know the reasons behind my demotion and mistreatment. I only knew that while many former captains were getting high-profile assignments, I remained at Central mainly as the OD during the entire mayoral campaign. However, I was determined not to allow these things to drive me away. It would take more than a bruised ego to send me packing. I was in this fight to the end.

27

The Campaign—1973

We got to stop all men
From messing up the land
When won't we understand
This is our last and only chance

—Curtis Mayfield, "Future Shock," 1973

A packed crowd of onlookers sat rapt in the Oakland Auditorium, listening to Bobby Seale, dressed in a black suit and black hat, announce his candidacy for mayor of Oakland and the candidacy of Elaine Brown, who stood next to him, for city council. As Chairman Bobby threw his hat into the raucous crowd, the curtain went up behind him, revealing five thousand bags of groceries stacked on the stage floor. Panthers stationed at the corners of the stage, dressed in powder-blue shirts, black slacks, and black berets, began giving out the bags of groceries to the waiting constituents. Another five thousand bags or more would be distributed at two other locations that same week.

Santa Rita and I had been put in charge of a squad of Panther monitors, all wearing the powder-blue shirts, black slacks, and berets. Given walkie-talkies, we had been charged with maintaining order and distributing the bags of groceries in an orderly fashion. Another security contingent wore leather coats and was obviously armed. With a few exceptions, the food giveaway at the auditorium went smoothly. I spotted one brother

231

loading up the trunk of his Cadillac with groceries, and saw a few people clutching three or four bags, running down the street. But at the giveaway later in the week in East Oakland, the monitors were almost completely overrun by overzealous crowds.

Preparing the bags of groceries was a huge logistical feat. Santa Rita, James Mott, and I had driven two freezer trucks down to San Jose to pick up the ten thousand frozen chickens purchased from Foster Farms. The poultry was then unloaded at the Berkeley Unitarian Church, where hundreds of nearly all white volunteers repackaged each chicken individually, in preparation for placement into waiting paper bags the night before the campaign kickoff. In the days before the event, ten thousand paper bags were laid out on the floor of the Oakland Auditorium. Joan Kelly and Carol Rucker coordinated the operation. Panthers spent hours putting canned goods, a sack of potatoes, a loaf of bread, a dozen eggs, and canned vegetables into each bag. The frozen chickens went in last. It took a tremendous collective effort to pull this off. There were many nights of no sleep, and long hours of work, but this is what we lived for: meeting, planning, organizing, fighting, and serving the people.

In the following weeks, the party opened up six campaign offices throughout Oakland, staffing each with the party's best organizers from around the country. Monday through Saturday more than two hundred comrades would be sent out into the city streets, to pool halls, street corners, liquor stores, churches, bars, and grocery stores. Wherever people gathered, we were there to register them to vote. The goal was to register every single eligible voter in Oakland. Party members also enrolled at many of the Oakland community colleges for the purpose of organizing the student populace. We had a substantial presence at Laney College and Grove Street College, where, through contacts, John Seale and Big Man Howard had acquired jobs in the administration. We enrolled the most comrades at Grove Street, including many brothers on the security squad who registered for tae kwon do classes. Formerly called Merritt College, Grove Street was the school where Huey and Bobby met and where they first began to organize. I was glad I was allowed the opportunity to enroll in psychology and history classes at Grove Street; it was the only time I got away from Central Headquarters.

Elaine Brown and Gwen Goodloe, the finance coordinator from the Los Angeles chapter, had enrolled at Mills College, an independent, all-female school. One of the first things Gwen and Elaine did was organize a party with the BSU on campus. They then selected a group of comrade brothers to attend for the sole purpose of hooking them up with the Mills sisters in order to better organize the campus. It was pretty comical at the party. Most of us brothers stood back, not really feeling up to this revolutionary dating game. Elaine and Gwen circulated, egging us on to mingle and meet the sisters. Elaine introduced me to the BSU president, Debby, from Los Angeles, and with Elaine's prodding, we developed a relationship that for me was strictly business. Yet to say I did not enjoy the assignment would not be totally true. Debby was a very nice sister, and the relationship allowed me some time away from Central and gave me the freedom to roam around the beautiful Mills College campus.

I had hoped to get an assignment coordinating one of the campaign offices, but instead I remained at Central, becoming the main OD and missing out on much of the campaign. The work during this period was intense. In addition to the campaign, we still had all the day-to-day party work to sustain, such as the school and the Survival Programs, as well as our new CETA Programs. The Comprehensive Employment and Training Act (CETA) was a federal government initiative to find work or provide job training for unemployed and disadvantaged people, especially youth. We had around twenty youth, some with gang ties, who worked in our CETA Programs. They were assigned jobs in different party facilities and also helped to launch the party's new SAFE Program, an acronym for Seniors Against a Fearful Environment. SAFE entailed the young people accompanying seniors to the banks and grocery stores and other activities. CETA was probably the best program ever to come out of Washington, DC, which is precisely why it did not last very long.

Manpower was sometimes short due to the needs of the campaign, which meant my having to pull security every night, sometimes going without sleep. Valentine and I often worked together on security, even though he had also been assigned to the clinic. We would compete to see who could stay up the longest. On one occasion both of us had gone three nights without closing an eye. Valentine was assigned to the upstairs window at Central, while I roamed the downstairs perimeter. I decided to go up to check on Valentine. I opened the door and could see him sitting in front of the window with the shotgun across his lap.

"Valentine . . . Valentine . . ." I whispered. There was no response.

I approached to see if he was asleep. When I looked at his eyes, I saw they were wide open, but he was dead asleep. He had snapped a toothpick in two and put the pieces in his eyes to prop his eyelids open. That was the funniest thing I had seen in a long time.

I was up three days straight during another week, and on the third night, after security detail ended at 2 a.m., I had to drive the big black truck over to West Oakland to pick up a truckload of papers. I remember getting on the freeway, but nothing else. I seem to have awakened just as I was exiting the freeway in West Oakland. My ancestors were watching over me that night, as on so many other occasions. I finished that task around 4 a.m., then headed to Mary Williams's house in East Oakland to prepare food for the Busing to Prisons Program, which was scheduled to depart at 8 a.m. Mary was Randy Williams's wife. I had already prepared the potato salad and was able to get Mary to fry the chicken for me as I finally dozed off to sleep.

Once, after yet another three-nighter, I took a shower and dressed up. I had been in Central for three days and three nights with the same clothes on. I needed to get out. I had one last function to perform. It was around 8:30 in the evening, and I had to deliver some papers to Huey's penthouse on Lake Merritt, where he had been living since his release from prison. The Central Committee had decided this housing arrangement was necessary for Huey's security. After handing the papers to Gwen Fontaine, now Huey's wife, I headed back to the office. At almost every intersection I fell asleep. I just needed to make it back to Central, yet I was so tired I could not keep my eyes open long enough to do even that. Somehow I made it, and immediately fell out in the back room upstairs.

Sleep deprivation was part of being a revolutionary. Up to this point, the only adverse effects had been a lot of grouchy attitudes and bad dispositions, which probably led to some faulty decisions. There had not been a fatality as a direct result of lack of sleep—not until one fateful morning.

Ever since the party's newspaper circulation had gone international, weary party members gathered in Distribution on Wednesday nights to work on the paper. On this particular Wednesday, as usual we had worked until 4 a.m.—and that was finishing early. Those who lived in other parts of the Bay Area would take long, sleepy rides home in one of the party vans. The longest trip was to Richmond, about thirty miles away. When Distribution Manager James Pharms asked for a van driver to take a group of comrades to Richmond, only one person volunteered. I had started to volunteer, but decided to let Cindy Smallwood take the keys.

Cindy was a fairly young sister with the disposition of an angel. Her lover, Andrew Austin, had been arrested back in New York, along with Ellis White. Andrew and Ellis had armed themselves as protection against the faction loyal to Eldridge and were subsequently arrested for carrying concealed weapons, a mandatory five-year sentence in New York. Cindy had remained faithful in her wait for Andrew, unusual in the party. Some days she and I would sneak away from the office to go for long walks, noting birds or vegetation we had not seen before. We had become close friends. She had a softness and tenderness about her that was as obvious as the morning sun.

Stretch Peterson, a brother from Philly, volunteered to ride shotgun with Cindy. After dropping off the comrades in Richmond, they headed back to Central. Fighting to stay awake, Stretch had succumbed to fatigue and dozed off. Cindy, exhausted from too many sleepless nights, fell asleep at the wheel and lost control. She was thrown from the van, only to end up beneath it. In the hospital she lay comatose for several days before life support was turned off and she was pronounced dead. Her death came as a particularly terrible shock because this had been a time of peace for the party. There was no war against the police, no shootouts or raids, which made her death that much more wrenching. At her funeral we all gathered to pay our last respects to a very beautiful angel, Cindy, the second Panther sister to expire; the first was Sandra, Geronimo Pratt's wife, found in a plastic bag on the side of the highway in Los Angeles, killed by the police. This was my ninth Panther funeral and by far the most difficult to bear. Cindy's family was devastated, for they'd had great expectations for their fallen angel. Stretch took it hardest of all the comrades, falling into depression and drinking, eventually returning to Philly. After about six months, though, he came back to Oakland.

During this period of relative peace, we experienced other kinds of losses as well. Early one morning, while on guard duty at Central Headquarters, I saw Harold "Poison" Holmes ram the party vehicle he was driving into the back of a station wagon driven by a gray-haired white man, right in front of the office. Poison jumped out and began firing his weapon at the station wagon. Then Poison climbed on top of the station wagon, yelling, "Bobby Seale for mayor!" with a glassy look in his eyes.

We quickly woke up the comrades and got everyone out of the back
door of the building, unsure what was transpiring. Within minutes, the
cops converged on the scene and arrested Poison. Had he taken refuge
in the office, the incident could easily have escalated into a serious confrontation with the police. What happened to Poison was something that
had been brewing for some time and was bound to occur among overworked, overstressed party members. Poison had snapped. He had
reached a point mentally where his reality had become distorted and
merged with irrationality.

The white man in the station wagon was mortally wounded by the
gunfire, and Poison was sentenced to five years in San Quentin. Poison
had always been a very high-strung, highly emotional comrade. He was
also a very good organizer and could articulate the ideology of the party
very effectively. And he demonstrated the fearlessness necessary to be a
soldier in the party. In 1970, he had been sent to New Orleans to assist in
organizing the chapter there. Shortly after his arrival, he was arrested by
the New Orleans pigs and subsequently beaten and tortured. He was
beaten severely, nearly losing a testicle. That incident had a tremendously
damaging impact on him. When he was finally freed, he was sent back to
Oakland. Then, in 1972, he went to China for three months with a delegation of Panthers and supporters, led by Huey and Elaine. After enduring
brutality and constant fear in America, to travel to a country totally supportive of our movement and revolution, where there was no worry of
arrest or fear of attacks, only to come back to America and face repression
was apparently too much for Poison. He had not been the same since New
Orleans, and after returning from China he appeared even more incoher-
ent. It was a sad way to lose a very good soldier.

Another brother from the trip to China also suffered a breakdown
and was sent back home to the Midwest. At the time, we were not aware
of the long-term effects of the tremendous amount of stress and trauma
that we were subjected to, or its impact on us and the party as a whole. A
sister from Philly was dealing with a lot of emotional stress and decided
to move out of party facilities. She rented a room on San Pablo Avenue
in a run-down part of Oakland. As OD, it was my responsibility to account
for all the comrades who worked out of Central Headquarters. After she
had not reported for duty for several days and no one had heard from her,
Comrade Bunchy and I went to check on her. We knocked on the door to

her room and did not get a response. We knew she had to be inside, so we kicked in the door and found our comrade sister in a very bad state. She had attempted to overdose on some sleeping pills. We immediately picked her up and rushed her to Highland Hospital. Thankfully, she fully recovered and moved back to one of the party facilities, and did not have any more problems after that incident. I think she just felt lost in everything that was going on but came to realize that her comrades were always going to be there for her.

There were other serious matters to contemplate as well. Comrade Fred Bennett was missing. With Randy Williams in prison, Fred had become the primary coordinator of the underground network and the party's weaponry. It was some time before his body was found, and details of his death emerged later. There was speculation that Fred might have been killed in retaliation for having an affair with Artie Seale, the chairman's wife. This was a ludicrous accusation, for the chairman was much more principled than that. Another scenario that circulated was that Fred had been killed by Jimmy Carr in the Santa Cruz mountains. Carr was a close associate of George Jackson while in San Quentin and after his release from prison had functioned at times as a bodyguard for Huey and also worked with Fred Bennett organizing the underground. Not long after Fred Bennett was killed, Jimmy Carr was shot dead in front of his house in San Jose.

Around this time, we also lost important members of the prison reform movement. Prison activist Popeye Jackson (not related to George) was assassinated on the streets of San Francisco. And attorney Fay Stender, Charles Garry's legal partner, was shot at point-blank range in her Berkeley home by a disgruntled former inmate and left for dead. Fay represented many prisoners pro bono, including George Jackson. I often drove to her home to deliver or pick up documents pertaining to my work with the Legal Aid Program. Fay was a tall, blond woman, always pleasant in demeanor yet very serious and devoted to her work, which was seeking justice for the San Quentin Six, the inmates charged with arranging the failed escape attempt that resulted in George Jackson's murder. Fay was not killed in the assassination attempt but was partially paralyzed and in constant pain from her injuries. Fearing for her life, she moved to Hong Kong, where she committed suicide in 1980.

Paul Morgan, a brother from the San Quentin cadre, worked with me on the prison program upon his release. He had burn scars on his face and neck, the result of a childhood accident. I enjoyed working with Paul, especially listening to stories about his experiences in San Quentin. He was gunned down in Berkeley near his apartment. The underground world of radical prison revolutionaries in Northern California was a dangerous, murky world where distrust and shifting loyalties were the order of the day. I could only sit back and observe all that was going on around me and wait for the next killing to occur.

One bit of good news during this unsettling wave of assassinations was that Elmer was finally released from Oregon state prison. Under the terms of his probation he was not allowed to leave Seattle for the next few years, so Elmer, our younger brother Michael, and Rosita Holland would undertake the rebuilding of the Seattle chapter.

As the mayoral race entered the final stretch, we were excited about our chances of toppling the white incumbent, John Redding. In deciding to run Bobby Seale and Elaine Brown for office, the party's objective was to raise the possibility among the Black populace that we could actually determine who occupied the mayor's seat as well as the city council in downtown Oakland. After preliminary polls were favorable to Bobby and Elaine, we began to think victory could be ours. However, a Black businessman named Otho Green, backed by the white Oakland establishment, also announced his candidacy for mayor fairly late in the race. This meant he might possibly draw a lot of the Black votes away from Bobby Seale. We tried to convince Otho Green to drop out, but he stayed in.

The morning of the elections, Panthers and community workers were stationed at key areas throughout the city with large banners, signs, and posters of Bobby and Elaine. The most significant strategic action that day was sending out vans driven by Panthers and community workers to senior centers and the homes of elderly people to escort them to the polls. We were not leaving anything to chance. Through the night and into the morning, we sat watching television coverage of the election, nervously awaiting the results.

The headline of the *Oakland Tribune* read: "John Redding Narrowly Defeats Bobby Seale." We had lost by a very narrow margin. The party and its members had run a magnificent, well-organized campaign. We had brought the Black community to the brink of victory. Black people who had never voted before cast a ballot for the first time. We had proven that the white control of city hall was coming to an end. We had also shown that the Black

Panther Party had a political machine that could not be matched—at least not in California. As for all the comrades at Central, we had come together from around the country and had overcome petty problems and monumental obstacles to run one of the greatest local campaigns in California history.

After the campaign was over, we loaded up the Chicago chapter's Greyhound bus and all the vans and cars, including all of the Panther children, and took a two-day outing to Clear Lake, northwest of Sacramento. Everyone was in great need of some rest and relaxation. It was the first time—ever—that we had taken a break from our work to do nothing but take it easy. Once we arrived, everyone broke off into little groups to hike or just walk around and relax. Daryl Hopkins, Tapps, House Man Lewis, and I rented a rowboat and grabbed a six-pack of beer, rolled up some joints, rowed to the middle of the lake, and just kicked back, not worrying about paper sales, driving duties, cleanup, or security. We had nothing to do but take in the trees and mountains, and enjoy each other's company without the usual stress of being a member of the Black Panther Party. Of course, there was still security to pull.

28

The Godfather on Lake Merritt

Twinkling twinkling grains
They do all sorts of things
While your inner mind is pleased
Your conscience is only teased
—Curtis Mayfield, "No Thing on Me (Cocaine Song)," 1972

"Aaron, you and Charles Bronson are going to Seattle with the chairman. He has a speaking engagement there. Be ready to go in the morning."

"Right on," I responded and hung up the phone. I was elated that John Seale had given me this assignment. I could get out of Central and go home, even if only for a few days.

The next day, with a .45 on my side, I was standing on the stage in Seattle, flanked by Charles Bronson, looking out at the audience, watching for troublemakers or would-be assassins. As Chairman Bobby spoke, it felt strange to be standing there. I had been away for what seemed like too long from the mild atmosphere of the Pacific Northwest. When I had left for Oakland, I was the defense captain of the Seattle chapter; now I was a bodyguard for the chairman and would soon be back in Oakland as the OD of Central Headquarters.

Later that evening, at the University Hotel, Chairman Bobby, Charles Bronson, and I were joined by Elmer, Michael, and one of Elmer's most

240

important recruits, Comrade Ron Johnson, a former member of the Nation of Islam in Los Angeles. We talked and drank long into the night before Elmer, Ron, and Michael left. My duties did not allow for me to leave the hotel, which meant I would have no opportunity to see my parents.

The next day we were at the airport, ready to depart for Oakland, when out of the blue two Seattle police detectives approached us.

"Aaron Dixon, we have a warrant for your arrest," said one.

"What for?" I asked, my heart beating faster.

"For driving with a suspended license," the officer replied.

They were polite, which was a change. Luckily, I was not carrying the weapon Elmer had provided me. I spoke briefly with the chairman and left with the officers. Within a couple of days, I was sentenced to six months in the city jail for driving with a suspended license. Where they had dug that up, I don't know. But it really didn't matter. My task now was figuring a way out of there.

While I was in jail, I began to do what all Panthers must do while incarcerated: politically educate the inmates. After a while, the guards caught on and decided to separate me from the rest of the inmates by putting me in an eight-bunk cell by myself. I didn't let that stop me. I continued talking to the inmates about their rights and why the Black Panther Party had stood up to the police, why our Survival Programs were so important to the people, and why it was imperative for people to come together to oppose this racist system of oppression. The guards demanded that I stop speaking through the bars, and when I refused they threw me into a padded cell for a couple of days. The padded cell was about the size of a small closet. You could not lie down or stretch out. I had to sleep with my feet propped up on the opposite wall.

After several trips to the padded cell, I decided to spend my time writing and reading and talking with my parents when I got the opportunity to speak on the phone. Poppy said he was going to talk to the judge to see if he could get me released. I didn't know if it would be possible, but I knew if it could be done, Poppy would do it. All I could do was bide my time. One day I decided to take all the mattresses off the other bunks and stacked them on top of one another near the window where the sun shined in. I would lie on the mattress stack in the sun and read, contemplate, and write. Sure enough, after a little over three months, I was free. Poppy had convinced the Black judge to release me.

After spending a couple days with Mommy, Poppy, Elmer, and Michael, I flew back to Oakland to resume my duties. It felt good to be back in the fold. I had needed a rest, truth be told, but I would rather have been resting under more desirable circumstances. I made it back to Central just in time for a series of changes.

Recognizing that we needed some form of recreation, the Central Committee made the decision to give the majority of party members Sundays off. Many of us had been working seven days a week for five to six years straight, and the idea of having a day off each week was happily embraced by everyone. On Sundays we would meet at Arroyo Viejo Park to play basketball and football. All the pent-up anger and aggression came out during the football games, resulting in numerous injuries, so it wasn't long before football was dropped from the Sunday plans. I do remember some basketball games. A friendly rivalry developed between the group of Valentine, Steve McCutchen, and me against Steve Long, Tim Thomson, and Bubba Young. We battled, rebounded, pushed, and shoved, often shooting for hours, as each of us showed off our technical skills. Steve Long and Tim Thomson were very good ballplayers. It was competitive but fun and great for relieving the stress we carried around.

Living at Central or some other overcrowded party facility was getting old. I got together with Melanie and Sherman, a brother from Los Angeles, and the three of us rented a three-bedroom apartment. After a year of sleeping on desks, in chairs, or in shared beds, it was good to have our own apartment, even though we did not spend much time there except to sleep. We were the first group to get an apartment, then other comrades began to follow our lead. On Sunday evenings, we would gather at the big house on 29th, where we prepared meals and played cards and other games while listening to the sounds of the Spinners and the O'Jays. Comrades also sometimes went to the movies or out to dinner.

One Sunday evening I took little Aaron Patrice to see the film *Papillon* with Steve McQueen and Dustin Hoffman. The film, now a classic, is about a Frenchman, Papillon, who is wrongly convicted of murder and sentenced to life in prison on Devil's Island in French Guiana, an almost unlivable place. He leads an unceasing struggle to be free, and, as a graying old man, he risks death to finally gain his freedom. Little Aaron was only four years old, yet he seemed to understand Papillon's unending desire to be a free man. I would watch this fim many, many times. I was captivated and related to his struggle to free himself from the cruel life of a prisoner in one of the most inhumane prison camps in existence.

With the election behind us, Chairman Bobby decided the comrades needed to focus on becoming a more disciplined force. Having spent four years in the air force, the chairman thought some of the methods used by the armed services would benefit the party as a whole. Everyone was summoned to the school auditorium for the orders. The chairman outlined the new expectations: at 3 a.m., the security person on duty at Central Headquarters would receive a call from June Hilliard or John Seale, informing them of the location of the morning exercise session. Security would in turn call all the Panther houses with the designated location where all party members were to report at 6 a.m. for calisthenics, followed by a two- to three-mile run. Then we were to return to our living quarters to clean up and shower. Beds had to be made military-style. Clothing, including socks, was to be folded neatly, and an inspection team would come by to check on the tidiness of the sleeping quarters, the cleanliness of the bathrooms, and whether socks and clothing were folded to military standards. Drinking alcohol and getting high were forbidden while conducting party business, which had always been a party rule, but it was now to be strictly enforced.

If you violated any of the new rules, you were summoned before a disciplinary board. This was a difficult new direction for many comrades, especially in light of what many of us had endured during the party's early years. We worked hard as it was. The calisthenics and the running were needed exercise, but the rest we could have done without. It really created more of a burden than anything else.

By 1974, it was obvious that Huey was moving in a direction that Bobby did not fully support. Huey, flanked by the thirty-man-strong security squad, had started to shake down the criminal elements in Oakland. Pimps, drug dealers, and managers of after-hours spots were now obliged to kick down some money or face consequences. This was not a counter-revolutionary tactic—in fact, many revolutionary movements throughout the world had operated in a similar fashion, taxing the illegal capitalists who profited off the community but did not pay into the system—but things began to get out of hand.

An unflattering story had run in *Jet Magazine* in May 1972, with Huey on the cover, sitting imperiously in a brown leather chair, very well dressed, labeled "Supreme Servant of the People," a title chosen by the Central Committee. It sent a very different message than the earlier pictures of him in his leather jacket, black beret tilted to the side, shotgun in one hand and spear in the other. This new image created doubts in the minds of party members and general public about Huey's real motives. As Valentine was part of the security squad, I would hear bits and pieces from him and others about what was occurring on the streets, and occasionally while members were in the field, people from the community would make comments. Around the same time, *The Godfather* was released, along with Huey's order for party members to see the film more than once.

Something was not right in Oakland. On one hand, the campaign and the programs at the school and the Son of Man Temple had been great developments for strengthening our relationship with the community. On the other hand, there was a dark side, an ugly side that had always existed, which lurks in the shadows of most militant organizations. That side was tilting the scales away from our goals of liberating Oakland. There was the tailor who was beaten up in Huey's apartment. There were rumors of prostitution and the attempted takeover of a rival nightclub. One day, twenty comrades were summoned to the LampPost. Gathered across the street was a band of street dealers, most of whom were armed. They were angry with the party because of the shakedowns and had intended to attack the LampPost, but they backed down when they saw all the comrades showing up.

Another evening, after dinner at Central, June called. "Aaron, get all the comrades in the truck and drive down to 7th Street in West Oakland to Lady Esther's Orbit Room. Immediately."

I got thirty comrades in the truck within minutes and hopped on the Nimitz Freeway. Five minutes later we were in West Oakland in front of Lady Esther's club. Huey and Robert Bay and several other Panthers emerged. Huey was talking to three dudes who had threatened him. June had us pile out of the truck and form a circle around Huey and the three dudes.

Huey, his coat draped over his shoulders, asked of his confronters, "So what are you going to do now?" He repeated this several times as the dudes stumbled and took off running. Many of us hardly ever saw Huey. He seldom came to Central Headquarters, as the Central Committee met at his home. If you had reason to see him, you needed to make a visit to his penthouse on Lakeside Drive or to the LampPost.

With the election over, there was a need for a new focus, an avenue to channel the energies of the throngs of uprooted Panthers. But instead of guiding the party in a new direction, as he had done so brilliantly for years, even while in prison, it appeared that Huey's intent now was to dismantle much of the party itself. Since its inception, the organization had attracted some of the best young people in Black America, and, I would argue, some of the brightest, bravest, toughest, and most dedicated citizens in America altogether. Even after the purge, the split, the police raids, mass imprisonments, and countless deaths, many of those comrades were still around. But gradually many would leave the fold, some voluntarily, some on Huey's orders. Some would even flee the party in an attempt to put distance between themselves and the madness going on in Oakland.

Bubba Young and Gwen Goodloe took off, as did Omar. Big Herm, who had managed Chairman Bobby's and Elaine's campaigns and now managed the LampPost, was run off. Carol Rucker and Kim Nelson, long-time party members and two of the toughest, hardest-working sisters around, split, along with Yvonne Carter, a sweet sister and the widow of Bunchy Carter. Big Malcolm moved to San Francisco and dissassociated himself from the party.

One day, Masai Hewitt, the minister of education, showed up at headquarters. During a Central Committee meeting, he had questioned Huey's tactics and opposed some of his moves in terms of the party's direction, and, as a result, was demoted. After that, he spent all of his time at Central, practicing martial arts or reading, not saying much or even showing the beautiful smile he had so often given comrades. Masai was one of the most principled comrades in the party. Warm and loving, he was also extremely committed and articulate about the struggles of oppressed people. He always carried a big black briefcase full of Marxist-Leninist books, and often quoted Mao and Lenin. He had traveled extensively throughout the world on behalf of Huey and the party. You could see in his eyes the hurt, the disappointment, and the humiliation he felt. Masai left without a word, not even a goodbye. Even the venerable Robert Bay was also gone.

Then came word that David and June Hilliard had been expelled. The rumor was that the Hilliards had plotted against Huey, but in the final hour, June, unable to carry out the plot, broke down in tears and confessed to Huey. Shortly after, Mojo, who seemed like he'd be around forever, was escorted out of the party, never to be seen or heard from again. Mojo had been in charge of the party's armament since Fred Bennett's disappearance. It had been rumored that Mojo was possibly a police informant because a large cache of weapons stored at the house on 29th had been confiscated by the Oakland police during a late-night raid.

For me, personally, things only got worse. I came in from the field one evening and was given word that Tanya had left for Seattle, taking Aaron Patrice with her. I was devastated. Aaron Patrice was my closest friend and weekend companion. Tanya had been working at the LampPost, and because of her late hours, Aaron spent most of his time with me when he was not in school. His constant bright smile always brought joy and amazement into my life. When I contacted Tanya in Seattle, she threatened to disappear and never allow me to see Aaron again. I sank into deep despair, wondering if I would ever be reunited with my son.

It seemed the party was falling apart. Huey's drug use and paranoia was dissecting and destroying the party brick by brick, comrade by comrade. Prior to Huey's arrest and imprisonment, he had not indulged in drugs, nor had he disrespected party members. But when he came out of prison, all the elements were there, waiting to ensnare him. At the time, cocaine was considered the hip new drug. Consumed by the stars, hip politicians, artists, players, and hustlers, it was a drug that made its users feel bigger and more important than they were. For Huey, next to the US government, cocaine became his greatest enemy. Now, without Chairman Bobby by his side, Huey slowly wandered down the path of no return.

Oakland in the early '70s was awash in the drug. Coming in through the port and as abundant as water, still labeled a "recreational drug," it was easy for cocaine to seep into people's lives, destroying its users and everything in its wake. I remember being ordered to leave Central Headquarters at 3 a.m. to pick up Comrade Bethune to take him to get Huey some coke. Everything came to a head shortly thereafter.

In 1974, a warrant was put out for Huey's arrest in the murder of a prostitute. The pimps and hustlers had also put out a $25,000 contract on our leader's head, and with many of the members of the security squad no longer in the party to protect him, Huey and his wife, Gwen Fontaine, disappeared. They eventually resurfaced in Cuba.

So many good soldiers had been expelled or run off—dedicated sisters and brothers, people who had been in the trenches from the early days into the peaceful times. Many were people I knew very well, including

Valentine. After Valentine refused to kiss Huey's feet at his orders, Huey broke the butt of a shotgun over Valentine's shoulder. Valentine was taken to the hospital. While waiting, he called Big Malcolm and asked him to bring him a weapon. But the party was taking no chances: after being released from the hospital, Valentine was put on a Greyhound bus to Seattle by John Seale and Flores Forbes from the Southern California chapter.

The most shocking development was the departure of Chairman Bobby Seale, his second wife Leslie, and his brother John. Huey may have been the party's figurehead and chief theoretician, but Bobby Seale was the heart and soul of the Black Panther Party. He was the organizational genius. It was hard to imagine the party without him. It was Chairman Bobby who had influenced Elmer and me to found the Seattle chapter. But the party and its purpose were much larger than any individual or any of its leaders. Those of us left in Oakland did not know what to expect.

I began to allow myself to wonder, to question why I was still hanging on.

29

Elaine's Rise to Power

Time is truly wastin'
There's no guarantee
Smile's in the makin'
You gotta fight the powers that be
　　　　　　　—The Isley Brothers, "Fight the Power," 1975

I remember sitting on a cement block outside the Oakland Community School, wondering about the future of the Black Panther Party. Almost all the party leadership in place at the inception of the Seattle chapter in 1968 was now gone, and only a few chapters were left—Seattle, Los Angeles, Chicago, and Dallas. Central Headquarters was down to 150 comrades from a peak of nearly 500.

Elaine gathered the remaining troops in the school auditorium and announced that she was in charge. We had assembled there on many other occasions for announcements and directives from the chairman and others, now gone. It was a somber gathering, yet there did not seem to be any doubt as to whether we could regroup and rebound.

Rise from the ashes is what the Black Panther Party did better than any other organization. It was in our nature always to recover, always to land on our feet. It was the spirit embodied in the party's philosophy, which was to dare to struggle, dare to win. The fight for freedom is one of the strongest desires on this earth, and with such a wind at our backs, we would provide the sails and ride this revolutionary vehicle as far as we could—and in most of our minds the ride would end only in victory or death.

Elaine laid down the strategy with confidence, empowering the rest of us. One of her first moves was to fill the vacancies on the Central Committee. Most of the new appointees were women, some of whom were the brightest and most commanding of the remaining party members— sisters like Phyllis Jackson from Tacoma, Norma Armour and Joan Kelly from Los Angeles, and Donna Howell from Boston, as well as Ericka Huggins, who was appointed director of the Oakland Community School.

Elaine had already begun to rebuild the military unit of the party by designating Comrade Bethune from Detroit as chief of staff. Big Bob from Boston and Flores Forbes were to be assistants to the chief of staff. I remember my first encounter with Bethune. It was at the child development center, the Panther day care at the big house on 10th Street in Berkeley, the same house where Tanya and I had stayed with the chairman and Randy Williams in '69. I remember how dutifully and gently Bethune changed the diapers of the Panther babies, wiped snotty noses, and fed the children. In that environment he had been so full of humility; now, he was head of all the military and disciplinary aspects of the party.

Bethune and Flores came to visit me at Central several days after Elaine's accession. I wondered what they wanted and why they were smiling.

"Hey, A. D.," Flores called out, sticking out his hand for one of his very soft handshakes. "Hey, man. You were chosen to be Elaine's bodyguard and to be on the squad."

"Good. Right on, man," I replied, unsure if I wanted this glorified position, knowing all too well the dangers of being on the security squad.

That night Flores came by the apartment where I was living with my new girlfriend, Lola. "Hey, man. Look through these books and let me know what kind of piece you want," he said as he handed me several issues of *Guns & Ammo*. He pulled out his piece and handed it to me. "A. D., I have a 1911 Colt .45."

The .45 automatic handgun was the preferred choice of most of the comrades; a few favored the Browning 9mm automatic. I finally settled on a Colt Combat Commander, which was shorter and more compact than the standard .45 automatic. With black rubber grips and a brushed silver finish, it was a beautiful weapon and would become my faithful companion for the next four years.

In the earlier years of the party, when the government was trying to annihilate us, every Panther was expected to take up arms and know how to use them, break them down, and clean them. There was no distinction between the day-to-day work and picking up a gun. As we shifted our focus to developing the Survival Programs and organizing in the churches, Black businesses, and political campaigns, the party began to shed the image of the urban guerrilla. In effect, we put our guns in the closet and instead drew upon the talents of our members to develop the programs and strategies for moving the community forward.

Now, the party's weaponry was largely the province of the security squad, focused on protecting the party leaders, ensuring the security of the party's facilities, and taxing the illegitimate capitalists, usually after-hours club owners or drug dealers. The toughest, most seasoned comrades were selected for the squad. I learned later that Flores, Valentine, and others had lobbied on my behalf for some time, but Huey had always objected. This had probably worked to my benefit, as the closer you were to the flame, the more likely to get burned. A handful of others were also newly recruited to the security squad: Clark "Santa Rita" Bailey; Tim Thomson; Allen "House Man" Lewis; Lamar and Leonard Donaldson, two brothers from San Francisco; George Robinson; Rollins Reid and Tex from Detroit; and Ellis White and his son Darnell White, who was the oldest of the Panther kids and now, as a young adult, was elected to be a full-time Panther. There was an attempt to reenlist Valentine, but we had no way of contacting him.

One of the first steps for Flores as head of security was making sure the party's arsenal was secure. Before the collapse, about a year earlier, the Oakland police had raided the house on 29th Street and seized a cache of weapons. The rest had been scattered throughout the East Bay and only a few people knew the exact locations. Flores slowly began to secure the party's illegal weapons, many of which had been left in deplorable condition. Working mostly in the dead of night, Flores traveled from location to location, cleaning, wrapping, breaking down, and concealing the armaments. He would take an assistant with him, constantly alternating assistants so no one aside from himself knew more than one or two locations of the weaponry. Over time, everything was successfully secured.

Going into my new position, I knew not to take Elaine's mood for granted. I vividly remember the second time we met, at Central Headquarters on Peralta, right after the split with Eldridge. Tension and paranoia were running high. That day I was the acting OD, filling in for Robert Bay and trying to coordinate the rides for the morning activities, a task that could sometimes be very complicated. The two most important rides were those to take the Panther children and staff to school and, equally important, to get the layout of the paper to the printers. Through no one's fault, the ride for the newspaper delivery was late. Elaine, who was the acting minister of information and had been working all night on the paper, lit into me with profanity. I had never been cursed out in such a manner. Having stayed up all night as well, I responded with my own barrage of profanity. Even so, the experience troubled me. Maybe I wasn't used to such volatile exchanges between comrades, or maybe it was the fact that the person I was arguing with was Elaine Brown.

On a fall evening, I reported to work on my first assignment as Elaine's bodyguard and driver. I had put on a suit and tie, as instructed, a cream-white, double-breasted suit. The engagement was the annual dinner of the California State Package Store and Tavern Owners Association (Cal-Pac), a large group of Black liquor store owners in the Bay Area. Former San Francisco 49er Gene Washington and his brother had founded the organization. Elaine, having announced another campaign for city council, felt it was highly important to garner the endorsement of Cal-Pac.

Elaine was an attractive person. She had a little-girl cuteness about her that men liked, yet when she opened her mouth she was an extremely articulate, decisive, and confident woman. She had facts and information to back up every point she made. I sat quietly as she addressed the audience of Black men, some of whom had been intimidated by the party in the not-too-distant past. Many of these liquor store owners had supported the Black lackey Otho Green, who had entered the mayoral race to draw votes away from Bobby Seale. Winning over these antirevolutionaries would not be easy.

After a dynamic speech and time spent talking with the leading members of Cal-Pac, it was quite evident that Elaine had won over not just Cal-Pac but, most important, the Washington brothers themselves, who owned the largest alcohol distributors in the Bay Area. The older of the two was Gene, a retired All-Pro. Another All-Pro, former Oakland Raider

Gene Upshaw, also endorsed Elaine's campaign. The Washington brothers not only threw their endorsement to Elaine but went on to sponsor many fundraising events for Elaine's campaign.

After the near-victory of Chairman Bobby's mayoral campaign, many Northern California politicians had taken note of the party's ability to organize the community and get people to the polls. It was safe to say the Black Panther Party had a well-run political machine. A handful of Northern California state representatives and local politicians began to approach the party in the hope of gaining access to our ability to get out the vote, as well as receiving our endorsement.

The most significant candidate looking for support was Jerry Brown, a very unconventional politician, who was running for governor. According to Elaine, Jerry Brown had worked with the Southern California chapter when he had served on the LA Community College Board of Trustees. The party gave Jerry Brown its support, and Elaine cultivated a political relationship that remained intact after he was elected governor in 1974. Upon taking office, Jerry Brown appointed as his right-hand legal counsel Tony Kline, who had also worked with the Southern California chapter as a law student. Elaine made frequent visits to Sacramento to meet with both of them. Jerry Brown was definitely not your normal, everyday politician. He turned down the traditional black limousine and driver, instead driving himself around in a light-blue '73 Plymouth. He also refused to live in the governor's mansion. He was a perfect fit at the right time for the party, and Elaine took smart advantage of this opportunity.

Within a year, Elaine had developed solid connections with many of the main power brokers in not only the Bay Area but Sacramento as well. Large corporations such as Clorox and its CEO, Robert Shetterly, a gray-haired white man who expressed an interest in the "new Oakland," soon became additional feathers in the party's cap. The time was ripe for Black political power in Oakland, and Elaine and the party represented the vanguard for the new Black politicos. The first victory for the party and the people was the election of John George, the party's longtime lawyer, as the first Black member of the Oakland/Alameda County Board of Supervisors.

Under the guidance of Elaine, Ericka Huggins, and Donna Howell, the Oakland Community School gained a reputation as one of the finest community-based private elementary schools (K–6) in the country. Many of the students were poor and living in the projects, but a few were from middle- or upper-class families. The staff, a combination of Panthers and professional teachers, created a loving, encouraging environment. Most of the students flourished, eventually progressing academically beyond their normal age or grade bracket. Panther Joe Abron, an engineering graduate from Michigan State, created an award-winning science program, and the music program, under Charles Moffett's genius direction, fielded an outstanding school band. The schoolchildren were provided with breakfast and lunch, and were picked up and dropped off by the school vans. Laundry services and clothing were provided for students from poor families.

Joan Kelly and Phyllis Jackson directed the Oakland Community Learning Center, housed in the same complex as the school. It gradually grew into an all-purpose resource for the community. With grant money, the center sponsored one of the first teen programs in Oakland, run by longtime community worker Johnny Stakes. The Teen Program engaged the most critical segment of the Black community: adolescents lacking the guidance and love to enable them to make it through the jungle of gangs, poverty, and racism. Employing several teens on the staff, the Teen Program blossomed, sponsoring weekly talent shows that allowed tremendously gifted young people an outlet for their creativity. The Teen Program also sponsored its own basketball team, coached by Panther Lonnie D, whose controlled coaching style bore a resemblance to that of Al Attles, the famed first Black coach of the San Francisco Warriors. Just like Attles, Lonnie D would walk around with a rolled-up newspaper in his hands. Two nights a week, the community center presented movie night, showing mostly Black flicks, charging fifty cents per person, and selling popcorn and hot dogs in the cafeteria.

Comrade Steve McCutchen from Baltimore, also known as "Little Masai," ran the Martial Arts Program three days a week. More than a hundred young students from the 69th Street Village housing project and the surrounding community would line up in the cafeteria in their white uniforms, performing their katas. This was probably one of the community center's most successful and most impressive programs. Not because it was teaching little Black kids how to kick and punch, but because it took these kids who were at high risk for gang- and drug-related activities and gave them discipline and purpose, as well as a strong sense of belonging.

Many notable and upcoming musicians used the auditorium for rehearsals: Lenny Williams, Frankie Beverly, Pete Escovedo, Sonny Rhodes, and John Lee Hooker. The community center also served as a meeting and conference site for many left organizations in the Bay Area, and it was not uncommon for the school to be visited by famous entertainers, such as Richard Pryor, or African dignitaries, including Sam Njomo of SWAPO, the Namibian independence movement.

The party received a large CETA grant that helped put about twenty comrades on the payroll, enabling them to afford to rent apartments or houses. This brought an end to the long-standing practice of communal living.

Elaine paid much more attention to the needs of the troops than had the earlier leadership. From the way things were progressing, it looked like we had a very real chance of capturing Oakland.

30

The Other Side of the Coin

There was a time, when peace was on the earth,
And joy and happiness did reign and each man knew his worth.
In my heart how I yearn for that spirit's return
—Pharoah Sanders, "The Creator Has a Master Plan," 1969

Enola Wilson, called Lola, was named by her retired military father
after the *Enola Gay*, the plane that dropped the nuclear bomb on Hiroshima.
In spring 1969 Lola had left home, at the age of fourteen, and joined the
Black Panther Party in Denver, Colorado. She survived the police raid on
the Denver office before being sent to work in the New York chapter, where
she worked under the tutelage of Sam Napier. On the chilly morning of
April 15, 1971, she left the Corona, Queens, Panther office, heading into
the field to sell papers. She left her son, little Damon, in the care of Sam
Napier. When she returned, she found the office on fire, Sam Napier dead,
and her son abandoned outside in the snow.

When I met Lola, in 1973, she was working in the party's finance de-
partment in Oakland. She was pregnant by a comrade from Boston, Pete
Alameda, who had left Oakland not long after the departures of Chairman
Bobby and Tanya and Aaron Patrice.

I befriended Lola. I brought her all the things she needed for her new-
born, and every evening I picked up Damon and Lola's youngest sister,
Valerie, from school, and brought them home. Soon after Lola had little

talie, we fell in love. She was sweet, kind, and highly intelligent. Our relationship blossomed so much and so quickly that we became the envy of other comrades. In the party, few relationships lasted very long.

Having grown up in a two-parent family, part of me yearned for a more traditional family arrangement. I think many comrades at that time wanted a more family-oriented situation, particularly if there were kids involved. Yet we understood that, as such, it would need to fit within the revolutionary framework of our lives and work. Lola and I and the kids functioned as a family unit within the larger Panther family. These were some of the first times since joining the party that I actually sat down to watch TV. We went on picnics and sailed on Lake Merritt. We had many good times together. In the back of my mind, though, I always worried how long these good times would last.

When not with Lola and the kids, I was doing party work, and most of that time was spent with Elaine. Working for Elaine was the most difficult job assignment I'd ever had or would ever have. She was an extremely demanding perfectionist and at times very difficult to work with. My day would start at 8 a.m. with picking up Janice Banks, Elaine's administrative assistant, who was from the DC chapter, then stopping at the newsstand on 14th and Broadway to pick up copies of the *New York Times*, the *San Francisco Chronicle*, and the *Oakland Tribune*. Next, we would stop at the home of Norma Armour, the party's finance officer, to pick up Elaine's $25 per diem. Then we would head to Elaine's penthouse on Caldecott Lane in the Oakland hills, where she had her office. When we got there, Janice would go through the newspapers and cut out any articles that might be relevant to the party for Elaine to read.

My attire was always suit and tie. My hair and grooming had to be neat and perfect. Elaine met with many corporate heads to solicit money for the school and the campaign. And there were numerous trips to Sacramento to meet with Governor Jerry Brown, his legal affairs secretary Tony Kline, and Speaker of the House Leo McCarthy, as well as the future speaker, Willie Brown, known as the best-dressed politician in Sacramento. There was the campaign trail and meetings in private homes and pool halls. Most weeknights I did not get in until 2 a.m. Saturday nights and Sundays I got to spend time with Lola and the kids.

While Elaine was making her mark on the political and social landscape of Northern California, another face of the party was at work in the underbelly. The military wing, or the "cadre," as it was now called, was also establishing a new identity for itself. Under the leadership of Bethune, Flores Forbes, and Big Bob, the cadre attempted to maintain the party's influence over the wild streets of the East Bay. That meant the continued taxing of illegitimate capitalists. I recall one early-morning excursion to ambush an individual who was resisting the taxation. Three of us waited in hiding outside the home of the owner of a large after-hours club who had stopped paying his dues. We wanted to send him a message. I was the driver, so when he came out, the others opened up with handguns. He returned fire, then retreated to his house and we took off.

Another time, two LampPost regulars, who fancied themselves hustlers, came into the restaurant. Over the course of their stay, they became disrespectful and boisterous, acting very insolent toward the comrades working that shift. Then they made some insulting references to Huey, Elaine, and the party and left. At the beginning of Elaine's reign, it had been established that we wouldn't take any shit from anyone. A couple of nights later, those two brothers learned the meaning of shotgun justice. Many late-night missions dealt with our enemies, and before long, respect was secured for Elaine and the party.

Sometimes the cadre gathered on Sundays to discuss discipline and other matters. We also went to the gun range to sharpen our aim, where we often encountered police officers at target practice. They were always looking to see what kind of weapons we were using, and we were always looking to see what kind of weapons they were using. We studied issues of *Guns & Ammo* to learn about the latest weapons or newest shooting stances, lifted weights, and practiced expanding our peripheral vision with eye exercises. Whether for business or pleasure, we spent a lot of time with one another. I became very close to many of these brothers, especially Tex, Big Bob, Flores, "The Duke" Perkins, House Man Lewis, Bruce "Deacon" Washington, and Tim Thomson.

In 1976, Elaine called up the remaining members of the Southern California chapter to Oakland. Only about fifteen comrades were left in the chapter at that point, and Elaine decided they could be of more use to us in the Bay Area. Repression by the LAPD had grown so great that by 1972, the entire Southern California chapter had been forced underground, operating from rented houses in the suburbs. For the past few years they had functioned almost totally incognito, dressing in Superfly outfits, the men wearing processed hair and big hats.

The Los Angeles cadre was a very colorful band of characters—Lemuel, Russell, Tony, Al Armour—but no one stood out like Simba, a fiery, expressive Vietnam vet who always made sure you knew he was from Texas and that he carried a snub-nosed .44 Magnum. He used to say to me, "A. D., you don't eat beef? Comrade, beef makes me mean, makes me ready to kill." He was as macho as they came.

These comrades were seasoned veterans and we could use the manpower. Besides, Elaine had an old score to settle with the Los Angeles coordinator, longtime Panther Jimmy Johnson. He was known to be abusive to sisters, including to Elaine during her days in Los Angeles. Upon his arrival in Oakland, Jimmy was ordered to Elaine's penthouse, where he was surrounded, beaten mercilessly, and expelled.

Corporal punishment had never really been established as a party policy. It just seemed to grow out of our circumstances and our paramilitary ideology. It was not widely used. As a matter of fact, most comrades were unaware of its existence. But under Elaine, anybody who committed a serious violation of policy or rule could expect a visit. And for those in the cadre, there was less leniency.

I understood Elaine's vision for the party, probably better than anyone else, but I also knew that she could be ruthless, particularly toward disobedient men. I had witnessed the male chauvinism in the early days, how Eldridge got away with beating Kathleen, and how brothers in leadership positions got away with things that the brothers in the rank and file dared not think of doing. Since her rise Elaine had changed all that, of course, and it was the men who bore the brunt of her anger. Some certainly deserved it. But some did not.

Elaine and I had been on the campaign trail day and night, constantly going from meeting to meeting. One night, on our way to yet another cocktail fundraiser, Elaine began to curse me out for something I had said or done. I made the mistake of responding with my own profanity, an echo of that incident years before.

The next evening I was told to report to Big Bob's apartment right away. When I got there, the lights were low.

"A. D., you got twenty-five lashes coming for disrespecting Elaine," said Bob in his low, sometimes gravelly voice. "Take off your shirt."

I had disrespected the current leader of the party, and, to be truthful, if she were a man I probably would not have responded the way I did. And that was something she detested, so now I had to accept my punishment. "Okay," I said to Big Bob, slowly and reluctantly taking off my shirt. I swallowed hard and looked at Big Bob, wondering what it would feel like to get twenty-five lashes with a bullwhip. I knew I could take a lot of pain, but could I endure this?

The large penthouse had several thick, wooden pillars in the living room. I grabbed the one in the middle of the floor and planted my feet, ready to receive my punishment. By the thirteenth lash, I began to feel the pain of the leather slicing into my back. I let go, hoping Bob would have some sympathy, hoping I could stall for some time in between strikes.

"A. D., put your hands back up," said Bob. He sounded a little irritated. I reached back up, grabbing hold of the beam, and the lashes continued.

The low lighting and the old-fashioned wooden pillars seemed to distort my reality, to alter time and space. For a split second I felt I was elsewhere—in another place, another time, in the hull of a ship or on some plantation. Then it was over. His job done, Big Bob gently began to swab my wounds with alcohol, telling me, "A. D., you can't sleep with any community sisters until your wounds have healed, okay?" The party had a strict code against telling the outside world about this and other issues.

"Right on," I said, glad it was over.

"You want some 'yack?" said Bob.

"Yeah, I'll have some."

We sat and sipped cognac and smoked a joint as my wounds burned fiercely. I knew Bob was only doing his job. He was one of the most honest, kindest persons around. There were also times when I found myself in Bob's position, meting out discipline to comrades who had violated a rule. It was the way things were in the party, particularly in the cadre. In truth, this kind of physical discipline was something we could have done without. But our willingness to use it, and our acceptance of it, was symptomatic of deeper issues having little to do with revolution.

I was temporarily relieved of my driving and bodyguard duties for Elaine and was replaced by Bill Elder from Detroit, "Still Bill," as we called him, a tall, handsome, bespectacled brother. Elaine went through half a dozen brothers in that role, finally settling on alternating between Bill Elder and me. I looked forward to the breaks from driving Elaine. It gave me more time to spend with Lola, as well as more time to read. I had discovered the books of Carlos Castaneda, and was drawn in particular to *The Teachings of Don Juan: A Yaqui Way of Knowledge,* one of the few nonpolitical books that I'd gotten into in a very long time.

For the first time since joining the party, I began to think outside a revolutionary context. But I could not allow my thoughts to stray too far from our mission. There was still much work to be done.

The End of the Line

Left to right: Me, Darren "The Duke" Perkins, and Louis "Tex" Johnson at the LampPost, 1975.

31

The Death of Deacon

Give me my freedom for as long as I be.
All I ask of living is to have no chains on me.
All I ask of living is to have no chains on me,
And all I ask of dying is to go naturally.

—Blood, Sweat & Tears, "And When I Die," 1969

The Oakland Community Learning Center had become
a popular hangout for young people in East Oakland, from the Martial
Arts Program to the CETA and Teen Programs to the movie nights. The
party always paid close attention to security; at any given time, there were
one or two armed members of the security squad at the center. As in any
ghetto in America, tempers could get hot and situations could get out of
hand quickly if not handled securely. There were a few problems, a few
incidents of gunplay, but we were always able to manage things. That is,
until one fateful Friday night.

The Teen Program had become such a success that we began to hold
teen dances at the center. The City of Oakland had outlawed teen dances
at schools and city facilities due to outbreaks of violence. Through our work
with the neighborhood youth, we felt we would be able to handle any problems that might arise. The first two dances came off without a hitch. We
checked every teen coming in for weapons and alcohol, and had armed security throughout the cafeteria to ensure the dances went without incident.

263

The first two went so smoothly that, for the third scheduled dance, Bethune gave the orders to drop the search; he also ordered security to disarm. That night, I was in charge of the security detachment. Tex, Deacon, Allen, and George Robinson were on duty with me. It was odd being on security and not being armed. But after all, these were kids.

Everything was going fine until the Brown brothers came in. They were two lanky, cocky, derby-wearing brothers well-known among the East Oakland youth. They belonged to a gang called the Derbies.

As an alternative to a pat-down, some of the comrade sisters had been assigned to dance with certain males to find out if they were packing. One of the sisters, Arlene, discovered that the Brown brothers were carrying weapons. She approached me and whispered in my ear, "Aaron, those two brothers have guns."

"Which ones?" I asked.

"The Brown brothers—the ones with the derbies."

"Okay," I said.

Allen and Tex were nearby, so I motioned to them and explained the situation. We slowly walked over to the two brothers, who apparently had been drinking before coming into the dance and were obviously intoxicated and talking loudly. I approached and asked them to turn in their weapons until the dance was over.

When confronted they became hostile and boisterous. Apparently, the alcohol was affecting their judgment—so much that they pulled out their guns. As we moved forward to disarm them, they began shooting. The sounds of the gunfire caused a panic, alarming the other young people. The situation turned chaotic as we scrambled for cover, some of us trying to usher the kids to safety. George slipped into the maintenance room where our weapons were locked up. In the meantime, two young people had been hit by gunfire. The Brown brothers backed their way out to the parking lot, where the younger of the two took off running toward the exit, leaving his brother behind. Comrade Deacon was able to sneak up behind the older brother, grabbing him and disarming him. Meanwhile, during all the chaos the younger brother returned, ran up behind Deacon, and shot him in the back.

I, along with several other people from the community, ran the shooter down, daring him to shoot us as we approached. We pounced on him and began letting out our rage. We beat him until we could beat no more. When I got back to the school, Deacon was already on his way to

Highland Hospital. The guns the Brown boys were carrying were only .22-caliber. We sighed with relief, thinking surely it would take more than a .22-caliber bullet to kill a comrade with a heart as large as Deacon's.

Santa Rita heard what happened and came to the hospital to stay with me as we waited for Deacon. When the doctor came out after several hours and told us Deacon was dead, we thought maybe he was joking, or maybe he was talking about another Black casualty. But it was true. Deacon was gone. He and I had been assigned to the security squad together. We were a two-man cadre, spending time cleaning weapons, pulling security. I had first met him in West Oakland after the split with Eldridge, when he was assigned to Central Headquarters after arriving from Philadelphia. He'd grown up on the mean streets of Philadelphia and, despite his small size, had quite a reputation among the gang members there. After joining the party, he had distinguished himself in battle against the Philly police. He was now a fallen comrade, leaving behind a small son.

That night, as I was lying next to Lola, I thought about how indiscriminate death was. It wasn't so much that we would be burying another comrade—that was something we were used by now—but the fact that Deacon had died during one of the more peaceful periods for the party. And he died at the hands of kids, our own community kids. His death also exposed me to my own vulnerability, which, up to this point, I had never really given much thought. We in the cadre were very close. We trained together, went out at night for business or pleasure together. At times it seemed we knew what each other was thinking. To lose someone as close as Deacon was painful.

Several nights later, three comrades entered Highland Hospital, the same hospital where Deacon had drawn his last breath. One carried a dagger and a hypodermic needle filled with battery acid, another carried a green duffel bag with an AK-47 inside. They hurried past a crowd of youngsters sitting in the lobby, gathered around the older Brown brother. Quickly, they went upstairs to the sixth floor and located the room where the wounded Brown brother was recuperating.

The dagger came out and was driven into the back of the victim several times as he weakly screamed out. The attackers rushed back down the stairs, past the unsuspecting crowd. If cops had made any attempts at stopping them, their orders were to let loose with the AK-47. This attempt to finish off the younger Brown brother was unsuccessful.

There would be other attempts, nights of sitting up in the safe house in West Oakland, sipping brandy while we cleaned our weapons, criss-crossing our shells and wiping them down with garlic—rumored to cause blood poisoning—as we waited for the clock to strike 3 a.m., when the streets were silent. Doors were kicked in as the hit team ran inside. We searched high and low for the Brown brothers but learned they had been sent away. Revenge is an unquenchable thirst. It is a bottomless pit to hell, an emotion both bitter and sweet, one that is never satisfied.

Deacon's funeral was held at the community center. Armed Philly Panthers stood at parade rest with their shotguns, wearing black berets and powder-blue shirts. It would be the last of the traditional Panther funerals as we bid our comrade farewell.

32

Oakland Is Ours

The world won't get no better if we just let it be
The world won't get no better
We gotta change it
Yeah, just you and me.

—Harold Melvin & The Blue Notes,
"Wake Up Everybody," 1976

The campaign for city council had been a rocky road for Elaine. Certain entities did not want her to be an elected official. She kept a rigorous schedule, moving between campaigning and running the party, being sure to maintain the party's funding at a high level. We thought victory was near and the city council seat would be ours.

Winning the seat would be putting one more piece of the puzzle in place. Many of us gathered at Elaine's campaign office in November 1975, waiting for the results, hoping our hard work would pay off. But Elaine was defeated by the white incumbent. The margin of defeat was small, but that was no consolation. We all felt the sting of losing the race, having worked so hard and set our goals so high. To be denied victory yet again was painful.

My job was challenging, yet I was determined to do it to the best of my ability. Although Elaine could be difficult for men to deal with and a tyrant at times, I saw a brilliant strategist, a perfectionist who never seemed to tire. Once she set her mind to something, it was done, no matter how monumental the task.

After the election, Elaine began spending a great deal of time in Sacramento. She knew the importance of developing her political connection to Jerry Brown and did not falter in that task. She became known and highly respected by many state legislators, a few of whom had been elected thanks to the party's political machine. Her influence and power in Sacramento grew so great that she was invited to the annual Passover seder held by an all-male group of Jewish legislators. Elaine, Willie Brown, and myself were the only Blacks in attendance. Not only was Elaine the only woman present, she was also the only woman who had ever been invited to this annual holiday celebration.

I sat back in the shadows and watched as these powerful men fawned over Elaine. She deflected every trite remark with quick wit. Her mind was working while they were playing. In Oakland, despite losing the election, Elaine had expanded the party's constituency, and she became a dominant figure in Oakland city politics.

When Governor Jerry Brown went to appoint judges for Northern California, he called Elaine for advice. Elaine selected a handful of Bay Area Black attorneys for judgeship, and they all knew the party was responsible for their being appointed. It was no surprise when Elaine was appointed to the executive committee of the Oakland Council for Economic Development. The council had been pushing for the construction of a freeway exit ramp into downtown Oakland. The hope was to entice the big developers to invest in reviving downtown Oakland, which had been slowly dying for the past ten years. This project could only move forward with the governor's approval. Eventually, Elaine was able to deliver on the freeway, thanks to Jerry Brown. Part of the deal she negotiated was for a thousand homes to be developed for the low-income families displaced by the ramp's construction.

In the summer of 1975 Elaine visited Huey in Cuba. After two failed campaigns to get Panthers elected to political office, Huey had devised another plan for capturing Oakland. History had shown that running a revolutionary for political office was not a sound strategy because the individual was either unelectable or susceptible to compromising his or her revolutionary focus. Huey had a new approach. Upon Elaine's return, at Huey's request, Elaine approached former superior court judge Lionel

Wilson about running for mayor of Oakland. If Wilson agreed, the party would run his campaign. Before Huey had departed Oakland, he and Lionel had become good friends. Lionel's son was heavily involved in the street life, and Huey had often looked out for him. Despite not having any real political ambitions, Lionel Wilson was a highly respected, very distinguished-looking Black man. He agreed to run, and his chances of success were high.

Lo and behold, the party ran Lionel Wilson's campaign and won, electing him as the first Black mayor of Oakland. The Panthers were finally in City Hall. Lionel knew very little about politics; however, with Elaine at his side, the future for Oakland was bright. Elaine was in the mayor's office almost daily, helping to shape his policy and strategy for improving conditions for Oakland's poor.

In return, Lionel was set to name two Panthers, Ericka Huggins and Phyllis Jackson, to the Port of Oakland Commission. The port was where the real power was concentrated. It was where the money was, and whoever controls the source of revenue controls the city. For years, cocaine had flowed freely into Oakland from South America. Now we could put an end to that. Elaine used to joke that, instead, "Now we'll have AK-47s coming in."

The city manager also became a stalwart of the party, and with these elements in place, we slowly began to make Oakland a city that would revolutionize American politics. We had seized control without a single shot fired. (Actually, there were some shots fired.) We began plans to re-create this process in other cities, such as Chicago, where a small cadre awaited orders, and Seattle, where Elmer had continued the work we had left behind.

Driving down Broadway one day, I was astonished to see Tommy Jones walking down the street. I immediately stopped to give him a ride. He mostly seemed the same, but a little unshaven, a little run-down, the tooth still missing on his left side. I was happy to see Tommy, but it was sad to see a former captain of the party looking like a drug addict.

"Hey, Aaron," he said, as he half-smiled. "I'm trying to get it together. Remember those good old days? Man, I miss those days."

"Yeah, I do too," I replied. My mind flashed back to the summer of '68, igniting memories of Matilaba, Landon, Randy, Robert Bay, and all the others who were prepared to shed blood for the people. I felt a bit of sadness for those days long gone.

"You take care," I said, and dropped him off at his destination.

Flores called one morning to tell me that Santa Rita had left. Santa Rita, a member of the party's vocal group the Lumpen, was a singer, a coordinator, an administrator, and a gunman; whatever needed to be done, he would try to accomplish it. And if he couldn't, he would tell you so. We didn't have too many brothers like him left. At one time we'd had scores of comrades like Santa Rita all across the country, but losing him now put more pressure on those remaining.

Santa Rita's departure planted a seed in my mind. He had left because he was just plain tired and disenchanted, and I think many of us who had been working so long and so hard were quietly feeling the same way, despite the many recent accomplishments. But the prospect of leaving something we'd devoted our lives to was extremely complicated, and there was always some new development, some unexpected challenge to test and renew our commitment.

And, in California, you never knew what to expect. There was always something strange going on, including all kinds of covert operations by the secret intelligence forces. Hands-down, the most bizarre experiment thought to involve the CIA was the phenomenon of Jim Jones, minister of the People's Temple, savior of the poor, the downtrodden, the sick, and shut-in. Jones owned a large church in San Francisco on Fillmore, around the corner from the former location of the San Francisco Panther office. The Nation of Islam had previously owned the building.

Elaine made it a point to meet with anyone of political significance in the Bay Area, and one of the weirdest meetings was with Jim Jones. He and his church had a lot of followers in the Black community, in particular a lot of older Black folks looking for a promise of a better life. Out in the field, we encountered many of his followers out collecting donations on some of the same corners in Oakland where we stood. Jim Jones wielded a considerable amount of power. He had contacts in the city and state governments and was able to procure funding and support for his militant "Help the Poor" platform. He even put out a newspaper. One of its issues touted a trip Jones had made to Cuba and a meeting he'd had with Huey. Even then, we felt his entire operation seemed very fishy, very strange. Nevertheless, his power was intruding on the party's constituency, so Elaine felt that a meeting was in order, at least to find out what he was up to, as he was operating in the Black community.

The Duke, Elaine, and I drove up to the church and were met at the gate by three gruff-looking brothers wearing big coats. It was obvious to us that they were carrying weapons. Inside, we were taken on a tour of the church. The building had an eerie feeling to it. In the cafeteria were several older Black workers preparing food. They acted very strange, very detached. On the top floor, we walked past a small room where a middle-aged white man sat at a table, operating a HAM radio with a microphone.

"That's our contact with Guyana," said our tour guide.

We were ushered into a room where Jim Jones sat, surrounded by little kids. He seemed to be white but fairly dark-complexioned, with jet-black hair. He boasted about his programs and the land his church was developing in Guyana. There really wasn't much back-and-forth dialogue. We all just wanted to get out of that place. The vibrations were unlike anything I had ever experienced. The people were almost emotionless, with little enthusiasm or joy. I don't think any of us was surprised at the massacre in Guyana two years later. Hundreds of Jones's followers died at after drinking cyanide-laced Flavor Aid. Comrade Russell Washington from Los Angeles lost five family members to this mass murder/suicide. At the time, unfortunately, we did not have the time or resources to explore the ramifications of Jim Jones's inroads into the Black community. We had our own contradictions to sort out.

Elaine often hosted parties for the comrades at her penthouse in the Oakland hills. We consumed large amounts of brandy, smoked plenty of weed, and danced away our emotions and pain. There was a sense that our time together was coming to an end. We all felt that the party represented the last hope for our movement, and Elaine had taken us to new heights. Yet I was beginning to wonder about my own future, my son Aaron, and my daughter Nisaa, who was somewhere in America—I had seen her only once. I felt trapped. At the same time, I also felt that here with these comrades was where I would always be, where I had to be, otherwise I would be no more. I often sat back and watched the comrades dancing wildly, as if in some kind of trance, as if these were our last dances together, the last dance of the Black Panther Party.

Several months later, Elmer was in a phone conversation with Ericka Huggins concerning the menu for the Breakfast Program in Seattle. A disagreement ensued, and Ericka accused Elmer of disrespecting her, for which Elmer was summoned to Oakland.

I was worried about what would happen to Elmer in this dispute. As just one example, Bobby Rush, deputy chairman of the Illinois chapter, had been summoned to Oakland by Elaine. He met with Elaine in Ericka Huggins's office at the school, which Elaine sometimes used for business. I, along with some others, hung around outside the office while he was being reprimanded. After several hours, Bobby Rush finally came out. The look on his face was of sadness and humility. I felt bad for him. He had endured the death of not only Fred Hampton, but at least four or five other Chicago Panthers and the imprisonment of many others. He had sacrificed his life, as we all had, now to be tossed aside like an old piece of meat, as if the years of blood and sweat meant nothing. At least he got away without physical harm, which is more than could be said of a few others. Simba had his legs broken before being expelled.

Being summoned to Oakland was like walking a tightrope over an ocean with sharks circling. One slip and you could be making a trip to the hospital. Luckily, Elmer was able to talk his way out of any physical action being taken against him; however, he was ordered to stay in Oakland. He requested to go back to Seattle in order to take care of some family business with his new wife, Dee Dee. A week later he called from Seattle to say that he wanted to talk things over with Huey and was not planning on returning to Oakland. Elaine was not pleased by Elmer's request, but she was hoping to persuade him to come back. The Seattle chapter was the longest-functioning chapter still in operation, and it played a major role in the plans to reinvigorate the party on a national level. With Huey in Cuba, it was not possible to accommodate Elmer's request for a meeting, so Elaine arranged to make a trip to Seattle.

Bethune, Elaine, and I caught a plane up north. Flores took a train to bring our weapons. We met Elmer at the Seattle chapter's community center, now located on 19th and Spruce. Tension was very high. Elaine wanted Elmer to come back to Oakland, but Elmer refused and kept requesting to speak with Huey. I attempted to persuade Elmer that it was not only in the party's interest but also in his own interest to acquiesce. I knew all too well that the people I was with could be extremely dangerous. While we talked, we kept hearing noises, even though the office was empty. Bethune wanted to investigate, but Elmer steered him away from the other rooms.

The conversation heated up, turning antagonistic. Elaine was not used to Panthers defying the hierarchy, but Elmer refused to back down. We could tell this would not be resolved in our favor, so Elaine, Bethune, Flores, and I decided it was best to retreat from a potentially volatile situation. With our hands on our weapons, we backed out. As Elmer confirmed for me years later, he had situated heavily armed Seattle Panthers, including our younger brother Michael, throughout the building. With tensions peaking and voices rising, a single move could have resulted in a bloodbath.

On the ride back to the hotel, I was silent. This event was devastating for me. Elmer and I had been like Mays and McCovey, like Johnny Unitas and Lenny Moore. We had always been as close as brothers could be, overcoming all obstacles between us. Secretly, I was proud of the way he had stood up to Elaine and Bethune, but I worried that this was not over. Back in Oakland, I was relieved of my duties with Elaine and presented with the choice between staying in the party or leaving. I was allowed a week off to decide.

I was not ready to leave the party. We had come so far. We were just a few steps away from securing total political control of Oakland. More immediately, I also wanted to stay around to keep my ears pricked up and my eyes open in case I detected a move to take Elmer out. As dedicated as I was to the movement and to the philosophy of the Black Panther Party, I was not about to stand by and watch my brother be eliminated. It had been discussed, and I knew that if they wanted to, they could do it. For reasons never divulged, it was decided against. There were bigger problems ahead.

33

Huey's Return

I come up hard, baby
But that's okay, 'cause
Trouble Man
Don't get in the way

—Marvin Gaye, "Trouble Man," 1972

One day, a group of mothers from the projects came by the community center, upset. Felix Mitchell, head of a new drug gang called the Mob, had taken control of the 69th Street Village, where many kids who attended the school resided. The mothers wanted us to do something about the drug infiltration, a growing problem that soon threatened to engulf East and West Oakland.

Felix Mitchell, only twenty-three, was smart and cagey, the perfect patsy for the Mafia to peddle their heroin. Huey hated the Mafia and had all but driven them and their heroin trade out of Oakland. Since Huey's exile, many of his enemies in the street life had begun to reassert themselves. Now, in Felix Mitchell, the Mafia had a front man whom they supplied with an endless flow of heroin and weapons, and there were plenty of gunmen around willing to join up.

Our first move was to send the Duke and Simba, both of whom had served in Vietnam, into the projects on a reconnaissance mission. The

274

information we got back was that these guys were well-organized, with rooftop lookouts and walkie-talkies. They were paying the little kids to act as lookouts and using some of the housing units to sell drugs. By all accounts, it seemed we were up against a formidable foe.

After several community meetings, it was decided that we would operate on two fronts. One front would focus on organizing the community, planning marches, demonstrations, and community meetings, and the second front would be military, involving the cadres. The machine guns were unearthed and assembled. We began casing the enemy's spots and they did the same to us, both sides anticipating and planning for a bloody war. To let them know we meant business, we shot up some of their safe houses. I thought I might not survive this dirty little war, that some of us would die. Death seemed close by, so close I could sense its cold breath waiting around the corner.

Fortunately, we had to put this operation on hold. Huey was coming home. In late spring 1977, our leader, Huey P. Newton, returned from exile in Cuba, prepared to stand trial for the charges leveled against him for the murder of a prostitute. Under Elaine's leadership, we had been able to realign the party's position in the community. The party's reputation was back to its original image as the champion of the people. We now had political control over the Oakland judiciary and city hall, and a heavy influence on state politics in Sacramento. Further, Elaine had been elected by the Northern California Democratic Party to be a delegate to the Democratic National Convention.

She also had forged an alliance with Reverend J. Alfred Smith, Oakland's most influential religious leader. They had collaborated on a broad agenda to address important issues in East Oakland, such as improving education, influencing the judicial system, and gaining electoral power. The Martial Arts Program, under the direction of Steve McCutchen, had been featured on the cover of *Black Belt* magazine, and many of the kids from the community who participated in the tae kwon do lessons had gone on to become instructors. These were the best days of that era, a time when we had a full complement of power and influence. Just three years earlier the party had looked to be on its last legs. Tremendous progress had been made under Elaine's leadership.

Despite our much improved position, I, as did probably many others, felt uneasy about Huey's return. I remember watching Huey, flanked by

Elaine, Big Bob, and Bethune, during the press conference held upon his return. I felt deep inside that maybe his return would backfire on us all. But I knew to keep that to myself.

Elaine found a nice home for Huey and his family on a cul-de-sac in the Oakland hills. Joe Abron, the party's technology expert, installed video monitors around the perimeter of the property. Finally, Huey and Gwen and the kids, Ronnie and Jessica, could relax after the pretty rough conditions they had experienced in Cuba.

Huey enrolled in a PhD program at UC Santa Cruz, where he was driven two or three times a week by Big Bob to attend classes. He also visited the Oakland Community School on occasion, talking about having an apartment built on top of the school building. In his home, he installed a Universal gym so he could stay in good physical shape. So far, it seemed Huey was making an attempt not to fall into his old habits, yet I still had an underlying feeling of uneasiness.

Lola had started working at the LampPost, which meant on weekends she got home late. This left me to watch little Damon and Natalie and Lola's youngest sister, Valerie. After the kids went to bed, I spent many Saturday nights watching *Saturday Night Live*. It was a revolutionary show for its time, filmed live with unknown performers, using sketch comedy to comment on the dysfunction of American politics and society. Even though Lola and I were still together, I had been seeing other sisters in the party as well as out, and it wasn't long before Lola started seeing other comrade brothers. This did bother me, especially when she started seeing Bethune, but there wasn't a darned thing I could do about it. Our relationship slowly began to go downhill.

It wasn't long before Huey's drug habit resurfaced, and his forays into the street life resumed. One night, while Lola slept peacefully, I was lying across the bed, watching the old gangster flick *On Top of the World* with Edward G. Robinson, and thinking how similar that portrayal of gangster life was to my own and that of the others on the security squad. I thought about how we were ordered to rob dope dealers and do many other things under the cover of night. I thought about my assignment at LaToure's after-hour speakeasy, where I sat with my back against the wall, .45 at the ready, eyes on the lookout for trouble, occasionally snorting a few lines of coke to keep up with the atmosphere. LaToure was later found shot to death, stuffed in the trunk of his gray El Dorado, courtesy of our mutual enemies. In the early days our enemies had been white pigs in blue, brown, or black uniforms. Now our enemies looked like us, dressed like us, and talked like us.

Suddenly the phone rang. I wondered who would be calling me at midnight.

"Hey, A. D. Grab your shoes and come up to the Name of the Game." It was Flores. "Shoes" was Panther code for weapon.

"Okay. Right on," I replied, then hung up. I knew that when Flores called, it usually was serious. I got up and grabbed my pants, shoes, and gun. For the past ten years, I had always placed these items within easy reach, on the floor right next to the bed.

When I got to the club, Name of the Game on Broadway, the Duke and Tim Thomson were stationed at the front of the club. Tex swaggered over to my car, his gold tooth showing as he smiled.

"Hey, A. D. The servant is in there meeting with the Mob and the Family."

I got out. Tex and I exchanged small talk, wondering why Huey would be meeting with these hoodlums. The Family was a rival drug gang to Felix Mitchell's Mob. Their most recent feud had left a handful of bloody bodies on the Oakland streets. They were known for jumping out of cars with machine guns. Their rivalry was so intense that the past couple of months had been reminiscent of the old Chicago gangster wars of the '30s during Prohibition.

Finally Huey emerged from the club, flanked by Big Bob, Flores, and Bethune. The rest of us followed them to their car and waited till they drove off. The next day I learned that Huey had given the two drug gangs an ultimatum: either they paid the party $50,000 a week, or we'd go to war. We had already begun preparing for this little war, but that had been intended to eliminate those vermin, not profit off them. Under Huey's influence, things were becoming unpredictable again.

A week later, I drove Elaine to the school to pick up her daughter, little Ericka. Elaine's time with little Ericka was limited, as it was for all of us with children, and Elaine tried to compensate by giving her daughter treats and taking her special places. I wasn't surprised when Elaine calmly asked for the keys to the Mercedes.

But something in her manner was unusual. I could not put my finger on it. When she told me she would be dropping me off and taking the car, I asked if she was sure, because she rarely went anywhere alone; Bill Elder, Bethune, or I would always be by her side. Elaine had a expression of peace and resignation I had never seen before. Hesitantly, I handed her the keys, looking forward to an unexpected, relaxing evening at home.

Several hours later, I was sitting at home watching the World Series. Reggie Jackson, Mr. October, had just hit his third home run, propelling the New York Yankees to victory. During his time with the Oakland A's, Reggie had lived in the same complex as Elaine. He always spoke with us whenever the opportunity presented itself. He was the epitome of the rebel athlete—defiant, bold. The phone rang as Reggie was rounding the bases, fist high in the air.

"Aaron, have you seen or talked to Elaine?" It was Ericka Huggins. I felt guilty, because I was supposed to know where Elaine was at all times.

"No. She said she was going to take little Ericka to get some ice cream," I answered, sheepishly. I hoped my answer sufficed. Ericka sounded very concerned, which worried me.

The next day, Tex and I went to the San Francisco Airport to retrieve the red Mercedes that Bill Elder and I had driven Elaine around in for the past four years. She was gone. Huey had felt threatened by Elaine's consolidation of power and her influence in Northern California politics. When she refused to give him access to the millions of dollars under her control through the Oakland Council for Economic Development, he threatened her unless she turned over control of the funds. Elaine had dedicated the last four years to building up the party's respectability, forging alliances that Huey, Bobby, and David Hilliard had been unable to forge. She had become one of the most powerful individuals in California. As much as Elaine loved Huey, in the end, he treated her just as he had treated the others that were run off from the party.

The day after her disappearance, Elaine took out a full-page ad in the *Oakland Tribune* to explain her departure to the people of Oakland. She did not reveal the truth—that Huey had fallen back into his old patterns. She instead cited her fatigue and expressed a desire to pursue her musical interests; Elaine was a very talented singer. The fact that she felt compelled to take out this ad demonstrated her importance to the people and the city of Oakland.

The following morning, keeping with the usual routine, I picked up Janice to go Elaine's penthouse, a place she had recently moved to on

Lake Merritt. Once we were inside the apartment, I told Janice that Elaine had left the party. It was a weird moment, because we didn't know whether to cry or laugh. As a matter of fact, we both yelled out in jubilation. Our reaction surprised us, but considering how difficult Elaine was to work for, maybe our joy should have been expected. I think we also realized that with Elaine gone, the party would fall. We both knew our own exit was imminent.

I had fallen in love with a young woman, a medical student at UC Berkeley, who worked at the clinic. Her name was Mildred, and she was a young woman of Black, Japanese, and Mexican ancestry from San Diego. She was attractive, intelligent, down-to-earth, and most of all, she was always happy and optimistic. I think we fell in love the first time we laid eyes on one another. With us there were no ulterior motives, no forced or hidden emotional reasons. We had a genuine attraction to one another. I felt as if she were in essence the girl of my dreams, as if she were my soulmate. My relationship with Lola was one of conscience; not that I did not love Lola, but I had been drawn to her out of my own weakness. I wanted to help her, to save her from unhappiness, and was looking to fulfill my own need for a sense of worth. I did not know what would become of this situation. I knew I loved Lola, but I knew also that Mildred and I had something special. With things in the party growing tense and uncertain, Mildred asked me if I would leave the party and go with her to San Diego. As much as I loved that woman, as much I sensed an opportunity for true happiness, I was not ready to cut my ties to the party.

I struggled to explain my inability to leave. Even though the writing was on the wall, I felt unable to make my escape. But events beyond my control would push me closer to the edge.

34

The Richmond Incident

Just a song before I go
A lesson to be learned
Traveling twice the speed of sound
It's easy to get burned
—Crosby, Stills & Nash, "Just a Song Before I Go," 1977

About a week after Elaine's disappearance, I was out in the field collecting donations for the sickle cell anemia program. It was the end of the workday, so I stopped at the Hofbrau on Telegraph Avenue in Berkeley to get my favorite dish, the turkey dinner. While I ate, I contemplated the future of the Black Panther Party. After my meal, I called Central Headquarters to let them know I would be coming in shortly to turn in the donation money.

Flores got on the phone. "Aaron," he said in his calm manner, "when you come in from the field, I want you to go home and get your shoes and meet me at the office by six. We have some work to do."

When I arrived at the office with my .45, House Man told me that Flores had already left, so I went back home to relax and spend time with Lola and the kids. The next morning I awoke feeling very strange, anxious, and extremely fearful. I sensed that something had gone wrong, something had happened.

Within minutes, Tex's girlfriend Naomi called. "Aaron, have you seen Tex?"

Her voice had a deep sound of concern, as if she suspected the answer. Since Tex and I were best friends and almost always together, she thought I surely would know his whereabouts. My stomach began to churn. I started to feel nauseated. Tex and I had been assigned together as a team after Deacon's death. He and I were inseparable buddies. For a while he had moved in with Lola, me, and the kids. We often hung out together. On occasion we skipped going out into the field, and instead went back to the pad and put on some Ronnie Laws or Gary Bartz, firing up a joint or two. As a young child, Tex had witnessed his mother stab his father to death, and that vision was always with him. We had both proclaimed that if something had to be done, we wanted to be together. If one of us were assigned to go out without the other, we always called, but I had not heard anything from Tex, not a word. That was not like him.

I opened the front door to be confronted with an ugly, overcast day. A light rain was beginning to fall. I picked up the Sunday paper and broke the rubber band. It opened onto a staggering headline, almost knocking me to the ground: **PANTHER FOUND SHOT DEAD ON RICH-MOND STREET**. I frantically scanned the article, looking for a clue, any clue that could tell me something, anything that would ease my fears. The dead Panther was identified as Louis "Tex" Johnson.

Outside my apartment, I gathered with Rollins Reid, House Man, and others in the soft rain as we tried to make sense of this disaster. We took long swigs of Johnnie Walker Red, trying to deaden the pain. Not only was Tex dead, but also Flores was wounded; he had gone into hiding. At that moment, I only wanted to kill the pain. I had already been numb for almost ten years, ever since the death of Welton Armstead, the first Panther killed in Seattle. For me, that was ten funerals ago. I just wanted to get fucked up, but it was no use. I couldn't forget Tex's smiling face.

I learned later that Huey had overridden Flores's assignment and replaced me with another comrade, who, in a panic, accidentally fired the fatal round that killed Tex. Tex was wearing a blue jumpsuit, which we often wore on missions of this sort. Also, several M-16s were found at the scene. The party attempted to distance itself from the debacle, later revealed to have been an attempt to silence a witness in Huey's upcoming trial. Tex's body went unclaimed. He lay alone on the streets of Richmond, California.

The following days and months would see the party sliding into a pit of no return. As a result of Tex's death and the aborted hit, a congressional investigation began to probe the internal activities of the Black Panther Party. In response, Huey sent several comrades from the security squad under ground, including Bethune. The horror of what had happened unfolded slowly. The night of the attempted hit, Nelson Malloy, a comrade from Winston-Salem who worked in the medical clinic, had been asked to take the wounded Flores to the emergency room. At the hospital, the nurse called the police. Flores and Nelson fled the hospital and caught a flight to Las Vegas, where we had just opened a branch community center. Huey sent a hit team to Las Vegas. They found Nelson and drove him into the desert, where he was shot several times and buried in a shallow grave, only to be discovered alive by passersby. Nelson was taken to the hospital and then went straight back to North Carolina. Tragically, he was paralyzed for life.

One evening, while I was sitting in the school cafeteria in what was to be my last political education class, Big Bob appeared in the doorway and motioned for me to come over.

"A. D., the servant wants you to go pick up all of the weapons and dump them in the bay. Here's some money for the U-Haul truck," he said, handing me a two-page list of addresses. "Get the biggest truck you can," he added, as I was heading out the door. Big Bob always seemed the same, no matter what was transpiring—no emotion, no digression, just straight ahead.

I looked at the long list of the locations of the weapons. I left immediately, taking James Aaron with me to carry out our final mission. For the next seven hours we crawled in attics, beneath houses, beneath porches, and in other odd, hard-to-reach places, gathering the entire armament of the Black Panther Party, with the exception of shotguns and hand weapons. At 3 a.m. we made our way to the middle of the San Mateo Bridge in a drizzling rain. We parked. James Aaron and I had said very little during our gathering mission. We both knew the end was near. We also knew that if we got caught with this illegal cargo we would both go away for a long time.

We occasionally puffed on a joint, trying to deaden our senses. So much had happened in such a short time. A California Highway Patrol car lazily drove by. After it was out of sight, we jumped into action, opening up the back of the long truck. We began to pull and toss crates, trunks, suitcases, AK-47s, M-16s, 9mm submachine guns, a .50-caliber machine gun, a long antiaircraft weapon, and endless trunks of ammo. We watched the party's armaments fall into the dark, cold waters of the San Francisco Bay. I came across my .30-caliber assault carbine, the twin of Elmer's, which we had purchased together. For a moment I stood and reflected on how we had spray-painted the carbines black, carving "All Power to the People" in the wooden stock, with our initials. I looked at the "A. D." one last time before I reluctantly tossed it in with the rest of the weaponry that had helped us to be the most feared and powerful political organization in American history.

Unloading the truck seemed to take us forever. The next night I was back at the bridge alone, discarding the remainder of the weapons. I made it home safely, exhausted, falling onto the bed, relieved to be done. Suddenly, something caught my eye in the closet. There were four beautiful, black M-16s with several clips and boxes of ammo, looking very seductive. Big Bob must have dropped them off. For a second I thought maybe I would keep these for myself, but I remembered the Panther oath we had all taken when we joined the party: *Obey all your orders in all your actions.* I knew this would be a dangerous time not to obey the orders given me. I jumped up and grabbed the weapons and ammo, drove down to the Oakland-Alameda Estuary, and tossed the sleek black weapons into the night, listening as they splashed into the water.

35

The End of the Line

Soul searching
Looking inside . . .
Soul searching
Digging a little bit deeper
Gotta keep on . . . Tryin'!
                    —Average White Band, "Digging Deeper," 1976

Tex's death had a heavy impact on all of us. His happy-go-
lucky, comical ways had put everyone at ease, yet he could be serious and
fearless when needed. He and Naomi had just started seeing each other.
Both of them had been moving from relationship to relationship until they
discovered their love for one another. Now, Naomi was walking around like
a zombie. For Lola, who was already unstable, his death was the defining
event that pushed her over the brink, from which she would never recover.
For her young mind, it was one too many losses, one too many contradictions. Something inside of her snapped. She slowly began to transform from
the person she was into someone she wasn't. Before Tex's death she did not
drink or smoke weed. She was always home with the kids in the evening.
She had always been conscientious and close to our little family.

We were all trying to dull our senses, trying to deny what was happening, that our revolutionary family was coming to an end and we would all

have to make a decision when to leave our slowly disintegrating army. When to step outside the tent and face life on our own. Those of us who were left were just barely holding on, functioning day to day, minute to minute.

Flores's absence was also felt. He had joined the Southern California chapter at seventeen. Flores was as smooth and calm as a clear morning sky. He was the only one in the security squad who never seemed to cross the line—he never got drunk, never overindulged; he followed the party line, yet was still flexible enough to allow others to bend the rules and policies. He had always treated me with the utmost respect.

We knew we were the last of the warriors, the last of a dying breed. We had become a strong force, feeling invincible at times. We had considered ourselves as eternal soldiers, always thinking we would fight the enemy to victory or to death. What we had failed to realize was that the enemy, at times, was us.

The once formidable Panther military might was now in ruins. For twelve years, people like Landon and Randy Williams, Field Marshal Don Cox, Orleander Harrison, Robert Bay, Geronimo, Valentine, and many others had maintained the military power and expertise of the party. All these comrades were now either imprisoned, dead, on the run, or disillusioned. The weapons themselves were at the bottom of the San Francisco Bay.

My mind in a daze, I felt no more enthusiasm, no more hope that we could continue to move the party forward. And, after all, that is what we lived for. Without the hope of a future, there seemed to be no more reason to live, no reason to exist. We had come so close to achieving something unprecedented in American history: the nonviolent capture of an American city by progressive revolutionary forces.

In late March '78, I was sometimes the driver for Huey, occasionally driving him down to UC Santa Cruz, where he was still pursuing a PhD in philosophy. During those drives our eyes would meet in the rearview mirror. He was distant, rarely speaking. I knew him more deeply than he suspected, especially the good in him and the complexity of his character.

He once asked me, "Aaron, how do you keep that inner tube from growing around your stomach? Mine is getting big."

"I stopped eating red meat," I answered, wondering if he would engage in conversation. He didn't. I wondered what was on his mind. What was he thinking about? I thought back to the time I first laid eyes on that baby face. He was behind steel-blue bars in the Alameda County Jail in

April 1968. Those were better days for him. Now it seemed nothing he did made any sense.

I wondered what had happened to him between our first meeting and his release from prison in 1974. In prison he had been brilliant in his leadership of the party, inspiring us to move forward against all odds. Many of us had thought that upon his release, Huey would set about correcting the mistakes others had made in handling the party while he was incarcerated, that he would set everything right. But something had happened to him. Huey used to joke, "A funny thing happened on the way to the forum. . . ." In the case of Huey P. Newton, whatever happened was deadly serious. Most of us will never know the truth.

There would be speculation that the government used some form of mind control or psychological experimentation on Huey while he was locked up in the California penal system. Maybe he never meant for the Black Panther Party to grow into a national and international organization. Maybe the party would have developed differently if the government attacks on us had not been so fierce that they led to the elimination of key leaders like Fred Hampton and Bunchy Carter, and the exile of important figures like Don Cox and Pete O'Neal. Maybe things would have been different if Bobby Seale had not been locked up in Connecticut upon Huey's release. According to many memos between J. Edgar Hoover and Richard Nixon, the government's goal was to eliminate the Black Panther Party by 1969. It was due to the ferocity and determination of the party and its members that we survived as long as we did.

It was a cloudy day when a knock came at my door, and there stood Randy Williams, broad-shouldered, muscle-bound from nine-and-a-half years in Soledad Prison. He had done his time as if it had been a stroll in the park, and at the conclusion of his sentence, he came straight back to the party, as if the revolution were still occurring. Poison had recently done the same.

"Hey, Aaron. Huey told me to come by to pick up the keys to the car and your .45."

I was not surprised or particularly concerned, for I knew this would push me closer to leaving. I handed him the keys. I picked up my Colt Combat Commander, the weapon that had been my constant companion the past four years. It was like giving up a part of me, something familiar and close. Reluctantly, I handed the gun to Randy.

"Oh, yeah," Randy added. "You are to report to the school for maintenance."

We barely looked at each other as he left.

The door had been opened, but it took one more incident to push me over the threshold. One evening soon after, I was part of a truckload of comrades dropped off in San Francisco's Broadway District, a popular destination for tourists and monied hipsters. We were passing out flyers for an event in support of Huey's upcoming trial. I went into a popular spot called Enrico's and began handing out flyers to the customers. I approached a table where a white couple and a Black gentleman were sitting.

The Black gentleman took one look at the flyer and jumped up and began a tirade. "Huey Newton is nothing but a two-bit gangster," he angrily yelled. "He's a murderer and a two-bit thug!"

I looked more closely at the man as I prepared to respond, and recognized the face of someone I had once admired. It was Bill Cosby. I had spent my late nights as a young teenager watching Bill Cosby and Robert Culp as tennis-playing spies on the TV show *I Spy*, a groundbreaking series for its time. There were very few if any Black actors in leading television roles, so it was a complete joy to watch this cool and funny Black cat on TV.

I was surprised at how short Cosby was in person. I was also shocked at his explosive anger and his disparaging remarks about Huey. After he finished his tirade I could do nothing but walk out. I had no defense of our embattled leader. Everything Bill Cosby said was true. The remarks had hit home for me. And coming from Bill Cosby made it worse—not necessarily because of what I had once felt for him as a performer, but more because he had gone on to represent everything we were against. He was fast becoming the poster boy for the new integrated America, the "me" generation that espoused get-rich individualism, stripping away the cultural communalism that Black Americans once had, communalism that put our elders, children, and community first. Cosby and others in the new Black elite would go on to become filthy rich pushing consumer brands like Jell-O in an almost minstrel fashion, with no political consciousness, no talk of struggle or change for humanity, as if Martin Luther King Jr., Malcom X, and the others had given their lives for nothing.

On the ride back in the truck I said very little. How had it all come to this? I felt both a great sense of sadness and smoldering anger. Sadness that the once powerful Black Panther Party was on its knees, its dedicated members scattered throughout the world, dead, imprisoned, or exiled. Anger that, without the party, there would be no more response to the Bill Cosbys of the world. They would be held up as the models for Black America, ensuring the end of what we had cherished, our families, elders, and communities.

The next day I was driving across the Bay Bridge, coming from a party demonstration in support of Synanon, a drug recovery program, which was under fire from the state and from former participants. Huey had ordered us to go to this demonstration. During the marching, I had no desire to be there. I no longer had any energy to represent falsehoods. As I made my way across the long, gray bridge, I realized it was almost ten years to the day that I had passed this way with Tommy Jones and Robert Bay, the two comrades who had ushered me into the party. We had stood together on that hot, muggy night on 7th Street in West Oakland, along with Orleander, Randy, and Landon, our black leather coats hiding our weapons as we defied the Oakland police. I thought about the many times I had ridden across the bridge with comrades, headed to the Frisco office or to the distribution center, to meetings, to the airport to pick up or drop off a weary Panther. Too many faces of too many beautiful men and women willing to stand strong against monumental odds, the constant arrests and attacks, the thirty-five dead comrades. We had won over the people with our programs, our beliefs in our leaders and ourselves.

"It's all over," I said to myself, looking out over the bay. I had held on until the end, and for me the end was now.

I arrived at the office and was confronted by Lonnie D, the acting OD. "Here's fifty papers," he said.

"I am not going out to the field," I responded. "I'm taking a leave of absence." I think that was the first time I had ever refused a direct order.

"You need to call Big Bob," Lonnie D replied.

I called Big Bob and he said to come over, so I headed to the house on 10th Street. Big Bob had just finished showering. His huge body was draped in a towel. Looking in the mirror, he shaved the whiskers from his face. I noticed his .45 in its leather holster, hanging on the door.

"What's up, A. D.?"

"Bob, I need to take a year off to rest and think things over."

There were some comrades that were fearful of Robert Heard, but I had always felt comfortable around Big Bob. He nodded and went into the other room. After a brief phone call he came back.

"Okay, A. D. That's cool. I talked to the servant and he said it was all right. Just stay in touch."

"Right on. I'll see you later."

I left. At that moment, I became a civilian for the first time in ten years. I had done it. I had successfully separated myself from the party without fully cutting myself off, which is more than I can say for most. The usual voluntary exit was made late at night or while out in the field, under the duress of fear. I was glad to be free, yet I was stunned by all that had happened. What I was going to do now, I had no idea.

I had been staying with a young lady named Pat McElroy. I met Pat out at a club one night and went home with her, eventually moving in. Lola and I had broken up, as she had fallen under the spell of Bethune. Part of me hated to leave her behind, but I had little choice. The party was the only real family Lola ever had. Pat was a free spirit like me. She was the perfect person to be with while I was making my split from the Black Panther Party.

I remember running down the street the following day, jumping up in the air as high as I could go, trying to touch the sky, feeling elated, feeling free, freer than I had ever felt.

That evening, though, the joy quickly turned to sorrow as I went through the old copies of *The Black Panther* lying before me: tattered pictures of Bunchy Carter, Fred Hampton, Chairman Bobby, the revolutionary art of Matilaba and Emory, and images of the New York 21 and of fallen comrades. I attempted to describe for Pat the memories from these past ten years of my life, and the significance of the pictures of these brave men and women I had grown to love. I turned to hide the tears slowly dribbling down my cheeks. I looked at the clock. It was 6 p.m., the time when all the comrades were returning from the field and probably getting ready to eat at Central Headquarters. I hurriedly grabbed the phone and dialed the numbers permanently etched in my mind.

"Central Headquarters, may I help you?"

"Hello, Lola."

"Hello, Aaron. How are you doing?" She sounded hard, trying not to show her sadness.

"Okay. And you?" I knew her too well. I knew she was hurt by my departure.

One by one, I eventually spoke to as many of my former comrades as possible. Later that night I deluged myself in drink and herb, trying to sort things out.

The following week I received a call from Al Armour, one of the members of the Los Angeles cadre.

"A. D. Come by. I want to talk with you."

When I got to Al's house, his bags were packed. "Take me to the airport. I'm going back to LA."

Al was one of the kindest people I had ever met. He had joined the party while attending college at UCLA. He was in the shootout when the Los Angeles pigs raided the chapter office in '69. He was a veteran soldier, a good brother, and he had just begun showing symptoms of multiple sclerosis.

"Aren't you going to tell someone?" I answered.

"No, man. Just take me to the airport."

I felt very close to Al Armour. He and I were similar in many ways, and he was as close as a brother to me. We had gone on several missions together, and, selfishly, I was not ready for him to disappear from my life. Reluctantly, I drove Al to the Oakland Airport, hugged him, and bid him farewell. I watched him hobble along with his bags, looking professorial in those big, thick eyeglasses covering a light-brown face as dear to me as that of Tex and Deacon and House Man and all the other comrades who worked in the trenches night and day, overcoming tremendous odds. That was the last time I would lay eyes on Al Armour.

Al's departure did not just leave me with a well of emotion. The very act of my taking him to the airport would sever my connection to the party, cutting me off permanently, leaving me alone and unconnected to anything. Big Bob and Lola had been driving in the opposite direction and had spotted Al and me heading toward the airport. When Huey found out, he was furious. He had Big Bob call me with a threatening message.

"A. D., Huey said you are helping people to leave the party. Therefore, you have twenty-four hours to get your mothafuckin' ass out of Oakland."

The words reverberated in my mind. Fear was the first emotion to surface, slowly replaced by anger. Huey's paranoia had reached its peak. Uncertainty, fear, and resentment fought for dominance of my mind, making it difficult to focus on any one thing, any single action. I hopped in Pat's '72 Datsun and drove deep up into the Berkeley hills to an isolated spot overlooking a deep valley flooded with green trees. The cloudy day was slowly turning to darkness. There I sat for several hours.

I had given ten years of my life to the party, the people, and the ment. Ten long years in the trenches, many sleepless nights, sacrificing everything, even my family, for the sole purpose of attaining the goals of the Black Panther Party. The party had been my life. It had become my family, replacing my biological family, relegating my parents to second place. Poppy had been my hero and my leader. Huey eventually took on those roles, in many ways becoming a father figure. It's never easy to cut yourself off from your family, no matter how much they have mistreated you, no matter how many times they have let you down. You hang on, hoping that someday, somehow, things will change. And it is even more painful, more devastating when they kick you out the door, slamming it behind you.

I did not really fear Huey, nor did I hate him. However, I was angry and disgusted with him, as a child may be disgusted with an addict father who has continually taken the wrong road, yet the child hopes, futilely, that someday things might be as they were before.

That night, I went back to Pat's house. There was no way I could leave Oakland. My connection to Oakland was all I had left—its people, its many visual signposts of my past. I decided I would not flee in fear, but I would need to be cautious. There weren't many comrades left, and I knew quite well their modes of operation. For several weeks I slept in dirty flop-houses in San Francisco, coming back to Pat's house during the day, waiting until things died down. During that period, one day I ran into Randy Williams in the Mission District. When he approached with a smile on his face, I knew not to have any fear. He said, "Man, I left the party. Huey's gone crazy."

I wasn't surprised when Randy told me Huey wanted me dead. We chatted for a few minutes before he went on his way.

One day while at Pat's house picking up some things, I saw something out the window that sent fear racing through my entire body. It was Big Bob in the black Lincoln Town Car. I watched as he slowly got out. I ran and grabbed my .38 and waited by the door. There was a knock. I wanted to answer. Part of me sensed that Bob was coming by for consolation, but the other part of me, the fearful, paranoid part of me, held back. Bob eventually drove off, leaving me to wonder not just about the purpose of his visit, but also why I did not open the door.

A week later I learned that Big Bob had broken down in tears, telling Huey he could no longer take it. He had hung on as long as he could, holding on to the family to which we had all pledged our undying love. When I heard this I was guilt-ridden for not having opened that door. It would be many, many moons before I saw the gentle giant again.

I remember when Big Bob lent me his copy of *The Book of Five Rings*, a guide to the way of the samurai. It was a book Huey had ordered us to study. Big Bob was the quintessential samurai: hard, soft, warm, cold, merciful, merciless. He was a huge presence, not just in physical size, but in terms of his humanity as well. In many respects our lives in the party often mirrored those of the samurai. We lived to fight and to die upholding a certain honor and a certain code, while all along living our lives as the freest of men and women. We fought for our warlord for the unification of our people, until the end. Now there was nothing more to fight for.

The end seemed to come so fast. We had passed through so many phases, so many ups and downs, always emerging victorious. The early days of self-defense, when Huey led armed, defiant young men and women against the racist police forces, set an example that spread through America and created an identity of resistance and rebellion that put Huey and the party in the international spotlight. In Seattle, people like LewJack, Bobby White, Bobby Harding, Mike Tagawa, Chester, Steve, and others armed themselves, as did thousands of others across America at the time, serving notice to the pig power structure that this was a new day. The retaliation from the police was swift, relentless, deadly. Our minister of defense was wounded defending himself and was sentenced to prison, a pattern that would repeat with many others across America.

We implemented services and programs for the poor, the needy, the downtrodden, capturing the hearts and minds of millions throughout the world. In response, the US government waged an unprecedented war, covert as well as open, against the Black Panther Party and its members in particular, and against the left as a whole. We buried many of our comrades. We left even more locked away for life in dungeons and prisons throughout the empire. Yes, we made grave mistakes that eventually contributed to our demise. But we were always able to rebound, rebuild, recoup our losses, and recruit new soldiers into the ranks. It was the incremental dismantling of the party by its own founder that sealed the end to the physical organization of the Black Panther Party, leaving us with only bittersweet memories.

For those returning to their families and communities, there would be no cheering crowds, no open arms, no therapy, no counseling. Marsha

Taylor, formerly Marsha Turner, committed suicide, I was told. The brilliant young woman who at age sixteen was national coordinator of the Breakfast Program had married Van Taylor, a captain of the San Francisco chapter, and they had left the party together around 1972. I heard that Calvin Bennett, a tall, dark brother from the Oakland chapter, who had worked security at the LampPost, had also taken his own life. Poison died homeless on the streets of Berkeley. Some fell into despair, joining the masses of walking wounded in America. Many eventually picked themselves up and dusted themselves off, and went on to become lawyers, professors, engineers, entertainers, filmmakers; many others continued their own forms of activism by becoming gang counselors or committing themselves to another cause; some went into politics. Many continued to do the work of the party in some form or another.

As for me, my own journey was not yet concluded.

36

The Last Hurrah

I'd like to fly far away from here
Where my mind can be fresh and clear
And I'd find the love that I long to see
Everybody can be what they wanna be

—Commodores, "Zoom," 1977

In April 1978, there seemed to be so many possibilities before me. Yet I felt constrained by my past, trapped by memories of glorious days and periods of anger and despair.

Poppy asked me to come back to Seattle and work for Boeing or go back to school at the University of Washington. Unfortunately, neither of those choices held any interest for me. I had no desire to leave Oakland. I was still numb and would remain so for many years. I just wanted to find a job and work and live normally as a twenty-eight-year-old Black man. After ten years of fighting for justice, organizing, packing heat, and living as dangerously as one could in America, I was ready for a new life.

My first opportunity for employment came from none other than Big Malcolm. We ran into each other on the Bay Bridge, and I followed him to his house in Daly City, atop the highest hill. His dining room picture window opened onto a full view of San Francisco and the East Bay. We sat down and talked and smoked some pot, renewing our friendship.

Malcolm was working as a project manager for the San Francisco Housing Authority, responsible for the contract hiring for the authority's renovation of the public housing projects. His wife, Jeri, had moved back to Alaska, leaving the kids with Malcolm.

"Dixon! Wha's goin' on, buddy? You finally got the fuck away from that crazy shit over there in Oakland." Malcolm was the same Malcolm I'd first met back in 1968, a man who never minced words. "Huey's a crazy motherfucker."

"Yeah, it was time for me to leave," I replied. "Shit was going too crazy for me." I paused for a moment, thinking, *This is a very sensitive time and subject for me.*

"Say, Malcolm, can you help me with a job?" I asked.

"Yeah, buddy," he responded. "You're right on time. The Housing Authority is hiring for youth counselors at the Valencia Gardens in the Mission District."

I was excited. That type of work seemed right up my alley—organizing and working with the future revolutionaries. I put in my application, got an interview, and was given a starting date. Finally, I thought, I could make some decent money and enjoy life. But it was not to be.

Before I could even start, the funding for the youth counseling jobs was cut due to an initiative on the ballot to roll back property taxes. Property tax funds paid for many social programs as well as teachers' salaries. My new job was lost, as were thousands of others. This kind of property tax initiative would become a new weapon of the right for cutting social spending. These initiatives would sweep across the country at a time when many of the cuts would result in the loss of frontline programs that might have helped stave off the crack epidemic just beyond the horizon.

Naturally, I was disheartened that the job didn't pan out, but I was used to such things. All was not lost. I ran into a childhood sweetheart, Carol Bushnell, who had chased after the very shy child I was in elementary school. The last time we had seen each other was back in 1971, while I was speaking at Portland State. We had a brief encounter and then lost contact. I learned from Carol that she had gotten pregnant and had a miscarriage, which surprised and shook me. Now, she was married with two children. Her husband helped me get a job as a tour bus driver for Lorries Tours of San Francisco. I drove a large minibus, picking up tourists at the various San Francisco hotels and depositing them at the San Francisco

Airport. They paid for the service and often gave me a tip. I picked up new passengers at the airport and dropped them off at designated hotels.

This was the perfect job for me after all the driving I had done in the party. I did not have to report all the customers, or the tips, which put some extra cash in my empty pockets. These were happy days for me, driving for Lorries, as brief as they were. The San Francisco summer sun was bright, the tourists were pleasant, and I was working, finally. I was feeling free.

One day after work, I went into the garage to chat with Dino, a brother from Texas with a twang to his speech. He was working for the company as a mechanic.

"Man, I sure wish I could drive. I was driving but my license got suspended," Dino sighed.

Being the type always willing to share how I beat the system, I responded, "I have a suspended license too, but they didn't check."

"Is that right?" he asked, giving me the side-eye, tilting his head.

The following day when I went into work, I was fired. My big mouth had cost me my dream job. I went into the garage to confront Dino. He caught me before I could start in.

"Baby boy," he said, "I am sorry about them firing you. I quit this mothafucker anyways."

He took off his overalls and we walked out of the building together. With his bug eyes and thick eyelashes, Dino told me, "Baby boy, don't worry." He said, "I am going to teach you how to hustle. Meet me down at the club under the Embarcadero at 9 p.m. sharp."

I was disappointed about losing a job I enjoyed so much. And I wasn't sure what to make of a character like Dino. For the past ten years of my life, most of my time had been in the company of revolutionaries, organizers, and militants. This was a new world to me, and I guess a new era as well.

That night, I met Dino at the club in Frisco's Embarcadero district. When I walked in, I almost didn't recognize him. There he was—in all his splendor, as if he had switched characters. It was like turning a page in a book. He was dressed in a brown pinstriped suit, a pink tie, and a brown brim, holding a pool cue.

"Baby boy. Do you play pool?"

"Yeah, I play a little," I replied, even though I hadn't played in many years.

"Let me finish this game," he said. He quickly disposed of the cat he was playing and started counting his winnings. Dino could obviously play some pool.

"Man, there is a lot of money to be made in these streets. I am gonna show you how to make some money," he said.

And that is how I, somewhat reluctantly, entered the "fast life." It was a colorful world, sometimes a very fun and adventurous world, and often a dangerous place to be caught up. The Vietnam War had stepped up the drug trade, heroin in particular, which meant more money on the streets, and more money flowing in the nightlife. The after-hours scene was a separate universe of pimps and their prostitutes, dope dealers, gamblers, white-collar criminals, and boosters, often sharing company with respected professionals and public figures. The fast life, as it is known in the ghetto, referred to the illegal subset of this world, and was a vibrant element of many cities. Oakland and Frisco were no different. It was our black market, a hidden economy that permitted Black people to survive and even thrive during very difficult economic and violent times. A community functioning within the larger community, the fast life had its own rules, laws, and morals. And violating one of these laws could be detrimental. It was an adult world, no kids allowed, a dynamic that would soon change.

Pat had already been part of this world. Her father was a longtime, old-school hustler, as was her mother, who also played the numbers and horses daily. Pat's mother entertained boosters and prostitutes at her house and frequently babysat their kids, along with taking care of a few foster kids. Yet most of Pat's seven brothers and sisters worked legitimate jobs, except for Marvin, the youngest son.

Marvin was a well-groomed and very sophisticated pimp. Though he could not read or write, he owned a fleet of fine cars, including Bentleys and Mercedes. An anomaly among pimps, he didn't allow his girls to walk the streets or use drugs or alcohol. He sent his girls to Las Vegas to work at the Mustang Ranch, and they would wire their money to Pat, who was Marvin's business support and confidante.

Pat transported the women from the Bay Area to Nevada. She helped Marvin with aspects of the business he did not have the skills for. Pat was beautiful and very intelligent, both sophisticated and down-to-earth. She had a knack for making money and acquiring nice things—mostly on the legal side. But from time to time, she dabbled on the other side. Such as the hot jewelry she'd buy and sell. Or the boosters who'd come by with trunkloads of stolen clothes that she'd buy for herself at a steep discount. And transporting her brother's cars or the women to Las Vegas. Like many Black people at the time, she had one foot in each world.

One thing Pat and I had in common was a taste for adventure. We both liked to take risks. When she wasn't working as a bookkeeper and I wasn't hanging out with Dino, she and I were out enjoying life. Or, rather, she was showing me how to enjoy life, as I did not have much experience in that area. We drove down to Monterey and Carmel, spending days at the beach; we hung out in Santa Cruz, sipping margaritas. Smoking pot on Union Street in San Francisco, visiting the clubs. Or going to the racetrack.

Although I was having fun, there was still a well of sadness inside me. My mind was attempting to understand and sort through the fallen house of cards that made up my life so far. The death of Tex, the sudden self-destruction of the party, and the painful separation from Lola and the kids and the other comrades: these things were always lurking in the back of my mind. I also felt the need and desire to connect with my two children, Aaron Patrice and Nisaa.

One day Dino called me over to his apartment in Frisco. He had a bunch of blank payroll checks he'd gotten from a girlfriend, a check protector machine, and a typewriter. We had bought several phony birth certificates from a skinny old brother with a storefront on Fillmore. For fifty dollars, he could create a legitimate-looking birth certificate with any name and birthdate you chose. Dino and I went down to the licensing department to get state IDs for the birth certificates. The following Friday, Dino typed up the checks, using the check protector to enter the amounts, and making them out to the names on the state IDs.

"So, baby boy, you gonna run these checks?" he asked. "I'll stay here since I did most of the work."

"Yeah, man, I'll do it," I replied. He handed me about ten checks and off I went. At the first eight banks it was a breeze. The checks ranged from $723 to $750, an average bi-weekly paycheck for an honest Joe—but I was no longer an honest Joe.

At the last bank I entered, on Pacific Street, the teller turned to the bank manager, who happened to be a tall, slender, light-brown-complexioned sister. "Let me call the company and check this out," she said.

When she turned her back to dial the phone, I quickly exited the bank. I remember laughing while running to the car to make my getaway. In my mind, I had conducted an assault on the financial symbols of the system, the banks and corporations. But, of course, these funds were not going to the people, per se. Dino and I split the take and enjoyed ourselves for a few days.

Late one Saturday night, Dino and I went over to Frisco to check out the late-night scene. We ended up at an after-hours club in Hunters Point, where I met an older sister who had spent some time in Seattle. Her name was Lydia, and we knew some people in common, hustlers of some kind. "So, Aaron. What are you into? What do you do?" she asked.

I answered confidently, "I am in the paper game."

She asked, "Can you cash a $37,000 check?"

"Yeah, I can cash it," I replied, as the concept of $37,000 ran through my mind.

"Give me your number and I'll give you a call," she said, and then split.

One morning I was lying in bed with Pat when the phone rang. It was Lydia. "Meet me on the corner of Union and 24th Street in front of the bank at 11:30," she said.

"Okay, I'll see you there." I put on my best suit and tie, combed my Afro, and left. I was a little nervous, yet more filled with a daring that at times bordered on stupidity. That was the way I was, and I was not ready to change.

I pulled up in front of the bank and sat in the car, reading the daily paper. The door opened. It was Lydia. A large woman with a scar on her cheek, she was what you might call "rough-looking," but she was as real as you get. And that is often what I looked for in a person.

"Hey, Aaron. Here's the check and ID. Go to the brother with the Afro. He is working with us. Call me when you're done, and get the money in cashier's checks."

"Okay," I said.

I casually walked into the bank and went up to the brother with the big Afro as instructed. I handed him the check; he turned to the manager, who okayed the transaction. And out the door I went with $37,000 in cashier's checks.

Afterward, I met up with Lydia in Burlington, a swank area outside of San Francisco. She lived in a big house in the hills with her daughter.

The paper game was her chosen profession. Aside from a prison stint, seemingly she had done well for herself. My slice of the pie was $13,000. In a short time, I had gone from cashing small checks to big checks, with bigger ones yet to come.

I was rapidly becoming embedded in this new world. The same emotional armor I had donned to protect myself as a revolutionary would be worn for this life of crime. My hanging with Dino in the nightlife was beginning to create tension between me and Pat. Besides, I had met a young, beautiful woman out at the club Long Island on Third Street. I found out that she was working for a young pimp I had seen in the after-hours clubs, who drove a brown Bentley. I eventually convinced her to give up prostitution and to try modeling.

With the money I made from the bank job, I decided to move out on my own. I got a nice one-bedroom penthouse in Alameda near the beach, picked up some fine furniture, and bought a 1974 Spitfire convertible, a little green two-seater. I also bought a quarter pound of coke, some cut, and a triple-beam scale. Taking up a suggestion of Pat's, I began selling coke in the after-hours scene. I often packed a long-barreled .38 in the small of my back, beneath the fabric of a nice double-breasted suit. In these after-hours clubs, you never knew whom you might run into.

Sometimes it was old comrades. While doing business in an after-hours club on Divisadero called the Living Room, I ran into comrades Ellis White, Russell Washington, and Dale Rosco. At first I wasn't sure how I would be greeted, but their smiles put me at ease. We chatted and smoked some weed. I sold them a gram of coke and we parted company. At another after-hours club where I was the coke provider, I ran into Captain Dexter Woods and John Brown, both formerly of the San Francisco branch. They had sided with Eldridge during the split. I hadn't seen either of them since that day at National Headquarters on Peralta Street back in 1972, when comrades were secretly choosing sides. John Brown was still wearing the brown brim that was his signature piece. Dexter was still sporting his smooth-looking Afro. We greeted each other coolly yet respectfully. I was pleasantly surprised that they came to my defense when an irate customer complained about the coke I had sold him, becoming belligerent. It so happened that night I had not bothered to pack any heat, leaving myself defenseless. John and Dexter interceded, and the matter was quashed. I was grateful to them for having my back. I had always respected them, regardless of the choice they had made in '72. And I know they respected me as well.

One day, out of the blue, I got a call from Lola. She needed a place to stay for a couple days, and spent them curled in a ball at the end of my king-size brass bed. This was not the same Lola I had known, who had a most beautiful smile and was as sweet as a bowl of sugar. The violent death of her mentor, Sam Napier, the death of Tex, and the disintegration of the party had a devastating impact on her young mind. On top of that, Bethune had viciously assaulted her because she was hanging out with some Rastafarians. That had, I think, pushed her further over the edge. She did not talk much, nor could I coax that beautiful, disarming smile out of her. It was terribly sad to see her like this. Eventually, she would take her younger sister Valerie, and her two children, Natalie and little Damon, to Jamaica, where they ended up living in the mountains in a Rastafarian commune.

I was spending less time with Dino as I accelerated forward in the fast life. A cat named Kenny Hampton rented a studio next to Pat's place. He had just gotten out of San Quentin and was a member of the Black Guerrilla Family. He was a crazy, grizzled-looking dude, but he was fun to be around. Kenny was very buff, with gray eyes and a short Afro, giving him the appearance of a dangerous man. We started hanging out together, going to the gym, sometimes sharing an Olde English 800. At the club Long Island, near Hunters Point, I met another brother named Donny, who had just gotten out of the service. He was a hothead. Soon he and his buddy, along with Kenny, started selling coke for me. The four of us cased out a dope house and a bank on Union Street with the intent of robbing them, but the plan never came together.

Meanwhile, Pat and I had concocted a scheme to embezzle from the company she worked for as a bookkeeper, over time totaling around $35,000. We opened up a PO box and a business bank account in the name of a phony company. A friend of Pat's who worked at the bank helped us set up the account. Pat would issue checks to the phony company on the PO box, and I would deposit them in the business account. A sister who worked for a large insurance company in Marin County gave us a check for $60,000, which we deposited in our business account, giving her a cut.

Even though Pat already owned a nice Cadillac Coupe de Ville, we decided to buy a new car. She wanted a Brougham, the finest in late '70s luxury cars, so we purchased a yellow, custom Brougham with a Rolls-Royce grill and a Continental spare tire mounted on the back. We also bought a safe for storing our illegal loot.

The more money we made, the lazier I became. I decided to move back in with Pat. The cocaine hustle had dried up, and I didn't exactly mind. I had never liked selling anything, except for *The Black Panther* paper, and I certainly didn't like selling cocaine. Pat, however, was not going to settle for mediocrity and began to put pressure on me to bring in more money. On a trip to Los Angeles, she had met a Jamaican who professed to have bales of marijuana for sale. I called him to set up a deal and paid his way to Las Vegas, where we arranged to meet for the transaction.

I flew into the city of glitter and lost dreams, wide-eyed with wonder at the excessive wealth flaunted by almost everyone around me. I checked into the hotel and waited for my contact to show.

He was a medium-sized, brown-skinned, average-looking brother with a slight accent, not intimidating in any way. He put me completely at ease. In the morning I gave him five grand and waited for my product. It never came. I frantically checked the streets and casinos, trying to track down the cat who had taken off with my money. In my panic, I even thought about contacting the police—but, after calming down, I realized that was not an option. Finally, I tucked my tail and returned to Oakland.

The more I thought about being ripped off, the angrier I got. I was not used to being swindled. In the party, we did not let such incidents go without retribution, so I put on my steel face, rented a Pinto, borrowed Kenny's sawed-off shotgun and took my long-barreled .38, and headed to Los Angeles to get my money back.

I checked into a hotel near the airport and began to try to track down my prey. After many calls, I managed to speak with a Mexican who said he also had been ripped off, and would arrange for the Jamaican to meet me at a garage next to his house in East LA at 7 p.m.

I arrived early and sat in the car with the sawed-off shotgun across my lap, waiting and watching. I was now a free agent, a solo operator, no longer part of a whole, no longer with the support of comrades who had vowed undying love, who were ready, willing, and able to give their lives in sacrifice for a comrade. I mulled over different scenarios. What if this were a setup? What if there were others coming? What if they were armed? In the party, in such a situation I would likely have suspended this kind of thinking and gotten on with the action, but my inner voice, the voice that had helped me to escape death on many other occasions, was speaking to me in a steady cadence.

I sat in silence. Out of nowhere, a black cat slowly walked across the street in a front of my Pinto. To me, that was a clear sign to abort this operation. I was mildly superstitious, but considered together, there were too many factors to ignore. I swallowed my pride, started the car, did a U-turn, and drove off.

I drove back to the hotel and put my artillery away. I went to a club down the street, sat at the bar, and ordered a margarita, trying to come to grips with my decision to retreat. People were dancing and having fun, and it occurred to me that one of the bartenders looked familiar. I was taken aback when I realized it was Brenda Dunge, my first love.

"Aaron, is that you? I heard you were dead!" she exclaimed when she saw me.

"No, I'm not dead," I responded. "How are you?" I asked, smiling and sipping my margarita.

"I left my family in Dayton, Ohio, and moved out here with my boyfriend," she replied.

Brenda was as beautiful as ever. After finishing her senior year in Seattle, she had gone back to Ohio, married her fiancé, and had two children. And now here she was in Los Angeles, looking for magic, a different kind of life, just like everyone else who came to La-la Land.

I gave her my number at the hotel and left. I didn't expect her to call, but part of me was hoping to have the chance to catch up with her. After all, she was my first love. But I never saw Brenda again.

A few days after I returned to Oakland, Pat was informed that the FBI had visited the bank that held our business account. She and I had given our oath to each other that we would not go to prison. Now we had to make a decision. In panic mode, we opted to sell her Coupe de Ville and Datsun and left the Brougham with Big Malcolm. My Spitfire had been stolen. We put our belongings in storage and rented a car for a long-distance getaway, swapping out the license plate to avoid being tracked down by the cops.

Greatly complicating matters, Tanya had finally decided to let Aaron Patrice, now ten years old, come live with me. He arrived in the middle of all this. And Mildred Center, the medical student who had volunteered at the Panther clinic, the only woman I had ever called my true love, got in touch to say she was coming to visit. She would be arriving at the San Francisco airport the same day Pat and I planned to go on the run. The timing could not have been worse. To have my son and to be with Mildred were two precious things I had dreamed of, even though I had done little on my end to make them happen. It was an excruciatingly difficult time for me, and no picnic for Pat either. My actions over the previous year and a half had been as reckless as anything I had ever done. We had both gotten caught up, and now we needed to figure a way out. Regrettably, rational decision-making was absent.

I called Mildred with some feeble reason as to why I could not keep our special rendezvous, and I told Aaron we were taking a trip to Texas. Pat's four-year-old son, Patrick, also came with us. That night, as we drove away, headed toward Reno, I glimpsed the fading lights of Oakland. As the hills and glow of Oakland disappeared, I felt a burden lift. I was leaving my Black Panther memories behind. Oddly enough, I felt some degree of freedom. Being on the run can do that to you.

Reno; Cheyenne, Wyoming; Denver, Colorado; and Albuquerque, New Mexico, all gave way to our party of runaway bandits and two kids. With Aaron Patrice and Patrick in tow, we attempted to enjoy the road trip as much as we could under the circumstances, staying in five-star hotels, swimming in the hotel pools. On the road, I started a regimen of pushups and situps, inspired by a *Sports Illustrated* article about a college football phenomenon, Herschel Walker. I also started taking pantothenic acid, a B vitamin I had read was good for reducing stress.

Our ultimate destination was Jamaica, where we could not be extradited for crimes committed in the United States, but we were first headed for Texas. Houston was experiencing the biggest economic boom in its history, fueled by the growth in the oil industry. People were relocating there from all over the country as well as overseas. Every day, contractors were cutting down acres of trees to make room for new housing developments.

We jumped in with the flow, renting a two-bedroom apartment in northwest Houston. Pat got a job in her undercover name, Amina Brown. I was using the name Calvin Worthington. Sadly and reluctantly, I realized that Aaron Patrice had to be sent back to Seattle. I could not ask him to live a life with his father on the run from the law. I started writing a short story about two runaway slaves heading West, a sort of parallel to what

Pat and I were going through. I had not picked up a pen to write in a creative fashion for almost ten years. The story seemed to beckon me, as if a hidden voice from the past were calling out to my creative side. However, the story was cut short, as was our stay in Houston.

We got word from Pat's mother that the FBI knew our location. Panicking, we put our furniture in storage in Houston, and took off for Beaumont, Texas, in the southeast corner of the state, to spend a few days with Pat's cousin, Evelyn. A petite, sweet Texan, seven months pregnant, Evelyn opened her home to us while we figured out our next move. The next day she took us on a tour of Beaumont. We tried to relax and get a feel for the town.

As Evelyn drove us through the Beaumont housing projects in the rental car, the Beaumont police began to follow us. Until now, we had gotten nary a glance from the authorities. We did not look like Texans, and why we ended up driving through the projects I can't recall. But it was enough to raise the suspicions of a small-time Southern cop.

When the red lights started flashing and the short burst from the siren began screaming, we knew we were in trouble. My mind started to spin. Evelyn stopped the car, got out, and waved back to the police car. Pat and I got out with little Patrick, acting nonchalant, as if this were just a routine stop.

Neighborhood residents were walking around, not paying us or the cops much attention, as Evelyn engaged in conversation with the officer. We knew that if the cops ran the license plate number they would discover the rental car and license plate did not match, and would eventually figure out that we were fugitives. Pat, I, and little Patrick began walking toward one of the buildings, talking to the residents, acting as normal as possible. Once we got to the building we ran inside, going down a long hallway to another door, exiting the building, continuing across the street and over an embankment until we came to a main road.

We caught a cab back to Evelyn's house, grabbed our belongings, and caught a cab to the train station. An hour later we were on a train to Chicago. We had barely escaped. Evelyn was our sacrificial lamb. We felt bad for putting her in this situation, but knew that if she were to be arrested, they would not hold her for too long.

On the train we got a private compartment. Pat and I did not say much on our journey through the Deep South up to Chicago. I wondered what little Patrick was thinking and feeling throughout this ordeal. The stress on Pat and me had been ebbing and flowing, and was definitely at high tide during this time. In Chicago I would have the opportunity to see relatives I had not seen in many years, although this was not exactly the occasion I would have chosen. But we had mastered the art of making the best of it.

We arrived in Chicago with our suitcases and caught a cab to my grandmother DeDe's house. Despite its being an unannounced visit, she was happy to see us. My grandmother was as gracious as ever. She lived alone in the large house on 71st and Calumet, the house full of memories of Grandada. He had passed away in 1968 while I was in New York, preparing to go the UN with Eldridge and the others.

There were so many childhood memories of Chicago in that house, memories of love and tradition, of childhood exploits and family unity. I thought about my father and his happy-go-lucky ways, always looking forward to the next adventure. My mother and her nurturing kindness. My brothers and my sister, and my cousins, Mark and Keith. How we used to run up and down these streets, dashing through the alleys in search of excitement, and forging alliances with the neighborhood kids. Those were sweet memories I had forgotten.

For now, we tried to make of most of this trip. My cousin Mark took us around to the tourist sites as well as local favorites. I visited with aunts and uncles and other relatives, not giving a hint as to the troubles that had brought me to the Windy City. I was no longer the quiet, shy, considerate little boy I had been so long ago. I was now a man trying to find my footing on shifting ground.

After several days, Pat connected with relatives in Louisiana and decided to go there for a while, taking young Patrick with her, with plans for us to meet up back in Houston. I spent time hanging with Mark, going on wild goose chases and odd adventures. Running low on cash, I began my hundred-dollars-a-day hustle, a con I had learned along the way. I would purchase a hundred-dollar traveler's check, report it stolen, and in the meantime cash it with my phony ID. Then I'd get reimbursed for the "stolen" traveler's check. This kept a little cash in my pocket.

Ma, my grandmother on my mother's side, took me to visit my grandfather Bop Bop, who had been stricken with Lou Gehrig's disease and was in a convalescent hospital on the outskirts of Chicago. I remember slowly walking into his room. I was not prepared for what I would see. There, in a low-lying bed, lay Roy Sledge, my grandfather, born in the same month as I was, and whom my grandmother and mother said I so strongly resembled. He could not speak or move a muscle. The degenerative disease had robbed him completely of his physical capabilities. When his gaze set upon his favorite grandson, the only thing he could do was release the tears from his brown eyes. I sat there, holding his hands, gently rubbing his forehead. Bop Bop had always dressed in a dapper suit and hat. He was a perfect gentleman and a man of few words, a man of respect and honor. He had taught us so many fundamental life skills—how to properly shine our shoes, how to be neat and clean and pick up after ourselves, how to be courteous.

I loved this man as I loved Grandada. I knew that Bop Bop would soon be joining him and the rest of our ancestors. I kissed Bop Bop on the forehead before I left, knowing I would not see him again in this lifetime. It was a very sad moment, yet I could shed no tears; it would be a long time before a tear would fall again from my eyes. I sensed that somehow, as crazy as this journey was, Bop Bop had been waiting for me to come say goodbye. Only a few days after my visit, he succumbed to the destruction of the horrific disease.

Ma was stoic, almost detached from the slow decline and death of her companion. She and Bop Bop were a contrast—he was the only one who could keep her judgmental ways at bay. He always did little special things for her. During his illness, she traveled the long distance by bus, standing at the bus stop in the freezing Chicago winter and then walking almost half a mile to the hospital to wash him and comfort him. When my mother found out the bus stop did not have a shelter or a bench, she called the Chicago Transit Authority to complain. Those trips took a terrible toll on Ma's legs and made it difficult for her to get around in her later years. I had not seen Ma or communicated with her since 1968, when my arrest led to Seattle's first large-scale rebellion and landed Elmer and me on the front page of the *Chicago Sun-Times*. At that point, she had disowned both of us. Even now, she was not particularly overjoyed to see me. I could only hope that our next meeting would be under better circumstances.

A few days later I was on my way back to Houston. As the Amtrak train roared through the flat heartland of Nebraska, Oklahoma, and finally Texas, I pondered my next move. I had no idea how I was going to connect with Pat, who was also on her way to Houston. I had no money left nor any place to lay my weary head once I arrived. All I had at my disposal was a gold and opal ring that Pat had bought me, and, unfortunately, I lost it on the train. I also had one last valid credit card, which I used to check into the Marriott in downtown Houston. After my third day, the front desk informed me I had only one more night before my card reached its limit. I still had not been able to locate Pat. I had to do something. I needed one last stroke of luck. The next morning, I dressed up in a nice suit, combed my hair neatly, and left the hotel, hoping for something to happen.

As I walked down the street, I saw a cute little sister with an Afro, bright eyes, and a curvy body. She smiled at me and I smiled back. I met her for lunch and she volunteered to pay. Her name was Sheila. I explained my situation, minus some details, and after her workday was over, she picked me up at the hotel and took me to stay at her place. After several enjoyable days with Sheila, I finally connected with Pat, but continued to see Sheila on the side.

Pat, Patrick, and I got another apartment. Pat got a job and I began looking for one. I had heard that Dino was in Houston, working for his father's excavation company. I drove out to the site where they were clearing land for the new developments. There was Dino, sitting on top of a backhoe, handling the heavy equipment like an old pro.

"Baby boy, how ya doin'?" he asked with a smile.

It was good to see Dino again, and see him working a legitimate job. He was, after all, no more a hustler than I was. He had gotten swept up in the California fast life just as I had. I am glad he was able to move on from California without any serious consequences. I said goodbye to Dino and continued on my journey.

I answered an ad for a youth program coordinator. Two Black women had received a large government grant for their nonprofit and were setting up a youth services bureau. They were so impressed with me that they hired me to develop and run the entire youth program. *Finally,* I thought, *maybe things are coming together for us.* Maybe we would eventually be able to reach our ultimate destination of Jamaica.

A girl Pat's mother had fostered came out to stay with us while she tried to kick a heroin habit. I should have anticipated that an addict and fugitives would be an unwise combination. One of Pat's cousins also moved in to help us pay the rent. At the time, all seemed well—we were like one big, happy family. Pat and I became known as "Bonnie and Clyde" to our associates. Pat and I began to feel at ease, which is always dangerous when you are on the run from the law.

I woke up early one Friday morning, looking forward to starting my new job the following Monday. I was excited about what I might accomplish with my new position and that the two women had enough confidence in me to offer me this opportunity to help build their organization. From my work with the party's Teen Program, I brought a lot of experience that could help these sisters get their program off the ground. Nevertheless, I was still cautious, given the circumstances under which I was living. Things could come crashing down at any time.

I went out on the porch and picked up the morning paper. The sun was bright and the day felt as if it would be a good one. Pat, however, was not feeling well and had decided not to go into work that morning. The constant stress was beginning to take a toll on her body.

I sat on the couch and opened the *Houston Chronicle* to read the news of the day. Suddenly there was a knock on the door. I got up and asked, "Who is it?"

The response startled me. "Is Aaron Dixon there?" No one in Houston aside from Pat called me Aaron.

I answered, "Aaron doesn't live here."

Then came, "Federal marshals. Open up."

In confusion, I ran upstairs to the bedroom and quickly woke up Pat. I pulled on a pair of pants and looked out the bedroom window, thinking perhaps I could escape down the tree next to the window. But there were three men in suits looking up. Just then, the front door burst open and marshals ran in with their weapons drawn, yelling, "You are under arrest! Put your hands up!"

It was over. There was no escaping now. Guns were put to my head as I was ordered to the ground and handcuffed. Pat was handcuffed as well. We were taken down to the police station and booked into custody.

I was transferred to Houston's Harris County Correctional Facility, where I was soon surrounded by Black and Latino inmates in a dark, dreary holding cell, and later moved to the southern tier, deep within the prison. The facility looked every bit like a dungeon. The food was atrocious. I found a worm in my beans, and was unable to stomach the green-and-yellow sausage. I ate very little during my stay.

One lone good aspect was that the facility was largely operated by the inmates, a common practice among Southern prisons, which meant we rarely saw the guards. Fortunately, I had just missed the harvest of the cotton fields by the inmates. After a week in that dismal place, the federal marshals came to pick me up. I never thought I'd be glad to see the feds, but that day I was elated.

Pat and I were reunited. Handcuffed and accompanied by the marshals, we boarded a plane back to the Bay Area. Pat and I said very little, just tried to comfort each other as much as possible. When the stewardess brought us dinner, we scarfed it down so quickly she brought over another plate.

Finally, this journey was over. Our year-and-a-half crime spree had come to an end. Now we had to pay our debt to society and put our lives back together. One thing was certain. We were not criminals—that is to say, we did not have criminal minds. But we got caught up in the thrill of materialism and the disregard for the law, like so many others in the "new" America. I had always been an adventurous, rebellious type, and in my ten years as a revolutionary, I had become addicted to the adrenaline rush of danger, of barely escaping death. It had become a key part of my identity. I had been on the other side of the law for so long that it was difficult for me to reenter what seemed to me a boring way of life, without danger or excitement. It would be something I would struggle with for some time.

I would eventually have to come to grips with my past, my anger, and my detachment. The end of the Black Panther Party had left a bitter taste in my mouth, as it had for many others. It would take at least a decade for the negative feelings to subside and the righteousness of what the party and its members stood for to resurface.

Pat and I were sentenced to a year in prison and five years' probation. She went to the Pleasanton Federal Correctional Institution and I ended up in Lompoc Federal Prison, along with John Dean, the former Nixon adviser involved in the Watergate scandal. When the dust had settled, Pat and I realized we had gone on the lam for nothing—although, over time, I began to wonder if perhaps it was not for nothing.

Maybe this strange journey had hidden meaning and purpose for me. Maybe it served to remind me that we must always remember and honor our ancestors, the people and places we came from. Maybe that is part of what happened to Huey. He stopped remembering. He forgot the sacrifices of our ancestors and all the others who paved the way for the emergence of the Black Panther Party. He had forgotten, as many of us did, that we set out to create a more humane world, for not just Black people but for white, brown, yellow, and red people, for the dispossessed and oppressed wherever they reside. We were ready to give our lives, and even to take lives if necessary, to secure a brighter future for all of humanity. We came up short. Yet the Black Panther Party's legacy is eternal.

It will live on, always, in the hearts and minds of those who stand for the truth, of those who stand for justice and are willing to do whatever is needed to create the world we all deserve to live in: a world free of poverty, hunger, greed, fear, and hate—a world full of love and abundance.

I have no regrets about my ten years as a soldier in the Black Panther Party. In the end it is the memories that make life worth living, particularly the good memories. My memories of Huey P. Newton are of a young, re-bellious, brave, captivating, eloquent genius who ignited a flame that will never die. My memories of the Black Panther Party are of men and women rising in unison to carry that flame, taking up a position of defiance, of sacrifice, and of undying love, infused with passion and determination to write a new, bold future for Black America. That eternal beacon will shine on, lighting the way for future generations and illuminating the past, helping us remember a time when the possibilities for humanity were endless.

Not Forgotten

May our collective conscience free Mumia Abu-Jamal, Chip Fitzgerald, Leonard Peltier, and the many other US political prisoners, including:

Sundiata Acoli

Herman Bell

Anthony Jalil Bottom

Veronza Bowers

Marshall Eddie Conway

Mondo we Langa (David Rice)

Ruchell Cinque Magee

Sekou Odinga

Hugo Pinell

Ed Poindexter

Russell Shoats

Herman Wallace

Albert Woodfox

…among many others

For information on how to help, please visit the website of the Jericho Movement, www.thejerichomovement.com.

Appendix 1

Poem written by my grandmother DeDe, published in a local Chicago paper, 1943

1943

How I miss your begging for pie,
And saying in fun, that from
sweets you would die.
I miss the gang who would come to
the door
Just as you started to scrub the floor.

There are many things I miss, since
you went away,
As I wander through the quiet house
each day;
Praying to Him, who is above
To send back to me the son I love.

The foregoing lines "To My Son"
brought in by Mrs. O. K. Glass was
composed by Mrs. Mildred Dixon,
6318 Langley Ave., Chicago, Ill.
Mrs. Dixon was a former Hendersonian and is the daughter of Mr.
and Mrs. John West on Plum St.

Mrs. Della Winstead received a
letter this week from her son, Sgt
Willie O Winstead, he is well and
doing fine. He is now stationed at
Fort Huachuca, Ariz.

Cpl. Ben Todd enroute to his home
in Russellville from a camp in Mich.,
spent Sunday with Mr. and Mrs.
Ed Phillips.

Soldier News

The expression of a mother's love
to her devoted son, Pvt Elmer Dixon
Jr., 644 Ord. Amm .Co. O U. T. C
Jackson, Miss., who is now serving
his country, follows:

TO MY SON

Oh, how I miss you my son,
And the tricks you played in fun.
I miss your loud laughter and tumbled
room
And your constant juggling of the
kitchen broom.

Appendix 2

Letter from Huey P. Newton to my mother, April 1971

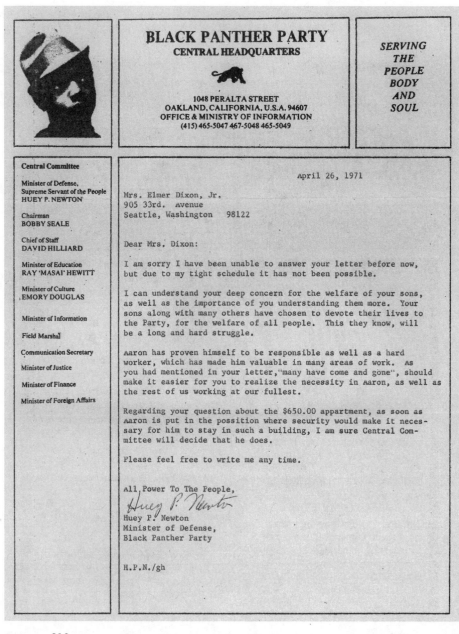

BLACK PANTHER PARTY
CENTRAL HEADQUARTERS

1048 PERALTA STREET
OAKLAND, CALIFORNIA, U.S.A. 94607
OFFICE & MINISTRY OF INFORMATION
(415) 465-5047 467-5048 465-5049

*SERVING
THE
PEOPLE
BODY
AND
SOUL*

Central Committee

Minister of Defense,
Supreme Servant of the People
HUEY P. NEWTON

Chairman
BOBBY SEALE

Chief of Staff
DAVID HILLIARD

Minister of Education
RAY 'MASAI' HEWITT

Minister of Culture
EMORY DOUGLAS

Minister of Information

Field Marshal

Communication Secretary

Minister of Justice

Minister of Finance

Minister of Foreign Affairs

April 26, 1971

Mrs. Elmer Dixon, Jr.
905 33rd. Avenue
Seattle, Washington   98122

Dear Mrs. Dixon:

I am sorry I have been unable to answer your letter before now, but due to my tight schedule it has not been possible.

I can understand your deep concern for the welfare of your sons, as well as the importance of you understanding them more. Your sons along with many others have chosen to devote their lives to the Party, for the welfare of all people. This they know, will be a long and hard struggle.

Aaron has proven himself to be responsible as well as a hard worker, which has made him valuable in many areas of work. As you had mentioned in your letter,"many have come and gone", should make it easier for you to realize the necessity in Aaron, as well as the rest of us working at our fullest.

Regarding your question about the $650.00 appartment, as soon as Aaron is put in the possition where security would make it necessary for him to stay in such a building, I am sure Central Committee will decide that he does.

Please feel free to write me any time.

All Power To The People,

Huey P. Newton
Minister of Defense,
Black Panther Party

H.P.N./gh

316

Appendix 3

Cover of *The Black Panther*, January 1971 (courtesy of Bill Jennings)

Appendix 4

Black Panther Party book list, 1968 (courtesy of Bill Jennings)

Black Panther Party
BOOK LIST

MALCOLM X	The Autobiography of Malcolm X
FANON, FRANTZ	Wretched of the Earth
NKRUMAH, KWAME	I Speak of Freedom
DAVIDSON, BASIL	The Lost Cities of Africa
APTHEKER, HERBERT	The Nat Turner Slave Revolt
Aptheker, Herbert	American Negro Slave evolts
	A Documentary History of the Negro People in the U.S.
Bennett, Lerone Jr.	Before the Mayflower
Bontemps, Arna W.	American Negro Poetry--Story of the Negro
Cronin, E.D.	Black Moses (The story of Garvey and the UNIA)
DuBois, W.E.B.	Black Reconstruction in America--Souls of Black Folk
	The World and Africa
Davidson, Basil	Black Mother, the Years of the African Slave Trade
Fanon, Frantz	Studies in a Dying Colonialism
Franklin, John Hope	From Slavery to Freedom--Negro in the United States
Frazier, C.F.	Black Bourgeoisie
Harrington, Michael	The Other America
Garvey, Marcus	Garvey & Garveyism--The Philosophy & Opinions of Garveyism
Herskovitts, Melville J.	The Myth of the Negro Past
James, C.L.R.	A History of Negro Revolts
Janheinz, John	MUNTU: The New African Culture
Jones, LeRoi	Blues People
Lincoln, C.E.	Black Muslims in America
Malcolm X	Malcolm X Speaks
Mwmmi, Albert	The Colonizer and the Colonized
Nkrumah, Kwame	Ghana
Patterson, William L.	We Charge Genocide
Rogers, J.A.	Africa's Gift to America
	World's Great Men of Color; 3,000 B.C. to 1946 A.D.
Wesley, Charles H. & Woodson, Carter G	The Negro in Our History
Woodward, C. Van	The Strange Career of Jim Crow
Wright, Richard	Native Son

Appendix 5

Information packet issued to all members of the Seattle chapter of the Black Panther Party, 1968 (contents reproduced as in original)

BLACK PANTHER PARTY
CENTRAL HEADQUARTERS
P.O. BOX 8641   EMERYVILLE BRANCH   OAKLAND, CALIFORNIA
845-0103   845-0106   621-1663   921-3860

POLITICAL EDUCATION KIT
for Black Panther Party Members

Primary Objective of Our Party
To Establish Revolutionary Political Power
for Black People

The Black Panther Party is an armed body for carrying out the political tasks of the revolution. Especially at the present, the Black Panther Party should certainly not confine itself to only fighting; besides fighting to destroy the enemy's military strength our Party must also shoulder such important tasks as doing propaganda among the masses, organizing the masses, arming Black people, helping them to establish revolutionary political power and setting up party organizations. The Black Panther Party defends itself with guns and force not merely for the sake of fighting but in order to conduct propaganda among the masses, organize them, arm them and help them to establish revolutionary political power. Without these objectives, fighting loses its meaning and the Black Panther Party loses the reason for its existence.

CARDINAL RULE: Have Faith in the People and Faith in the Party

MOTTO: We Do Not Want War. We Are the Advocates of the Abolition of War, But War Can Only Be Abolished through War, and in order to Get Rid of the Gun, It Is Necessary to Pick Up the Gun.

Power to the People
Black Power to Black People
PANTHER POWER

NATIONAL FUNCTIONAL
STRUCTURE OF THE BLACK PANTHER
PARTY LEADERSHIP

1.	Minister of Defense	Huey P. Newton
2.	Chairman	Bobby Seale
3.	Minister of Information	Eldridge Cleaver
4.	National Headquarters Captain	David Hilliard
5.	Minister of Education	George Murray
6.	Field Marshalls	Don Cox
		Chico Deblin
		George Ware
7.	Minister of Black Culture	Emory Douglas
8.	Minister of Finance	Melvin Newton
9.	Prime Minister	Stokely Carmichael
10.	Minister of Justice	Rap Brown
	Communications Secretary	Kathleen Cleaver
	Minister of Foreign Affairs	James Forman
	Minister of Black Religion	Father Neil
	National Captain of Women	
	Asst. National Captain of Women	Betty Carter

BLACK PANTHER OFFICERS OF SEATTLE

AARON DIXON	CAPTAIN
CURTIS HARRIS	LT. OF DEFENSE
WILLIE BRAZIER	LT. OF EDUCATION
BOBBY WHITE	LT. OF INFORMATION
ELMER DIXON	CAPT. OF MILITARY
BOBBY HARDING	HEAD OF CENTRAL STAFF
NAFASI HALLEY	LT. OF FINANCE
KATHY JONES	CAPT. OF WOMEN
JOYCE BRUCE	LT. OF WOMEN

UNIT LEADERS

UNIT COORDINATOR   ELMER DIXON

#1 – Elmer Dixon
#2 – Aaron Dixon
#3 – Richard Noble
#4 – Billy Connar
#5 – Chester Northington

#6 – Joe Atkins
#7 – Curtis Harris
#8 – Gary Owens
#9 – Artis Parker
#10 – Lawrence Smith
#11
#12

SECTION LEADERS

Steve Phillips	#1	Yesler to Day
Bobby Harding	#2	Union to Yesler
Buddy Yates	#3	Union to Madison
Richard Noble	#4	Projects

CENTRAL BOARD
SEATTLE BLACK PANTHER PARTY

Aaron Dixon	EA 5 8794
Willie Brazier	EA 4 4091
Joyce Bruce	EA 4 4817
Elmer Dixon	EA 5 8794
Nafasi Halley	EA 2 7291
Bobby Harding	EA 2 8817
Curtis Harris	EA 5 9018
Kathy Jones	EA 3 7304
Richard Noble	PA 5 7461
Steve Phillips	EA 5 8563
Bobby White	EA 4 4817
Buddy Yates	EA 5 5127

Other Important Phone Numbers

Dr. John Greene	EA 9 8105;	home: EA 5 3456
ACLU	MA 4 2180	
County Jail	MA 2 5124	
City Jail	583-2376	
Bail Bonds	MA 2 6633	
Model Cities	583-5700	
Lawyers:		
Mike Rosen	EA 5 6230	
Gary Gayton	EA 2 1960	
Chris Young	EA 4 5492	

BLACK PANTHER PARTY PLATFORM AND PROGRAM

1. **We want freedom. We want power to determine the destiny of our black community.**
   WE BELIEVE that black people will not be free until we are able to determine our destiny.

2. **We want full employment for our people.**
   WE BELIEVE that the federal government is responsible and obligated to give every man employment or a guaranteed income. We believe that if the white American businessman will not give full employment, then the means of production should be taken from the businessmen and placed in the community so that the people of the community can organize and employ all of its people and give a high standard of living.

3. **We want an end to the robbery by the white man of our Black Community.**
   WE BELIEVE that this racist government has robbed us and now we are demanding the overdue debt of forty acres and two mules. Forty acres and two mules was promised 100 years ago as restitution for slave labor and mass murder of black people. We will accept the payment in currency which will be distributed to our many communities. The Germans are now aiding the Jews in Israel for the genocide of the Jewish people. The American racist has taken part in the slaughter of over fifty million black people; therefore, we feel that this is a modest demand that we make.

4. **We want decent housing for shelter of human beings.**
   WE BELIEVE that if the white landlords will not give decent housing to our black community, then the housing and the land should be made into cooperatives so that our community, with government aid, can build and make decent housing for its people.

5. **We want education for our people that exposes the true nature of this decadent American society. We want education that teaches us our true history and our role in the present-day society.**
   WE BELIEVE in an educational system that will give to our people a knowledge of self. If a man does not have knowledge of himself and his position in society and the world, then he has little chance to relate to anything else.

6. **We want all black men to be exempt from military service.**
   WE BELIEVE that black people should not be forced to fight in the military

service to defend a racist government that does not protect us. We will not fight and kill other people of color in the world who, like black people, are being victimized by the white racist government of America. We will protect ourselves from the force and violence of the racist police and military, by whatever means necessary.

7. **We want an immediate end to POLICE BRUTALITY and MURDER of black people.**
   WE BELIEVE we can end police brutality in our black community by organizing black self-defense groups that are dedicated to defending our black community from racist police oppression and brutality. The Second Amendment to the Constitution of the United States gives a right to bear arms. We therefore believe that all black people should arm themselves for self-defense.

8. **We want freedom for all black men held in federal, state, county and city prisons and jails.**
   WE BELIEVE that all black people should be released from the many jails and prisons because they have not received a fair and impartial trial.

9. **We want all black people when brought to trial to be tried in court by a jury of their peer group or people from their black communities as defined by the Constitution of the United States.**
   WE BELIEVE that the courts should follow the United States Constitution so that black people will receive fair trials. The 14th Amendment of the U.S. Constitution gives a man a right to be tried by his peer group. A peer is a person from a similar economic, social, religious, geographical, environmental, historical and racial background. To do this the court will be forced to select a jury from the black community from which the black defendant came. We have been, and are being tried by all-white juries that have no understanding of the "average reasoning man" of the black community.

10. **We want land, bread, housing, education, clothing, justice and peace. And as our major political objective, a United Nations-supervised plebiscite to be help throughout the black colony in which only black colonial subjects will be allowed to participate, for the purpose of determining the will of black people as to their national destiny.**
    When, in the course of human events, if becomes necessary for one people to dissolve the political bands which have connected them with one another, and to assume, among the powers of the earth, the separate and equal station to which the laws of nature and nature's God entitle them, a decent respect

to the opinions of mankind requires that they should declare the causes which impel them to separation.

We hold these truths to be self-evident, that all men are created equal; that they are endowed by their Creator with certain unalienable rights; that among these are life, liberty, and the pursuit of happiness. **That, to secure these rights, governments are instituted among men, deriving their just powers from the consent of the governed; that, whenever any form of government becomes destructive of these ends, it is the right of the people to alter or to abolish it, and to institute a new government, laying its foundation on such principles, and organizing its powers in such form, as to them shall seem most likely to effect their safety and happiness.** Prudence, indeed, will dictate that governments long established should not be changed for light transient causes; and, accordingly, all experience hath shown, that mankind are more disposed to suffer, while evils are sufferable, than to right themselves by abolishing the forms to which they are accustomed. **But, when a long train of abuses and usurpations, pursuing invariably the same object, evinces a design to reduce them under absolute despotism, it is their right, it is their duty, to throw off such government, and to provide new guards for their future security.**

RULES OF THE BLACK PANTHER PARTY
CENTRAL HEADQUARTERS
OAKLAND, CALIFORNIA

Every member of the BLACK PANTHER PARTY throughout this country of racist AMERICA must abide by these rules as functional members of this party. CENTRAL COMMITTEE members, CENTRAL STAFFS, and LOCAL STAFFS, including all captains subordinate to either national, state and local leadership of the BLACK PANTHER PARTY will enforce these rules. Length of suspension or other disciplinary action necessary for violation of these rules will depend upon decisions by national, state or state area, and local committees and staffs where said rule or rules of the BLACK PANTHER PARTY were violated.

Every member of the party must know these verbatum [*sic*] by heart. And apply them daily. Each member must report any violation of these rules to their leadership or they are counter-revolutionary and are also subjected to suspension by the BLACK PANTHER PARTY.

THE FOLLOWING RULES ARE:

1. No party member can have narcotics or weed in his possession while doing party work.
2. Any party member found shooting narcotics will be expelled from this party.
3. No party member can be drunk while doing daily party work.
4. No party member will violate rules relating to office work and general meetings of the BLACK PANTHER PARTY, and meeting of the BLACK PANTHER PARTY, ANYWHERE.
5. No party member will use, point, or fire a weapon of any kind unnecessarily or accidentally at anyone other than the enemy.
6. No party member can join any other army or force other than the BLACK LIBERATION ARMY.
7. No party member can have a weapon in his possession while drunk or loaded off narcotics or weed.
8. No party member will commit any crimes against other party members or BLACK people at all, and cannot steal or take from the people; not even a needle and a piece of thread.
9. When arrested BLACK PANTHER PARTY members will give only name and address and will sign nothing. Legal first aid must be understood by all Party members.
10. The Ten Point Program and platform of the BLACK PANTHER PARTY must be known and understood by all Party members.

11. Party Communications must be National and Local.

12. The 10-10-10 program should be known and understood by all members.

13. All finance officers operate under the jurisdiction of the Ministry of Finance.

14. Each person to submit daily report of work.

15. Each sub-Section Leader, Section Leader and Captain must submit Daily reports of work.

16. All Panthers must learn to operate and service weapons correctly.

17. All Leadership personnel who suspend or expel a member must submit this information to the Editor of the Newspaper pertaining to suspension, so that it will be published in the paper and known by all chapters and Branches.

18. Political Education is mandatory.

19. Only office personnel assigned to respective offices each day should be there. All others are to sell papers and do political work out in the community, including captains, section leaders, etc.

20. COMMUNICATION — All Chapters must submit weekly reports in writing to National Headquarters.

21. All branches must implement First Aid and/or Medical Cadres.

22. All chapters, branches, and components of the BLACK PANTHER PARTY must submit a monthly Financial Report to the Ministry of Finance and also the Central Committee.

23. Everyone in leadership position must read no less than two hours per day to keep abreast of the changing political situation.

24. No chapter or branch shall accept grants, poverty funds, money or any other aid from any government agency without contacting the National Headquarters.

25. All Chapters must adhere to the policy and ideology laid down by the CENTRAL COMMITTEE of the BLACK PANTHER PARTY.

26. All branches must submit weekly reports in writing to their respective Chapters.

POCKET LAWYER OF LEGAL FIRST AID

This pocket lawyer is provided as a means of keeping black people up to date on their rights. We are always the first to be arrested and the racist police forces are constantly trying to pretend that rights are extended equally to all people. Until we arm ourselves to righteously take care of our own, the pocket lawyer is what's happening.

1. If you are stopped and/or arrested by the police, you may remain silent; you do not have to answer any questions about alleged crimes, you should provide your name and address only if requested (although it is not absolutely clear that you must do so). But then do so, and at all times remember the fifth amendment.

2. If a police officer is not in uniform, ask him to show his identification. He has no authority over you unless he properly identifies himself. Beware of persons posing as police officers. Always get his badge number and his name.

3. Police have no right to search your car or your home unless they have a search warrant, probable cause or your consent. They may conduct no exploratory search, that is, one for evidence of crime generally or for evidence of a crime unconnected with the one you are being questioned about. (Thus, a stop for an auto violation does not give the right to search the auto). You are not required to consent to a search; therefore, you should not consent and should state clearly and unequivocally that you do not consent, in front of witnesses if possible. If you do not consent, the police will have the burden in court of showing probable cause. Arrest may be corrected later.

4. You may not resist arrest forcibly or by going limp, even if you are innocent. To do so is a separate crime of which you can be convicted even if you are acquitted of the original charge. Do not resist arrest under any circumstances.

5. If you are stopped and/or arrested, the police may search you by patting you on the outside of your clothing. You can be stripped of your personal possessions. Do not carry anything that includes the name of your employer or friends.

7. Do not engage in "friendly" conversation with officers on the way to or at the station. Once you are arrested, there is little likelihood that anything you say will get you released.

8. As soon as you have been booked, you have the right to complete at least two phone calls — one to a relative, friend, or attorney, the other to a bail bondsman. If you can, call the Black Panther Party, EAst 3-6280, and the Party will post bail if possible.

9. You must be allowed to hire and see an attorney immediately.

10. You do not have to give any statement to the police, nor do you have to sign any statement you might give them, and therefore you should not sign anything. Take the Fifth and Fourteenth Amendments, because you cannot be forced to testify against yourself.

11. You must be allowed to post bail in most cases, but you must be able to pay the bail bondsman's fee. If you cannot pay the fee, you may ask the judge to release you from custody without bail or to lower your bail but he does not have to do so.

12. The police must bring you into court or release you within 48 hours after your arrest (unless the time ends on a week-end or a holiday, and they must bring you before a judge the first day court is in session.)

13. If you do not have the money to hire an attorney, immediately ask the police to get you an attorney without charge.

14. If you have the money to hire a private attorney, but do not know of one, call the Bar Association of your county and they will furnish you with the name of an attorney who practices criminal law.

Index

About the Author

Aaron Dixon is one of the co-founders of the Seattle chapter of the Black Panther Party. He has since founded Central House, a nonprofit that provides transitional housing for youth, and was one of the co-founders of the Cannon House, a senior assisted-living facility. Aaron ran for US Senate on the Green Party ticket in 2006.